# CRITICAL ACCLAIM FOR
## *CALYPSO BLUE*

"Len Buonfiglio enjoys the ex-pat life in sun-drenched St. Pierre, running a bar and staying out of trouble. But trouble finds him, and that's a damn good thing for readers. *Calypso Blue* is the next best thing to booking a ticket for a Caribbean vacation."
—James R Benn, author of
the Billy Boyle WWII mysteries

"Paradise never felt so seedy. Silverman gives us murder, blackmail, kidnapping, and colorful characters to keep us guessing. A knockout from a single rum punch!"
—Fabian Nicieza, Edgar-nominated author of
*Suburban Dicks* and co-creator of Deadpool

"Brian Silverman's delicious and heady crime thriller, *Calypso Blue*, is addictive, smart and peopled with unforgettable characters. This book grabs hold and won't let go."
—Peggy Townsend, author of *The Beautiful and the Wild*

# CALYPSO BLUE

# BOOKS BY
# BRIAN SILVERMAN

*Freedom Drop*
*Calypso Blue*

# BRIAN SILVERMAN

# CALYPSO BLUE

A Len Buonfiglio/Caribbean Mystery

The characters and events in this book are fictitious. Any similarity to real persons, living or dead, is coincidental and not intended by the author.

Cover design by Zach McCain

ISBN-13: 978-1-970861-30-3

*Rosa Theresa Silverman, the only daughter of Italian immigrants, much to the dismay of her Calabrese parents, pursued a passion for art. That passion took her to college and there she met a man and started a family, putting the things she loved so much to the side to take care of her husband and children. Even while chasing three boys separated by just four years, she would find time to create. As one of those boys, I never cared much for art or valued what she was creating. It was more about what she gave me for school lunch—things expected from a mom. As I got older it became obvious, even to my primitive eye, that what she was putting on canvas and in the kiln was both bold and beautiful. And as I experienced my own struggles of creating something from nothing, I appreciated more the sacrifices she made to do what she did. This book is dedicated to the creative influence in my life, my mother.*

# AUTHOR'S NOTE

If you subscribe to the digital music service, Spotify, you will find each of the three playlists listed at the beginning of *Calypso Blue*'s three parts. They can be found under the title of the playlists. Hearing them while reading might enhance the overall experience or detract from it. The choice is yours.

# PREFACE

# A

## Dreamland 2001

*John Saint John was up early. It had stormed the night before and that didn't help his sleep any. Earlier that day he visited a man on Gravesend Avenue, a man whom a colleague put him in contact with. It took almost ten days to get it, but now the man had what Saint John requested...what Saint John wanted. He had his gun.*

*That night he tossed and turned, thinking about what must be done the next day. He kept the gun in a small black plastic bag—the kind you get at a bodega when buying a can of beer. Saint John didn't like guns. When he preached at the Faith Palace Baptist Church on Union Street, a Sunday side job he cherished, he railed against the gun violence that plagued the streets of Brooklyn. And now he was a hypocrite. But he was also only a man—and a father. And as such had to do what a man—what a father—had to do to protect his family.*

*That was what he kept telling himself as the storm raged both outside and in his head that night. The morning was clear and, unusual for early September, there was a slight hint of fall in the air. He put on his maintenance department uniform and slipped the black plastic bag into the canvas backpack he carried to work every day. Before leaving, he went into the bedroom where his daughters slept. He kissed them both: eleven-year-old Jasinda and fourteen-year-old Miriam. His wife had already left the house, working to care for an elderly woman who lived in Brooklyn Heights. With their parents' busy schedules, the two girls learned to fend for themselves. They were good girls. He thought about their half-brother, who lived on the little island where Saint John was from. The boy was almost twenty now. His mother could not control him. He was often in trouble. He had a bad disposition. A quick temper. St. John regretted every day that he was not there to guide the boy, spiritually and morally. But it was a choice he made when he left the island for New York. When he fell in love with another. It was something he had to live with.*

*He hovered over Miriam, staring at the calm in her face as she slept. He hoped when she woke that calm would remain, that she would in time lose the frightened, tormented gaze that had occupied her face since that day on Eastern Parkway. But he didn't think so. He was worried about her and that was why he had to take care of this thing. He couldn't let what happened to her stand without retribution. She had to see that her father loved and cared for her...and would die for her if necessary.*

*The 3 train, even at six in the morning, was crowded, but he was fortunate to get a seat. He clasped his arms around his broad chest, hugging the backpack tight to him. He could feel the sharpness of the gun in it. It was as if it were radiating heat. He had the earphones of his portable cassette player plugged into his ears. He was listening to the sweet voice of Marcia Griffiths. She was singing that beautiful song about a dreamland. He needed to hear her voice to help settle him—to calm him for the day ahead.*

*He got off at Fulton Street and walked across to the North Tower, where he worked. He knew that the financial offices on the top floors were already busy working the overseas markets. On his way in he saw Stanley Clement coming out of the Tower, his shift finished. Clement was short and rotund with very dark skin and a hairless head. The two acknowledged each other. Clement, originally from the Caribbean island of St. Kitts, lived on Lincoln Place, also in Brooklyn.*

*"Rain hard last night," Clement said to Saint John.*

*Saint John nodded. "Beautiful day today."*

*"It is," Clement said, staring up at the blue sky and then into Saint John's face. "My friend get you what you need?"*

*He nodded again but said nothing. He didn't tell Clement why he needed the gun. He didn't tell anyone what happened to Miriam and who did it to her, not even his wife. They would know soon enough. He wanted all his people to know.*

*"A pity we need such things in this country," Clement said with a shake of his head. "Quiet day for you, I think. I see you at church tomorrow evening."*

*"Yes, sir, and thank you."*

*Clement nodded and shuffled toward Fulton Street, from where Saint John had just come.*

*Saint John went into the maintenance entrance to the North Tower and took the service elevator down to the basement, where he had a locker. He put the backpack in his locker and double-checked to make sure he spun his combination lock to secure it. He glanced at the work assignment board in the adjoining maintenance staff lunchroom. He saw that he had to go check a water leak in the kitchen of the law offices on the sixteenth floor.*

*As he rode the elevator up, he thought about his decision to keep his daughters and his wife in New York. Now he knew he made a mistake. He should have already sent them all to the island, where he would soon join them. He had thought there would be more opportunities in New York than on his tiny island. But here there was evil, promiscuity, and bad boys with guns. But that just confused him more because the irony was that the gun he had in his locker was not to be used on a bad boy with a gun from New York. It was to be used on a man from the island. His island. Evil was everywhere. He knew that from his biblical studies. But the island where he was raised was different, or so he thought. He had made his decision. His wife and the girls would move as soon as possible—while it was still early in their school year. He had already told his sister that they were coming. She was now making the living arrangements for them. There was much more to do.*

*After a quick inspection, he discovered that a gasket was loose under the commissary kitchen sink on the sixteenth floor. He tightened it and checked to make sure a new washer or bolt was not needed. Then he felt the floor shake violently under him. He pulled out from under the sink.*

*"Earthquake?" a young woman asked him as she poured herself a cup of coffee.*

*"Certainly feel so," Saint John said. "This building steady though. No worry here about a little New York earthquake."*

*She smiled at him and took her coffee back to her desk. The small walkie-talkie he carried on his belt was beeping. He picked it up.*

*"Saint John," he said into it while he listened to the squawk coming from his supervisor, telling him to check on some fire damage on the ninety-first floor. He sighed; Clement said it was going to be a quiet day. He didn't think so. And he was actually glad of that. It would keep his mind off what he had to do after work.*

*There were people huddled in groups and talking quietly as he walked through the office to the elevator bank. The elevator seemed slower than normal but finally arrived and was empty, which was also unusual for the morning. It was rush hour. Usually the elevators were packed. He tried to think if it was maybe a Jewish holiday and that was why it was quiet. He wasn't sure.*

*As the elevator ascended rapidly, he thought he should call his son on the island. He should alert him that his half-sisters and stepmother were moving there. The boy's mother was dead.*

4

*He had no family there. Now he would have a family. He would have people who cared for him. He hoped that would soften him and dull the rage that seemed to consume the boy.*

*That Marcia Griffiths song was in his head. "Dreamland." He thought for sure that it was written about the island where he was born. The place where he hoped to soon return. He was humming to himself as he rode the elevator up.*

*The elevator stopped on the ninety-first floor and the door opened. Just as Saint John was about to step out, thick metallic smoke streamed into the elevator and immediately filled his lungs, knocking him onto his hands and knees. Before he lost consciousness, his mind went to the image of his daughter Miriam, her costume torn, her hair disheveled, wandering Eastern Parkway late into the night of Labor Day. Then he realized that the gun in his locker would never be used. There would be no retribution.*

*"My babies," he whispered faintly before the hot thick smoke melted his lungs.*

# B

# Land of Promise

The dream always starts with the air thick with smoke. I am running up subway stairs while trying hard to clear my lungs. But my legs are like lead weights. I'm carrying a body over my shoulder. I do this multiple times. Taking body after body up the subway stairs as I strain to breathe. I attempt once again to go back down into the smoky subway tunnel, but this time I'm stopped. Held tight by strong arms. Don't they know there was someone I left behind? Don't they know that was the only reason I was in that tunnel? Those bodies I pulled from the smoke, I didn't really care if they lived or died. They were in the way. I took them to safety only because I needed to clear a path to get to her. She was still down there. But I couldn't save her like I saved the others.

Sometimes I wake up right there at that point in the dream, but most times the dream continues into a second part—when I fall asleep again. In part two of the dream, I'm in the kitchen in my house in the Bronx, in the neighborhood where I grew up. My wife at the time, Kathleen, is there with my young children, my daughter Kasie and my son, Luke. I'm holding a big silver key. One of those old-fashioned door keys. On the key are the words "New York City." I don't know what to do with such a key.

"The keys to the city, The June First hero. What a man." I see the lips of my ex-wife move and hear her words. But the voice sounds nothing like hers. It's a masculine voice. It sounds like my own voice. And the tone is sarcastic; the words spoken with derision.

"I didn't want this," I plead to her.

"You wanted it all," I hear her say, again in that strange voice.

I stare at the key that I know will unlock nothing. "No."

"You're a bastard." Her words are hot. So hot it's as if they singe my flesh.

I shake my head. "No...I'm a hero." My words are weak, barely uttered.

"What are you, Daddy?" Kasie, the older of my children, asks.

When I look at my daughter, I see my ex-wife's face on her six-year-old body. The masculine voice replaced now by a child's.

"Daddy? What are you?"

"I'm a bastard." I say this now in a loud, clear voice. So loud, that sometimes I wake up saying it.

The dream dissipates after that, or an alarm, usually set on my cell phone, wakes me. On this morning it's the latter, I had set my alarm the night before and now it is buzzing, rousing me from that dream. But it stays with me while I shower and then when I feed my three dogs. I think about it when I go to the big window of my house on the Caribbean island of St. Pierre where I live now, so far from that house in the Bronx. I stare at the Atlantic Ocean. Alone and without my family. I wonder what triggers the dream. I try to remember the last time I had it. I can't. There is no pattern. I have no idea what ignites it.

I put music from one of my playlists on. The music I choose could be arbitrary. I have many playlists. But this one is a deliberate choice—made by the one I left in that subway tunnel. I tell myself it will help me shake off the effects of that unsettling dream. Her name was Nura Azar and the playlist she made for me so long ago I titled "Nura's Island." It was the playlist I listen to more than any of the others. I put it on shuffle. The song that queues up first is Marcia Griffith's "Dreamland." Nura called the island we both envisioned a land of promise. But it could have been a dreamland too. I got to see her land of promise. She never did.

I need to get going. I need to start my day. I don't have time to dwell any further on the dream and why it came to me again. And I'm grateful for that.

I have an old black Jeep—I've had it since I moved to St. Pierre. It serves me well on the steep and winding roads of the island. My house is on what is called East Road. It is one of St. Pierre's major roads, if you consider a narrow, two-lane, semi-paved road as something major. It connects the east Atlantic coast with the Caribbean Sea on the west coast. I drive from my house toward Garrison Harbor. The Blue Star ferry from St. Vincent will arrive soon and I have to be there to collect my twice-weekly delivery of beer—cases of Carib, Heineken, Dragon Stout and the non-alcoholic Vitamalt. It's a Tuesday morning and, as I knew I would, I see Livingston Harrod slowly maneuvering down the road's steep slope to where he works as caretaker of the Glad Tidings Seventh-day Adventist Church. I pull over as always and open the passenger door for Harrod, who, by now, expects the lift down the hill.

Harrod settles himself into the Jeep and turns to me. His face is grave. "Sassy hurt the Lord bad," he says in a somber tone.

I look at him as I drive down Center Road toward Garrison, St. Pierre's capital. His eyes are staring straight ahead. The windows of my Jeep are open, letting in the morning air. "Lord Ram?" I ask, but I know there really couldn't be any other Lord he is referring to on St. Pierre. Or any other Sassy, for that matter.

"Mmhmm," Harrod, who is bone-lanky and, I estimate, in his late seventies, nods. "They say he not gonna make it. That what I hear on the radio." Harrod then remains silent until I drop him off.

I sit in the Jeep watching Harrod hobble toward the church. "Sassy, she hurt the Lord bad," was what he said. I ponder those words for a moment. But only for a moment. At the time, they mean nothing to me. And then I drive on to the harbor.

# PLAYLIST ONE

## Tubby's Calypso Jams, Soca, and Such

1. King Tubby Meets the Rockers Uptown, Augustus Pablo
2. Abatina, Calypso Rose
3. Ten to One is Murder, Mighty Sparrow
4. Bee's Melody, Lord Kitchener
5. Man Smart, Woman Smarter, The Duke of Iron
6. Never Ever Worry, The Great Honorouble Lord Pretender
7. Sugar Bum Bum, Lord Kitchener
8. Congo Man, Machal Montano and Mighty Sparrow
9. In de Congaline, Burning Flames
10. This de Place, Patrice Roberts
11. Pump Me Up, Krosfyah
12. Big Belly Man, Mac Fingal
13. Cloud Nine, Lyrikal
14. Down de Road, Krosfyah
15. Same Boat, Calypso Rose

# 1

## The Fete

The *Blue Star* was just pulling into the dock when I arrived. I parked the Jeep and headed over. Tito, co-owner of the Bougainvillea Hotel and head chef of its four-star restaurant, was already waiting for his delivery, as was Sam Suraj of the Yacht Club. I nudged Tito from behind. Tito, whose last name I never learned, turned, grinned and hugged me with his meaty tattoo-adorned forearms. "Lennie, hola, and good morning," he said.

"Good morning?" Sam Suraj questioned Tito's jovial greeting. "How this a good morning when the Lord lay dying in St. Elizabeth hospital?"

"Yeah, I heard about that," I said. The ferry began to unload passengers and cargo.

Janell Vincent, who worked on the ferry, placed the cases of beer at my feet. "Such a glorious man and songsmith. We cannot lose Lord Ram."

I piled the boxes onto the hand truck I'd brought with me. "Any word on his condition?"

Suraj looked at me as he assembled the supplies he needed for the bar at the Yacht Club. He just shook his head.

I said goodbye to Tito and wheeled my supplies to the Jeep, piling the boxes in the back.

I turned on the radio to the one local AM/FM station (it worked on both frequencies) that broadcast from Garrison. I recognized the distinctive, gravelly voice of Lord Ram as soon as the radio came on. The song was one of his recent calypsos. The voice was weaker and even more gruff than usual. It was hard for me to understand what he was singing about—something to do with the price of goat meat. Like the thousands of other compositions he'd sung over his sixty-year career, the goat meat most likely represented something else. What it could be, I had no idea, but I was not from St. Pierre—or the Caribbean. I was a transplant on this island. What he was singing about was directed to his fellow Peteys, the term used for those living in St. Pierre, as well as those natives who now lived in cities like Toronto, London, and my hometown, New York.

"Today it will be Lord Ram all day," the somber, deep voice of the radio announcer intoned. "While we listen, let us pray for a speedy recovery for the King of Calypso. St. Pierre's own. The power of prayer, I know, will heal the great man and we will all, soon, once again, see and hear him entertain us with his genius."

I turned the radio off and drove up Windy Hill Road and pulled the Jeep into one of the three parking spots of the Sporting Place, the bar I opened soon after I arrived on St. Pierre. My partner in the venture, Tubby Levett, had his old '09 Toyota in one of the other spots. Before I could get out of the Jeep, Tubby was at my car door.

"You heard?" Tubby asked.

"How could I not?"

"Busy day here, Mr. Len," Tubby said.

"You think?"

"I know," Tubby said.

We loaded up the hand truck with the cases of beer and I wheeled them into the bar.

"I already call Mike to tell him to come," Tubby said. "But I think today we need more than Mike."

I looked at Tubby, my best friend on the island. Tall and lean, he was the furthest thing from being rotund, despite what his name implied. "What is it I'm missing here?"

"The word already out," he said.

I had no idea what word he was referring to. But that was nothing new for me from Tubby and from St. Pierre where it seemed I was in the dark, even after nearly a decade of living here. "What word is that?" I asked, because Tubby wasn't volunteering anything.

"Someone say that this the place to fete Lord Ram. This the place, to celebrate the great man and send him the vibes that will heal him."

Tubby had an answer for most everything, but that wasn't the answer I wanted to hear. "And who is that someone?" I asked, eyeing him suspiciously.

"Not me, Mr. Len."

"Not you? Then who?"

"I don't know, but that the word I hear, and you know when I hear the word, it usually accurate."

I pondered that. There was a flow of inside information on the island that, despite my years here, I was not privy to. It wasn't that social media or texting was uncommon; it was as common here as anywhere, but information also came in other ways. Maybe from a brief chat with a taxi driver or fisherman. An exchange between open car windows. Or at a church service, or during a dominoes game at a roadside rum shop. So despite all the twenty-first century technological advances that the island shared with the rest of the world, that was how most vital news traveled on St. Pierre.

As Tubby predicted, by eleven that morning, the deck was overflowing with customers. Tubby, Mike, our third bartender when we needed a third, and I were behind the bar quickly mixing up rum punches and opening bottles of beer.

Andrew Patrick and Langston Neely, both postal workers, were sitting at the bar, their eyes downcast.

I opened a cold bottle of Carib for each of them. "No mail today?" I asked, looking from one to the other.

"Sick today," Langston said, apparently speaking for both of them.

"Ah no can work with the Lord lying over at St. Elizabeth," Andrew added. "The people can wait a day for dem damn mail."

"They say it just a matter of time," Langston muttered.

"Where do you get your information?" I asked, noticing another group entering the bar, attendants from St. Pierre's national park at the base of Mt. Hadali.

"Minerva from the hospital where she work in the kitchen. She text my wife," Langston said.

"What St. Pierre without Ram?" Andrew asked no one in particular.

"They say the Queen smash the Lord head with a Dutch pot," Horace Fancy, a retired customs officer, chimed in.

Fancy's wife, Owena, who was by his side, shook her finger at her husband. "Who tell you such rubbish?"

"I hear it from dem two," Fancy pointed down to the Brown brothers, Niles and Edwin, who worked at the island's small aggregate quarry. But they, like most everyone else on the island it seemed, were also not working today.

Niles nodded. "They say the pot hold a chicken fricassee the Queen make special for Lord."

Owena laughed. "I know that is rubbish for sure. The Queen no can lift a heavy Dutch pot filled with chicken fricassee and smash the Lord's skull with it. No she cannot."

"That Sassy stronger than you think," Niles said, his voice louder to compete with the rising decibel level in the bar. "And when a person get fired up with anger, they even stronger. It's the adrenaline, you know."

Langston moved between the group at the bar, displaying a photograph on his cell phone. "Barrington just text from police headquarters. He say it not a chicken fricassee in the pot, but a cook-up with goat."

Fancy shook his head and threw up his hands. "Now I know that not correct because I remember the Lord telling me many years ago that goat meat was for savages. That's what he said. The Lord's words. I remember them like it yesterday."

His wife stared at him, open-mouthed. "Man, Lord Ram tell you no such thing. That man not know Horace Fancy."

"The Lord know who I am," he said. "He talk to me at the airport that time he bring in the case of whiskey he buy in Scotland. It was I who clear that for him. Ram know Horace Fancy."

"Maybe they quarrel over Queen making a goat cook-up when he wanted chicken in de pot?" Langston queried.

"So she threw the heavy pot at the old man? She try to kill the man over what in the Dutch pot?" Owena said, shaking her head in disbelief. "She a big star too. Why she risk all that to hurt an old man?"

Another group entered the bar. All the indoor tables were now occupied and the crowd on the deck was reaching overflow capacity. Squeezing through the bodies at the bar was Rondell Myles. Myles, a local music promoter who booked soca acts into small venues around the island, and who was also one of the producers of the island's low-key Christmas Kaiso Fest, was waving at me to get my attention.

"As you can see, Rondell, it's kind of busy in here," I said, leaning close to him. "What is it you want?"

"Yes, very busy. I see yours is the place for those to come to pray for the great man."

I smiled and looked around the bar—at the bottles of Heineken, Carib, and the small glasses of white rum that were blanketing the tables. "I don't see anyone praying in here, Rondell."

"Mr. Len, you been on this island long enough to know that we Peteys show our respect to our loved ones with a fete. We try to turn a sad time into a happy one."

"And my Sporting Place has been chosen as the site of the fete to celebrate the grave condition of Lord Ram?"

"Yes, exactly," Rondell said.

"And who anointed it so? The 2020 Club on Marvell Road is much bigger and better equipped to handle a fete than my place."

"The 2020 Club never have use for the Lord. You know King Delight, one of the owners of that place, and the King and the Lord—well you know those two true enemies both on and off the stage."

I noticed a group of six from Windward Savings had just come through the door and were making their way to the already two-deep bar. I turned to Tubby and Mike. Tubby shook his head and looked down.

"They close the banks," Rondell said.

"And someone spread the word to come here?" I asked Rondell.

"Not just I, Mr. Len. Other people say you have a fete up here on Windy Hill to pay tribute to the magnificent Lord Ram. You know that sometimes, on this little island, events just happen. There no planning."

"No planning?" I looked at Rondell suspiciously. I knew he had other motives. He was well aware that the Sporting Place could not accommodate a fete on such short notice. He smiled at me as if he knew what I was thinking. That I was well aware of his plot would not deter him.

"In half an hour I can set up tables and add another small bar outside in the back. I get my good friend Edison Aloo to work the grill and make his famous spicy chicken. I have Tony X bring his music and play the songs of Lord Ram exclusively. The girls come and help serve and clean up. Nothing to worry about, Mr. Len. We make this a real fete worthy of the great man himself."

"We?" This was Rondell's way of proposing a business arrangement.

"Worry about nothing, Mr. Len. I charge at the door. For that we give them beer, rum punch and chicken. We'll work it out when this over. I'm a fair man. This you know."

I didn't know that, and with the din of people in my bar clamoring for beverages, I didn't really have time to think on it. We needed help. I couldn't turn away the citizens of my adopted island because I wasn't able to handle a crowd. How would that affect my status as a foreign interloper here? Tubby had been listening in to Rondell's proposal. I looked at him.

"No choice," Tubby said to me. "We must do this."

I knew Tubby was right even though I wasn't happy about it. I nodded my compliance to Rondell. He beamed a broad glistening smile and hustled out.


Within the hour, just as Rondell promised, there were tables and chairs set up outside on the lawn surrounding the upper deck. Tony X had his mammoth speakers connected to my electricity and already the calypso of Lord Ram was blasting from them. I could smell the charcoal from the hollowed-out oil drum converted into a smoker that Edison Aloo used to barbecue his chicken. Rondell brought a few men he knew to help with setting up—getting the beer bottles and other beverages into big coolers filled with ice. It was if they were all at the ready and waiting for Rondell to give them their cue to begin work. As if there was no doubt that I would approve of his proposition.

The last pieces of Rondell's ploy to arrive were the "girls" he promised to help serve and shuttle drinks from the bar to the customers. Sonia Pitts, outfitted in very short jean shorts and a tight white T-shirt with lettering that read MYLES APART, Rondell's company, emblazoned across her chest, was one of the girls. Sonia was an ambitious young dancer who was part of a local troupe whose major production was the native re-creation shows for the cruise-boat crowd. The troupe also performed every Monday at the Tamarind Tree Resort manag-er's cocktail party and on Thursdays at the Lime House. The two were St. Pierre's two largest hotels.

Following Sonia inside and wearing the same Hooters-like outfit was, to my surprise, Betta Baptiste. I stopped in the middle of mixing a rum punch to look at her. Her eyes caught mine for an instant and she looked down and away. I finished pouring the rum punches into glasses. When I looked up she was at the bar, a tray in her hand waiting for me to put the glasses on her tray. "Paolo is with Mama," she said to me in a soft voice, referring to her young son.

I put the rum punch-filled glasses on her tray. She kept look-ing at me trying to gauge if I was judging her in any way on how she was dressed. I wasn't. She was a single mother. I understood that a young woman needs to work. Who was I to tell her what that work should be? "Well, that's good," I muttered.

Tubby shouted from the other end of the bar that we needed to make another round of rum punches. Betta quickly took the tray of drinks and began to pass them out to those who paid the admission for this impromptu fete. The rush at the bar on this night reminded me of those Friday happy hour two-dollar Mai Tai specials at Harry's Hula Hut on the Lower East Side in the mid-1990s—one of my first gigs.

Tony X had cranked up Lord Ram's biggest Carnival hit, "Ram de Back Door," on the fifteen-foot speakers. The music was so loud, I was sure the pounding bass was probably reverberating down Windy Hill Road and most likely could be heard all the way to Garrison Harbor. The music was acting like a siren call—a summoning to the Sporting Place to pay tribute to Lord Ram.

I was pulling cold Caribs from the ice chest and opening

them rapidly when there was a loud, collective clapping and a happy yell over the music. I looked up from my work to see that just about everyone was on their feet dancing, hands in the air and hips swaying.

I opened the Sporting Place with the idea that it would be the island's first sports bar. We had four televisions: two over the bar and two mounted on the back walls. The main draw, of course, was when there were international sporting events: Grand Slam tennis, the World Cup in soccer, the Olympics, NBA basketball and championship boxing along with, sadly in my opinion, the travesty of UFC fighting. But Peteys would come also to watch local West Indian cricket, soccer, and track and field. Once we were established, Tubby thought, and I slowly came to agree, maybe we should dedicate a night to music. We decided to do slow-jam Thursdays where couples could come and listen to soca, reggae and old-school R&B. There would be some dancing on those days, but we never packed the place like it was today, when bodies were right up on each other, moving to a heavy bass sound.

I could see Betta in the dancing crowd, holding her serving tray above her head, a smile on her face as she swayed her hips like no other. Sonia was right up against her moving her own hips, both girls coaxing the others to keep the flow going.

"We put on a true bacchanal," Rondell yelled to me as he pushed to the front of the bar, a self-satisfied smile on his face.

"Who was I to doubt you, Rondell?"

I looked back at Betta and noticed she had stopped dancing.

"Keep your mind on your work, old man," Tubby teased as he nudged me. "She out there reveling with the others. You know you can't belly up to her like we can."

I looked at him and then quickly looked back at Betta. I wasn't thinking of going belly-to-belly, back-to-back with Betta. No...something else caught my eye. I was tall, but I had to rise up on my toes to see better. I wanted to know if what I thought I saw—the pale, bald dome of someone I once knew, someone we both knew—talking to her. And a pale, bald dome would surely stand out in this crowd. I looked around, straining to see from my spot behind the bar, but now Betta and whoever she had been talking to were obscured by the others surrounding them. There was no sight of that pale head. Maybe I imagined it. I realized I hadn't eaten all day and had been so busy I didn't even think about drinking water despite the intense heat in the crowded bar. For a moment I felt lightheaded, my head spinning from both dehydration and hunger. Maybe it was a lack of nourishment that had me seeing things? I glanced through the crowd again. Betta was in the back, working now, gathering empty bottles and glasses.

"What's wrong?" Tubby asked, noticing the look on my face. "You good?"

"Yeah, I'm good." But I wasn't so sure. Sweat was running down my face. It was hot inside the bar, but not so hot that I should be dripping.

Tubby opened a bottle of water for me. "You need to drink," he said. He waved to the girls.

I took the bottle and sucked down the water even though I knew that wasn't what was making me dizzy. It was that I thought I saw a ghost. Someone I hadn't seen in years. That I was possibly seeing things had me off balance more than anything. But I never had that problem before. Maybe I needed my eyes checked. Or maybe it was my head that was a little off and that was troubling. I wasn't young. No, I was closer to being old than the opposite. And that was becoming a frequent thought in my head: my health, mortality, and death itself. They say age is just a number. I needed to keep my mind off my number.

When I looked out at the crowd again, I saw Betta, this time pushing through the crowd, a plate of food in her hands. She came up to the bar and put the plate in front of me—a barbecued chicken leg, cabbage and two grilled plantains. "Please eat," she said, looking up at me for just a moment before she disappeared into the crowd.

After the food I felt better. I forgot about what I thought I saw in the crowd and plowed through the evening without further incident.

It was a bit past midnight—the fete had been going since four in the afternoon. I saw Myles smiling broadly, happy with what he had accomplished, and chatting with three men. I gestured to him and he came behind the bar.

"We are wiped out here," I said. "The beer. The rum. It's all just about gone. When does this end?"

"No worries, Mr. Len," he answered cheerily. "I send Dickens down to the garage to pick up more."

"You want to keep this going? It's late, Rondell." I stared at him. "How are you going to make money if we keep pouring the drinks?"

"We start a cash bar now. Tell them what they paid up front was good only until midnight."

I stared at him. He was serious. I was about to tell him that it was over, that I was closing up, when Superintendent Keith McWilliams of the St. Pierre Police Department moved through the crowd. McWilliams leaned his imposing frame over the bar. "A word, Buonfiglio."

Tubby looked at me and I at him. We both wondered what this meant. I nodded and walked with him outside. He was in uniform: gray pants and a short-sleeved, gray button-down shirt with a pocket covered by his badge. The pants had red piping down the side seam and the sleeves of his shirt had thin red stripes. He carried his hat in his hand.

"Are we disturbing the peace, McWilliams?" I asked. McWilliams and I had a wary friendship. He knew that, since coming to St. Pierre, I was helping his fellow Peteys find justice in places his small department did not dwell. But I tried to work with McWilliams when I could. I knew he was a good man and St. Pierre was lucky to have him in charge. Still, we jabbed at each other whenever we crossed paths in mutual investigations—not that I would ever consider myself an investigator. He was a professional. I was nothing more than a bar owner out to do some good in my adopted home.

"No, Buonfiglio, a fete is a good thing under the circumstances. But I have news now and I know your place here is where most be today. I would like to relay that news, if you don't mind, before unnecessary rumors begin to circulate."

"You mean like Queen Sassy hitting Lord Ram over the head with a Dutch pot filled with a chicken fricassee?"

"Exactly, Mr. Len. We do not want that."

"Of course. I'll tell Myles to cut the music. Say what you need to say."

"Thank you, sir," he said, switching from referring to me by my last name to the more formal use of "Mr. Len."

We headed back inside. McWilliams stood behind the bar. People were curious and starting to wonder what the police superintendent was doing here. Myles was looking at me.

"Tell Tony to cut the music," I said to him.

He glanced at me and then at McWilliams. "Why?"

"Just do it," I said.

McWilliams gave Myles a look along with mine and he scampered off to the DJ setup in the back of the bar. We waited a moment and then the music was off. The bar was quiet except for some last laughs and chatter. Soon all eyes were on McWilliams.

"I would like your attention," McWilliams said to the crowd in his deep baritone. He waited a moment to continue. Almost immediately, the bar was silent. "I would like you here to be the first to know that at ten forty-nine this evening, the great Lord Ram passed from this life to the next. St. Pierre's most magnificent citizen is dead."

There were gasps from the crowd and then soft sobbing could be heard. "She kill he!" someone yelled from the back of the bar. That started more grumbling and shouts.

"Quiet now," McWilliams said. His face was stern as he surveyed the crowd, and the murmurs and chatter immediately stopped. "Lord Ram die from an accidental fall in his home. There will be more—official details—in the days to come along with the news of his funeral arrangements once they are determined by his family. Thank you for celebrating the great man. Please peacefully respect his memory and those of his loving survivors."

Almost before McWilliams finished speaking, people were starting to flow out of the bar. I knew McWilliams well enough by now to guess his motives. He hoped that after hearing his statement, when the word would quickly begin to spread about Ram's death, there would be no wild claims of murder or anything else. But McWilliams also understood that there would still be rumors and doubt. He was used to that on St. Pierre. Like anywhere else, the Peteys were often skeptical of their government and what they were told.

McWilliams put his hat on and came out from behind the bar. He nodded at me and left.


The bar was emptying. People were whispering, some were crying, and in less than ten minutes everyone except for Rondell Myles' crew were gone. Soon Tony X had his speakers packed up and loaded onto his truck. On his way out, Edison Aloo said he would come for his grill tomorrow. Myles came behind the bar with the cash box under his arm and a wad of Eastern Caribbean bills in his hand. He gave me the bills.

"If you think it's not enough, you just tell me, Mr. Len. Don't be shy. I always want to be fair."

"I'm sure you do, Rondell," I said.

But I wasn't planning on counting the money. After replenishing my beer and rum supply, whatever was left over would go to Lord Ram's favorite charity. If he didn't have one, I would find an appropriate donation.

I saw Sonia Pitts waiting by the door for Myles. I wondered for a moment if Myles was going to drop her off and then go home to his wife and children, but I knew better than to wonder too long on that. Betta came to the bar and looked at me. "You worked very hard," she said in her quiet voice.

I shrugged, remembering how much harder I used to go at it back in the days when I was hustling to make the bars I owned in Brooklyn work. "I'll drop Tubby at his place and then take you home," I said, coming out from behind the bar. Tubby's wife, Lysah, had come earlier with a friend. She left a couple of hours ago to be with their young children, taking Tubby's car. I could feel Tubby's eyes on me when I said I would take Betta home. Whenever he pushed on how I really felt about her, I told him it was nothing more than friendship. Tubby, however, was very intuitive—he was good at reading people. And I was an easy read. He knew there was more, that our history was about friendship, but underneath it all, there was a quiet, unstated and unconsummated yearning.

"No...no..." Betta said almost anxiously. She shook her head at me. "It out of your way, Leonard."

There—she said it. "Leonard." Only Betta could get away with that without a growl from me.

"I drop her at her home," Rondell Myles said as he moved, smiling, to join Sonia at the door. "She on the way. For you, Mr. Len, up on the East Road, is out of the way."

Betta looked at me and nodded. It was almost as if she was relieved that I was not going to drive her home. I wondered about that.

Tubby and I made sure the bar backlights remained on, but everything else, the overhead fans and the televisions, were off. The back deck door was locked, and we double-locked the front door on the way out. Tubby got into my Jeep. He sat back in his seat as I headed down Windy Hill, not saying anything. I'm sure he was as tired as I was, but that never stopped him from talking.

"Why McWilliams come and tell us that news?" he asked me after the silence.

I glanced at him. "Why?"

"That man not come to the fete to announce that Ram die unless he have a reason."

"Maybe he didn't want people to spread any unfounded rumors. I guess he wanted to make it clear that Lord Ram did not die, you know, under unusual circumstances."

"Now the people do the opposite, Mr. Len. And McWilliams know that. He come so we all can speculate more on how Lord Ram really die."

"What are you talking about? You need some sleep, Tubby."

"I need sleep, yes, but I know that McWilliams come to our place to put doubt in others' minds about how Ram die. Everyone there know that."

"See, now, Tubby, what am I supposed to think about that? McWilliams comes to tell us that Lord Ram died peacefully from natural causes, and you say he did that as kind of a…I don't know…subliminal message that he didn't."

"Subliminal…yes, that's the word. Exactly, Mr. Len."

"Are you trying to make my head explode?"

He hissed again at me. "How many years now you live here and still you don't understand us? You find out soon what I'm talking about."

"What's that supposed to mean?"

"Nothing, Mr. Len. It mean nothing. Just remember I talk to you here about this when you come to me for some help."

I looked at him and then back at the very dark road in front of me. I pulled up in front of Tubby's house. There was a light on outside near the entrance and I could see a light through the front window in his kitchen. His wife and children, I assumed, were sleeping. Tubby started to get out of the Jeep.

"Did you notice any other white men at the bar tonight?"

"White men? Like you?"

"Yeah like me, wiseass. I know we stand out in a crowd here. You would have noticed."

"Besides your pale skin, I only see that Marcus, from the

medical school, who date Corrine Tonsil who work at the hospital. He have very light skin and he not as pale as you. And he not white. Why you ask me this?"

"It doesn't matter," I said. "See you tomorrow. No rush. I expect we won't get any business till later."

He nodded. "With Ram's death, people done with celebrating until his funeral. But remember what I tell you about McWilliams."

"How can I forget?" I drove off, heading to East Road and my house.

# 2

My three dogs, the Spotted One, the Gray One, and especially the Puppy, were happy to see me after being away all day. I filled their bowls with dry food, and they went at it lustily as I poured myself a shot of rum. The rum was from Martinique and called *vieux*—or old. It went down as smoothly as cognac. I bought the bottle off a boat, a floating gourmet market of duty-free goods that avoided St. Pierre's import taxes. The boat serviced a few of the island's better restaurants and when I had the urge for, maybe, a big wedge of Parmigiano-Reggiano, or a few cans of good pomodori pelati to make sauce with, Tubby and I would skiff out to the boat. I had only a few shots left of the rum, reminding me that I needed to get out there the next time the boat was anchored offshore.

My back was achy and my knees were stiff. There was a time when a night like the one I had just experienced at the Sporting Place was an everyday occurrence. When I started up the bars in Brooklyn there was never a letup. I was on my feet twelve hours a day, at least six days a week, until the bars were established and I could hire others to fill those demanding roles. Since coming to St. Pierre, I had gotten complacent with my body and health. It's not that I was sickly or aging any faster; I just wasn't doing the things I knew I had to do to prolong what time would eventually take from me. For whatever reason, maybe it was just island life, but I had been slacking on my conditioning. I needed to keep up with my training—the Muay Thai I had once mastered, but now practiced only occasionally, usually with Tubby's urgings. He was eager to learn the art and I didn't mind working with him. My enthusiasm—and ambition—to stay fit, trim, in shape was waning. I had to try to reverse that.

I took my drink to my chair facing the dark Atlantic. I slumped down into it as the Gray One nuzzled his snout to my thigh and I stroked his head. Seeing that, the Puppy, a female, jumped up onto my lap. I noticed that water was spraying off my big picture window. It had been a stifling day and now it was raining. The sound of the rain was like hard, quick gun-shots as it pounded my roof. And then, within a minute or two, it stopped.

I knew I should have wondered what Tubby meant, what he said to me about McWilliams signaling the opposite of what he told the crowd, that Lord Ram's death wasn't an accident. But it was too much for my tired brain at that moment. Instead I thought about Betta and how she so quickly and uncharacteristically refused my offer to drive her home.

I'd known Betta Baptiste since I came to St. Pierre. I knew her when she had a small room on Front Street that she shared with a friend and entertained male visitors to the island. I happened to be one of those visitors when I first visited St. Pierre, back before I decided to make it my home. Betta was a temptation, there was no doubt about that; it was just that at the time, after leaving New York, and my family, that part of me was an empty hole. I would bring her to the restaurant at the Lime House Hotel for a steak dinner. It was the only restaurant on the island that served steak. And we would talk. Or I would talk, and she would listen, her eyes always probing mine. When I brought her back to her room, she would invite me in. She would ask me to stay with her. But I never did. Our quiet talks had revived the feelings of intimacy that had been dormant for too long, and I very much wanted to accept her offers. But I just couldn't. Not that way.

Not long after those weekly dinners, Betta met another man who became more to her than someone she simply entertained. He said he would take care of her, and he did. Until he didn't. Soon after they were married, he left her with child. The monthly checks he sent to her sustained her, so she never had to go back to the small room on Front Street. And they helped feed and clothe her son, their son, Paolo as if that, sending checks, was enough to make up for what he did to her.

There were just a few drops left in my glass. I finished them off and thought about how a man could just desert a woman he said he loved. How could he desert his young family. I wanted to judge, but knew I couldn't. Not after what I did to my own family.

The rain was gone. I could hear the waves down below. The usual white noise. The balm that helped me to sleep every night. And after the busy day, those waves did their job again.

# 3

I was even more stiff the next morning and knew that the only way to loosen up was to stretch and maybe go through some of the training exercises I used to do regularly when I was competing. I went outside to my backyard near the tamarind tree. I stretched out my lower back, quads, and hamstrings, flexed out my calves, and then grabbed my jump rope. I skipped rope for about ten minutes in one-minute intervals, and then got on the still-damp ground and did pushups on my knuckles. I was breathing hard, but it felt good to push. I followed with burpees as the dogs looked on curiously. It was a rare sight these days to see me workout like this. My closest neighbor was a quarter of a mile away, so I didn't have to worry about prying eyes, wondering what the old man next door was up to.

When I finished, my shirt was soaked through with sweat. I took it off and went inside, the ceiling fan whirring. That and the constant breeze from the Atlantic kept the house mostly cool. I had air conditioner units in each of the two bedrooms, but only used them when I had guests or when the humidity was off the charts. I gulped down water and made myself some breakfast.

I had the radio on in the kitchen as I fried two eggs. The morning disc jockey for St. Pierre's one local station spoke in a clear baritone. His delivery was slow, mannered, and filled with deliberate pauses to emphasize certain words. "*On...this...day,* we…all of us who call St. Pierre our home…mourn the death of a…*great*…man. This man…known to all as *Lord*…*Ram*, they say pass…peacefully. *We*…can only *hope*…that…is the case."

"We can only hope that is the case?" What did that mean? Was it more of that nonsense that Tubby was talking about on the way home, that McWilliams, though he announced that Ram died of an accidental fall, was inferring the opposite. I shook my head. I didn't want to think about that.

I tuned out what the disc jockey was saying as I gathered my food on a plate. The droning finally concluded and one of Lord Ram's big hits came on. This one was titled "Mr. Senior." I listened to the lyrics through the scratchy recording. The song must have been one of Lord Ram's earlier efforts. In it, he lamented how a young schoolgirl taunted and tempted a respectable man of the church with her "rosy cheeks and brown thighs." I knew that some of the earlier calypso tunes cloaked sexual innuendo in their lyrics. There was one hit, I knew, by a famous calypsonian about a doctor's "needle" that always "frightened" his female patients, fearing he wouldn't find the right place to "plunge it in." Lord Ram was a master at weaving sex innocently into his songs, and despite the church-going ways of many of his fans, those lyrics helped make him the legend he was.

I downed my eggs and coffee while listening. I heard my phone ding. I was getting a text. I got up, turned off the radio and checked to see what was written across my phone's screen.

The text was from Tubby. *Did you order a case of vermouth?* I stared at it. Vermouth? Was he kidding?

Using my fingers and thumbs, clumsily as usual, I typed: *Stop busting my balls.*

I refilled my mug with coffee and sipped as I stared out at the ocean. I knew I'd get a reaction from Tubby, and it took less than a minute. He was faster with his thumbs and fingers than I was.

*When I bust your balls, you feel it,* he typed. And then added.

*A box of Italian vermouth sit in front of our door this morning when I open up.*

I took a breath, staring at the words on my phone. Liquor was never delivered to the bar. I had to go to the harbor and get it off the ferry like I did the previous day when my cases of beer arrived. I ordered my liquor from a distributor in St. Vincent and occasionally used one in Barbados. But one thing I never ordered was vermouth. I know it was used as an ingredient in martinis, but we didn't do martinis at the Sporting Place. There were some visitors who came off yachts and heard about our place and the view of Garrison Harbor, and once in a while there would be a request for one. I could improvise with a vodka or gin martini, but if they wanted the real deal, I suggested they visit the Bouganvillea, the island's most exclusive lodging and restaurant. In either case, I didn't even have martini glasses stocked in the bar. So if I did make a mock "martini," it would have to be served in a Collins glass, the same that we used for rum punches, our biggest seller besides beer. We also had rocks glasses, wine glasses, and shot glasses. That was it. We didn't serve draught beer at the bar, but if someone wanted a glass with their bottle of beer, they would also have to have it in a Collins glass. I remember one man who was visiting from Brazil and insisted that he have a glass with his beer, that it was the only way he drank his beer. My job was to serve our customers and please them in any way, so I offered him a Collins glass. He shook his head. "Too big," he muttered. "The beer get warm in such a big glass." So I took out one of each size glass we had. He examined them, shrugged, and had his beer in a shot glass. I watched him pour from the bottle, refilling the small glass after almost every sip.

I wasn't sure how to respond to what Tubby had texted about the vermouth. Instead, I typed: *What are you doing there so early? We didn't have to open until this afternoon.*

I waited and then: *No school today. Busy at home.*

I knew Tubby well enough by now, just as he could read me

as well as anyone. I knew that since there was no school today, his three school-aged children and his two-year-old would all be home with his wife. She carried the heavy domestic load in the family. Tubby was industrious, as hard a worker as I've ever known, but I also knew when it came to family responsibilities, watching his children, whom he really adored, and setting rules and boundaries for them, was something he preferred to leave it to his wife. So with a full house today, he wanted out, and used any excuse to get it.

There wasn't much to say about the vermouth. We would figure it out later.

*I'll be there in a couple of hours,* I texted. I was sure business would be slow today while the news of Ram's death spread throughout the island. The fete was done. Now, for most Peteys, it was time to grieve until the next day came, when it would be time to celebrate again. And I was sure that day would come, though whether before or after his funeral, I had no idea.

# 4

Only Tubby's old Camry was in the Sporting Place's parking lot when I pulled in. We had no customers, but Tubby had the televisions on. He was looking at his phone, ignoring the golf tournament from New Jersey on some sports channel. I noticed the box on the bar. Tubby didn't look up from his phone. I peered into the box and then pulled out a few of the bottles. They were ornately labeled, each different from the others. Each bottle had a different colorful illustration depicting various Caribbean island scenes and people. I thought that unusual for Italian vermouth. You would think the illustrations would portray where the vermouth was made. The label and name of the vermouth were written in Italian.

"You know where it come from? Who bring this to us?" Tubby asked, looking up from his phone.

I thought I might know, but I didn't answer. I kept looking at the beautiful illustrations, the artwork that made-up the bottle's label. The one I held featured palm trees and a beach scene in vibrant colors. There was an old man sitting under a palm tree playing a guitar. Looking closely at it, the man could have been Lord Ram—or it could have been anyone. The name of the vermouth on the one I held, written in cursive script was *Bellezza Nera*, I looked at another bottle which featured the illustrated image of a black woman. It was a depiction of someone I knew. The resemblance was too true to be just a coincidence. Below the illustration was the scrawl of the artist's signature, which I could not quite make out. I put the bottles back in the box.

"Is this a joke?" I asked, looking at Tubby.

"What joke? I tell you, Mr. Len, this at our door when I open up."

"You didn't see who put it there?"

"I already tell you no, that's why I ask you. You okay? I know yesterday was busy, but something not right with you. What kind of drink vermouth that a man put a woman of color on the label?"

I couldn't answer that. I examined it more closely. The bottle itself was dark brown; I assumed the vermouth inside was dark red as others I knew, which meant it was sweet vermouth, as opposed to dry. White, dry vermouth was more commonly used in martinis, which is what I thought was in the box when Tubby texted me. Sweet vermouth was used in European specialty drinks, including the famous Negroni. We carried Cinzano in our bars in Brooklyn and during my last years there, the Negroni became a thing with some of the tattooed and pierced hipsters and their mates. Those same hipsters, from what I have been told, now come to the bars with strollers along with a new crowd of young hedge funders, IT specialists, and craft startup folks, all of them pouring into Bushwick and Williamsburg, raising property values and gentrifying the neighborhoods at warp speed.

I put the bottle back and sat on a stool. I looked around the Sporting Place. Not twelve hours earlier, it was as crowded as it had ever been. Now it was empty. The two overhead fans were buzzing, and Tubby had opened the screened windows to help air out the smell of spilled beer. Even though I'm sure he mopped up, that smell tended to linger. Being on the incline of Windy Hill Road, we were blessed with constant breezes from both the Caribbean, less than a mile away, and the Atlantic, only two miles in the other direction. Our view was of the

Caribbean and Garrison Harbor, a semi-circle at the port of St. Pierre's capital city. The blue water was surrounded by eighteenth- and nineteenth-century structures fortified with red-tiled roofs to absorb the elements. The view was one reason I choose this site to build on; after opening, I realized I needed an outdoor space to take advantage of that view. Tubby and I built a spacious deck in the rear of the bar that turned out to be a valuable investment. The deck and that view was now a stop for almost all the island tours, and it was listed on sites like Yelp and TripAdvisor. We would get a heads-up from tour guides or taxi drivers that they were bringing a group, and Tubby and I prepared for them with pitchers of rum punch and cold beer.

I heard the sound of tires on the gravel of our parking lot. I peered from my seat at the bar out the window to see a police car from St. Pierre's limited fleet. I watched as Keith McWilliams stepped out of the car, but dressed as a civilian in jeans and a dark blue polo shirt. He walked slowly to the bar's entrance and as he pushed open the door, Tubby got up from his seat at the table. He drifted back to the bar where I was, both of us curious about the visit from the out-of-uniform McWilliams.

"Morning, gentlemen," he said, giving us a slight smile. A smile, slight or not, was a rare sight on McWilliams. I only knew him as a very serious man. He had to project that in his role as the island's police superintendent. The smile usually only appeared when he was making fun of me, jabbing at my own earnestness in pretending to solve a crime, something I knew was really out of my league.

"Is it still morning, McWilliams?" I kidded.

He glanced at the watch on his wrist. "Ahh, you are correct, Mr. Buonfiglio, we have passed midday and are now into the afternoon hours."

"I see you are off-duty. Or are you?"

"Oh yes, sir," he said. "Absolutely off-duty. The official vehicle is my only means of transportation today. My wife took the family car. She and her mother wanted to go pay their respects over at Belmont Farms."

I looked at Tubby. He nodded. "The place where Lord Ram born," Tubby said. "I know many go there today. I hope they clear the road."

"We have a patrol there all day. Officers are there to maintain proper traffic guidance," McWilliams said.

Belmont Farms was on the northeast corner of St. Pierre. I had driven past it many times on East Road, the mostly narrow two-lane road that encircled the twenty-two-square-mile island and connected with West Road at the roundabout in Garrison. When I first arrived on St. Pierre, I took an island tour with Rawle Johns, a man who was said to be the island's best tour guide. The tour took pretty much all day. Johns, a very big man with a soft high tenor voice, pointed out all the places of interest, including Belmont Farms. We pulled over in his van and got out to look at the stone memorial claiming the spot as where the great Lord Ram, whose given name was Orandy David, was born. Johns told me that Ram was born in a shack with nine other children. His "God-given" talent helped him break the cycle of poverty and made him an international calypso star. That was the popular legend of Lord Ram's rise to fame.

John's words were still fresh in my mind as I thought about that tour several years ago. The man was an ambassador for the island, always presenting it in the best light when he conducted his tours. But like Lord Ram, Johns was also now gone. Unlike Ram, he did not go peacefully. Thinking about Johns, I had a feeling McWilliams was here on business, official or not. But I played along with the charade. "What can we get you this afternoon?"

"I'm sure you must have a few Caribs left from yesterday's fete," he said. "And please join me."

I bent down to the stocked refrigerator. We were rarely without St. Pierre's favorite local beer. I took two bottles and opened one for him and one for me. He looked at me as he lifted the beer. He went to his pocket with his other hand and pulled out a few EC bills. I waved them away.

"No, I insist. I am here on my own time."

"Your own time or not, these are on me," I said.

He nodded. "Can we go enjoy the view? It's a beautiful afternoon, despite the sadness in the air."

I looked back at Tubby, who was watching the interaction with interest.

"We can." I came around from the back of the bar and the two of us went out to the deck. McWilliams closed the screen door and looked back at Tubby.

"I would like to discuss something with you that is very sensitive, Buonfiglio. Something you must not discuss with anyone else."

My eyes went back from the deck to the bar. I shook my head. "Tubby works with me, McWilliams. Here and elsewhere. And whether you want this to be kept a secret or not, Tubby will find out what we discussed. Better you let me talk to him confidentially than have him hear whatever you have to tell me from secondhand sources."

He sipped from the bottle. He was hesitant. "I know Mr. Levett is an honorable man. He has done very well here, still..."

"I trust Tubby like a brother, McWilliams. Don't talk to me if you can't accept that he will know as well."

He took a breath and another sip and then nodded. "So be it."

I waited for him to speak. There was a nice breeze coming off the harbor. It was summer and the rainy season on St. Pierre, but that just meant there was a bit more humidity than normal and that each day we could expect some rain that could last one minute or half a day. While the rest of the Caribbean waded cautiously through hurricane season, St. Pierre was below what was considered the hurricane belt. That didn't mean there was no chance. I had heard stories of the devastation of a hurricane that did hit the island in 1984, but that was the last one.

"Mr. Buonfiglio, I usually warn you off of meddling in affairs that concern the law here on St. Pierre," McWilliams finally said. "But now I must do the opposite. I am here to ask that you get involved in something that I cannot. Or let me say, I will not."

I looked at him. He was right. I didn't expect this. The few times I've been involved in criminal matters, he would try to dissuade me from pursuing them. He was in charge of law and order on St. Pierre, and wanted to keep it that way. Outside interference was not welcome, and although our relationship was checkered, it was not hostile. That was not McWilliams' way. He was low-key yet commanding. He didn't need to bark at the small fleet of officers he had, or at anyone really. He just did his job as best he could and that meant keeping outsiders like me from getting into his business.

"I came here last night to tell the people who were at the fete that Lord Ram died. But I did not want to give out the specific circumstances of his death beyond what I said about him his falling. I didn't want to add fuel to the fire of gossip and innuendo. I wanted to reassure them that there was no foul play involved in the man's death. As you know, there really is no greater figure to represent St. Pierre than Lord Ram. His status as an international star gives all of us so much pride. We are a tiny nation and our accomplishments on the world stage are negligible. But not so with Lord Ram. He was a calypso superstar, known worldwide. And he is—was one of ours."

He paused to take a sip from the beer and stare out at the harbor. I still was not sure what he was trying to say but, remembering that Tubby immediately understood the mixed messaging of McWilliams' little speech the night before, I was starting to get an idea.

"What were the specific circumstances of his death, McWilliams. Can you tell me?"

He nodded at my question. "The official statement is that he die from a blow to his head from a fall in his kitchen. The man was ninety-five; everyone know Ram not what he was. That he had become feeble the past few years. Some even questioned his state of mind. Had dementia taken over to the point where he could not function normally? We do not know that and there will be no autopsy. It is true that those with dementia have trouble walking, their balance not quite right. My wife's father suffered from it until his death. I see what it do to him. It is very plausible that Lord Ram trip over his own feet in his kitchen, smash his skull against the floor or kitchen counter, and the hemorrhaging in the brain kill him."

"Sounds plausible to me." I was waiting for the other theory that he was pondering, and I knew was coming.

"On the other hand, the cerebral hemorrhage could have been induced by a very strong blow to the head. Maybe Lord Ram did not trip over his own feet? Maybe someone take something hard and smash his skull with it?"

McWilliams made sure to look hard at me when he said those words. It was obvious he wanted me to believe that this was actually what happened without stating it.

"You're the investigator, McWilliams. Have you surveyed the crime scene, dusted the place for fingerprints? Found that blunt object that might have killed him? Seen any evidence that maybe Lord Ram did not die from a fall? And to tell the truth, even if the man fell and cracked his skull, I wouldn't consider that a peaceful death, would you? To me, dying peacefully means you go to bed, close your eyes and it's over. Am I wrong?"

He grinned. "I never use those words," he said. "I never say 'peaceful.'"

"No, but you kind of implied it last night."

"Maybe so." He smiled at me. "And you are not wrong, Mr. Buonfiglio. That is how we all want to go when the time come. We all want to die peaceful."

"Yeah, when the time comes." We looked at each other. "But you are telling me this why?"

"I'm not sure why, really. Yes, I am the investigator as you say. I have surveyed the crime scene. No, there was no dusting of fingerprints. The medical examiner confirmed that he die from trauma to the brain. Bleeding. But how this happen was not pursued further. And I find no evidence of a blunt object or anything else. Yet my years have taught me many things. This tell me that I'm not so sure the death an accident." He pointed to his stomach...or in this case, I think he meant his gut. "And I'm here talking to you because, as far as those who I work for, the citizenship of St. Pierre and its government, this is a closed case. Lord Ram is dead. He will be celebrated as the great local hero and that will be the end of it."

"And again I ask, McWilliams, what does this all have to do with me?"

He was searching for words. I could tell he was uncomfortable asking and telling me all this. "I know we've had our little differences the past few years when you...hmm...offer your help to others here. But despite our differences, I've come to admire your methods. I think we've developed an understanding. You know the boundaries and haven't pushed beyond them."

"Yeah, well, I grew up with some respect for law enforcement. You do a good job here, McWilliams. And I really don't try to get into your business. This is my business." I gestured to the bar. "The other stuff, the less I have to deal with, the better. It's not something I want or ask for. Things seem to just happen."

"No, you do not ask for it. I believe you. Which is the purpose of my visit here. I am asking you now to do what I cannot. I cannot leave this as is. If there was a wrong done and I do not pursue it, how do I look my children and grandchildren, if I ever see them now that they live in London, in the eye? How do I sleep at night knowing there was an injustice not addressed? Even if it is not I who investigates, at least I will know I did

41

what I could."

"Meaning using me to do your work?"

"I ask it as a favor, nothing more."

"Uh-huh, and if find out something. That there was injustice here. Will it be addressed?"

He looked out at the harbor. "Let me just say, it will put my mind in a different place. I promise nothing more."

I marveled at his calm, steady tone. He never showed any real emotion, though he was admitting that he was very uncomfortable with the official results of the inquiry into Lord Ram's death. I thought for a moment about what he was asking me. I got involved in mostly small-time disputes or crimes, nothing as high-profile as this. What was I becoming here on St. Pierre that the superintendent of police would call on me to ask me to help solve a crime? Even in the few cases I did resolve I always thought I just stumbled on answers and results. I never ever believed that I had the skills of an investigator. And I wasn't lying when I said I did not want them—that all I really wanted was to run my bar.

"Do you really think I can help you in any way? I'm not a cop. I'm not a detective. I don't have any of the resources you have. What can I do that you can't?"

He gulped down most of the remains of his beer. He waited a moment and then burped. "Excuse me, Mr. Buonfiglio." He stood up.

I stood up with him. Apparently the meeting was over. He wasn't going to answer my last question. He had asked what he came to ask. It was up to me now to decide what to do.

"If you insist, I have my wife make curry goat for you. She is an excellent cook." He grinned. He was making fun of how the women on St. Pierre, when they want my help on a sensitive matter, bring me one of their home-cooked specialties.

"Don't think I won't, McWilliams. I know of her stellar cooking reputation, and I see you have not gone unfed."

He laughed out loud this time. He went into his pocket before we headed back inside to the bar and handed me a business card. "On the other side," he said. "My personal cell phone number. You call and we can arrange to talk somewhere, maybe at your place. Some resources can be arranged. It won't hurt to ask. Anything you learn, please come to me first. I trust your discretion with this."

"Alright, McWilliams." I looked at the card as I walked with him back into the bar. Tubby's eyes were boring into us.

"Good day all. My regards to your wife, Mr. Levett," he said to Tubby and then walked out into the bright sun toward his car.

# 5

"This about Ram and how he die?" was the first thing Tubby said to me once McWilliams' police cruiser pulled out of the parking lot.

"You ask me, Tubby, when you already know?"

"I tell you so. But why that man come in here to talk to you about it? That is the mystery."

I smiled. "And maybe I'll keep it a mystery."

He sucked through his teeth.

"Now McWilliams want your help? That why he come here in civilian clothes?"

"You know more than I do, Tubby. Not that I'm surprised."

"Maybe so, but what I don't know is why he ask you for help when you a clueless senior in these matters."

"What matters are you referring to? And stop with the senior routine. You know I can still roundhouse my foot up your ass before you even think to block it."

"That change soon enough. I'm working on that. And the matters I refer to are the matters that concern people from this island. That involve those who born here and know the ways we do things."

"You never stopped me from involving myself in those matters before, Tubby."

He looked at me. "You know I did. I don't know why you do these other things. We have a nice bar here that people come to. Why you need to think you have to prove yourself beyond that?"

I thought about what he said. Was that really what I was doing? Was I trying to prove that I was someone different than who I am? Or was it something else? Maybe it was a feeling or an obligation I thought I had. Or was it a sense of guilt over what had become of my life since that June day several years ago? Of what happened that day and what it did to me? To my family? Either way, I couldn't just say no to the superintendent of police when he was enlisting my help. And who knew, maybe one day he would return the favor.

"McWilliams asked me nicely," I said. "How could I refuse?"

That brought on another hiss from Tubby.

"Be careful with this, Mr. Len," Tubby said now with seriousness. "We talking Lord Ram."

"Yeah, I know that, and that's why you're gonna help me, aren't you?"

"Help you? Without me, you like that Pink Panther."

"What Pink Panther?"

"I forget he name. The one who bumble all the time trying to solve the crimes."

"Oh yeah, him. What was his name?" I Googled on my phone. "Clouseau, Inspector Clouseau."

Tubby laughed. "You better not be like Clouseau on this."

"Well, if you give me a little clue about where to start digging, Tubby..."

"You always must start with the young wife. Don't the cops first go to the husband of the murdered wife?"

"You watch too much *Law &Order*, Tubby. I thought you'd tell me something I don't know. And what am I supposed to do, just go interrogate her? This is Queen Sassy we're talking about. Why would she talk to me?"

"No one say you have to help the man. Tell him no. That the best thing in all this. Leave it alone."

Why couldn't I leave it alone? Why did I feel a sense of obligation to McWilliams? And a feeling that if there was a wrong done, it should be exposed? But I had no idea how to go about it. I really didn't need this now. Things had been running smoothly at the bar. My life, though mundane, was cruising along without incident. I kind of liked it that way.

Tubby held up one of those bottles of vermouth. He was staring at the label. "Someone know our island paint this picture," he said as he looked at the illustration on the label.

"Yeah, seems so."

"But what we supposed to do with this stuff?"

I got up from the table where I was sitting. "Here, let me show you."


I searched under the bar where the few bottles we rarely used were kept. I knew I had a bottle of Campari there. I think I bought it at one of the duty-free shops in Barbados on a trip back to New York a few years ago. I really don't know why I did. Campari was not a desired beverage on this particular tropical island. I found it buried behind a bottle of ouzo that I also never used. The bottle was dusty and the top was sticky.

"That look a little too sweet, Mr. Len," Tubby said, examining the bottle of Campari and the bright red liquid inside.

"It does, doesn't it," I said, knowing that it was the opposite of sweet.

I opened one of the bottles, put my nose to the top, and sniffed. My sense of smell was acute, maybe too much so. If someone was smoking a cigarette two blocks away, I knew. It was both a godsend—it helped in my cooking and enhanced my sense of taste—and a curse, for obvious reasons. What I sniffed out of the bottle smelled like what I remembered as vermouth. This one had a rich, agricultural fragrance. I had no idea what ingredients went into the making of vermouth, but this Bellezza Nera was extremely floral. I looked again at the label. In the fine print, it mentioned that Bergamo was its place of origin. Besides the obvious big cities like Rome, Florence, Venice, Naples, Milan and Palermo, I wasn't familiar with all the many cities and towns of Italy. But I did know of Bergamo. I knew that Betta received her monthly checks from there. And that made me pause.

"Now what you do?" Tubby asked. "You drink that on the rocks? Straight? We never even have the stuff when I work at the Yacht Club."

The Yacht Club was just a small bar off the harbor and close to one of the adjacent lagoons. And the boats that came and docked at the lagoon were very rarely yachts. Yet Sam Suraj, who owned the bar, called the place the St. Pierre Yacht Club, despite that it was nothing like a yacht club.

"Patience, my good friend," I said. "Let me display the skills I had as a bartender so many years ago." I filled a shaker with ice, added an ounce of the Campari, an ounce of the sweet vermouth, and grabbed a bottle of Beefeater gin, adding an ounce of that to the mix. I shook it all up and poured into one of our rocks glasses. The color was deep red.

"Is that it?" Tubby asked, reaching for it.

I pushed his hand away. "Wait." I looked in the small refrigerator behind the bar. I knew we had oranges in there, as we sometimes used them in rum punches. These oranges were green and very thick-skinned, littered with pits, kind of a reflection of the island where they were grown. I cut off a slice, picked out the pits, and added it to the drink. "Now you can try it."

Tubby took the drink and sipped. He grimaced and almost immediately spit it out. "How a man drink something so bitter?"

"Many men do, Tubby. And women too. It's a Negroni."

"Yeah, Mr. Len, only a bitter man like you would enjoy such a drink."

I laughed. "Despite my nature, Tubby, the Negroni is not my preferred cocktail."

"You think we sell this here on St. Pierre? Never." He filled a glass with water and rinsed it in his mouth to wash out the taste.

"You are right, Tubby. We won't. But then what do we do with all that vermouth?"

"Anything but make a drink such as this."

# 6

The next day, an apartment complex-sized cruise boat happened to find its way to Garrison Harbor. Within minutes, Harold Boothe's army of taxi drivers pounced on the cruisers who were shuttled off the big boat and onto the island. The savvy drivers sold half-day and full-day tours of the island. Both options offered them one of the best views on St. Pierre. And along with that view, the island's best rum punch. So, despite the continual mourning of the death of Lord Ram, we were very busy at the Sporting Place.

Once the cruisers had their drink and their photo-ops and returned to their big boat and off to the next island, the bar cleared out. I told Tubby to go home and have dinner with his family, something I knew was a rare occurrence. He protested, but not very strongly, agreeing that it was probably the right thing to do. So I was left alone to close the place. Before shutting down the bar's lights, I saw the case of vermouth lying there. With the exception of the bottle I had already opened, the one with the illustration of the man playing the guitar on the beach that I left front and center among the other bottles behind the bar, I grabbed the box and carried it into the small office behind the bar.

When I got into my Jeep and started it, the jazz playlist was still queued on my phone and immediately went to the Bluetooth. I heard the jingling of piano keys. I glanced at the screen of my phone that I had on the mount in the Jeep. The display read "How Could You Do a Thing Like That to Me," *Erroll Garner, The Complete Concert by the Sea.* Listening to the great jazz pianist had me taking a slight detour before going home. At the roundabout, I went due north up a narrow road. I slowed my Jeep as I approached the house—Betta's house. It was where she lived now with her young son, Paolo.

From a distance, I noticed there were lights on inside. It was almost midnight. Why wasn't the house dark? I pulled up in front, leaving the Jeep to idle, and stared at the little house. I was tempted to get out and knock. To see Betta. To ask why she wasn't asleep. Could she be reading? On her laptop? She could be doing anything, and none of it was my business. I saw shadows in the lights from my seat. Not the shadow of just one person. Not the shadow of one woman and one small child. Multiple shadows. I strained to try to see more but couldn't. Again, what business was that of mine? She was just a friend I cared about. Nothing more. That's what I told myself as I quickly pulled away, got back to the roundabout, and took East Road home.

I was normally an early riser, but for the last few months I was up even earlier thanks to the whining of the Puppy, who demanded some pre-sunrise attention. I got the puppy from a litter belonging to a nutmeg and cocoa farmer, Edvin Petit, who was a Sunday afternoon regular at the Sporting Place. Petit would come to the bar alone, leaving his wife and many children and grandchildren at home, to watch golf while very slowly sipping a Carib beer. If golf was not on, he would ask if I could switch one of the televisions to another sport, like bowling, darts, or even that thing called cornhole. He enjoyed sports with snail-like paces. Anything that was too frenetic—

American football, the NBA, or UFC crap—he would plead for me to change the channel. One Sunday he mentioned that his mongrel just had a litter. When I expressed interest in possibly taking one of the pups off his hands, he smiled, which was a rare occurrence for him. He told me I could take any or all of them. He had enough around his farm. I went over to his farm soon after and took a look at all the pups. I quickly narrowed it down to the two with brown coats. When I learned that one of the little ones I was eyeing was female, my decision was an easy one. Petit pleaded with me to take a few of the others, but I already had two dogs, both male. I once had a female mutt with a brown coat. I liked that dog very much and thought of her often. She was fiercer and more loyal than the males. I could never replace the brown one who was gone, but this little one with a copper-colored coat, I hoped, would end up being just as loyal. Just as fierce.

The Puppy was growing quickly. Every morning I lifted her up and off me; I had noticed that she was getting a little heavy for this routine. The other dogs, the Gray One and the Spotted One, didn't bother with me like the Puppy. They knew the routine. After cleaning up and making coffee, I would get around to filling their bowls with kibble. It was then they would show up from their lazy meanderings around my small lawn.

I heard barking while I was getting dressed. The only time the dogs barked was when someone was at my door, which wasn't often. I quickly pulled on a T-shirt and headed out of my bedroom to the front door, nudging the dogs gently away so they wouldn't scare whoever was there. It was later than usual for me to be getting up. I opened the door and was surprised at the sight of a girl standing on the other side, holding an aluminum tray. She was most likely my daughter's age, or maybe even a couple of years younger. I might have seen her before somewhere, but I didn't think so. Idling on the road in front of my house was a big black SUV with dark-tinted windows. Her ride, I assumed.

"Mr. Len?" she asked. Her voice matched her age. I guessed mid-to-late teens.

"The one and only," I said, and seeing that she was just a kid, I reined in my usual contempt at hearing a stranger address me that way. I'd been on the island going on close to ten years and was addressed as Mr. Len pretty much since I arrived despite my many protestations to be called something else.

"I brought you pone," the girl said, holding out the tray.

I looked at her. She looked at me. She had wide dark eyes. I detected just the slightest teasing smile on her face at what she said. "You brought me pone?"

"Uh-huh," she said, that same smile intact. She *was* teasing me. "Cassava pone."

"And why are you bringing me cassava pone?" I asked.

"Because my mother told me to," she said.

"And who is your mother?" I asked.

"Kindra Alexis," she said.

My face was a question mark. I didn't know a Kindra Alexis.

"Queen Sassy," she said and then waited for that to sink in.

It wasn't early, but it was too early for me to comprehend what was going on now.

"Queen Sassy made cassava pone for me?"

"Of course she didn't make it for you. My mom doesn't cook. But someone, I think one of my aunts, brought it when everyone came to pay their respects. She told me to bring it to you. I'm Teesha."

"And you are Queen Sassy's daughter?"

"Yes, Mr. Len."

I shrugged and reached for the tray. I did like cassava pone but taking it would mean something else. It would mean Queen Sassy, or rather, Kindra Alexis, wanted something in return. I knew the pattern. If someone wanted my help, the best way to get it was a food offering. I could refuse it, but I hadn't had breakfast and I was getting hungry. Cassava pone would be the perfect complement to the dark coffee I was about to brew, a small batch straight from the mountains of the nearby island of St. Lucia. In a way, this was my good fortune. Now I had an in to see Queen Sassy.

"Thank you, Teesha, and tell your mother I appreciate it. Do you know why she is giving me the pone?"

She laughed again and ignored my question because the Puppy had made an appearance around my ankles. "Ohh, how cute, "she said, bending to her knees to pet the Puppy. "I love dogs," she said, looking up at me now with a dazzling toothy smile.

"She's a charmer," I said, and then realized that this young girl's father had just died. From her cheery mood, she didn't seem to be grieving. Still, I couldn't forget my manners. "And my condolences on your father's passing to you and your mother."

She looked up at me and shrugged. "He was old," she said to me, not looking up from the Puppy whom she continued to pet.

He was old? That was it. You get old and you die. That was the expectation. I didn't know how to respond to her. But he was old, I thought. What did I remember them saying, that he was ninety-five or ninety-six when he died? This girl, his daughter, couldn't have been more than seventeen, which meant she was conceived when Ram was around eighty. I heard on the radio that Ram had many children, grandchildren, and great-grandchildren. He wasn't just a prolific songsmith, I thought to myself, while trying to think about what it must be like becoming a new father at eighty.

Done with the Puppy, she stood up and gave me another smile. "Yeah, okay, I should go now. See ya, Mr. Len."

I watched as she practically skipped to where that black SUV was waiting for her. I watched until she got in and the car disappeared down the road before going back inside the house.

Back inside, I got the coffee going, and opened up the tray and had a look at my breakfast. I knew that a sweet dessert wasn't the best way to start my day, but I was feeling lazy and didn't want to make a healthy but disgusting protein shake or eggs. I dished some of the pone onto a plate and poured a cup of black coffee. I sat in my chair facing the big picture window overlooking the Atlantic. The cassava pone was delicious, but I knew it came at a cost. What would Lord Ram's widow want with me? I remembered what Tubby said about how to proceed on this and as usual, he was correct. First go to the widow, he had said. It seemed that now she had first come to me.

# 7

The Sporting Place parking lot was full, which meant that there were already cars in the three spots. I thought about that often and sometimes Tubby did too. We wondered if maybe we should mark one of the spots "reserved for owner," but we never did and that was probably for the best. So on this day and others, I had to park my Jeep up the hill and walk down. I was surprised at the crowd at the bar. It was just past noon on a Friday. I guess after word got out about the fete and how we handled it, our reputation on the island, and with the tour guides who worked the cruisers, was further burnished. We weren't really equipped for large crowds. If this continued, we would have to make some changes, get more help, something. Seeing the crowd, I now regretted my breakfast choice. I needed something more substantial to get through this day.

"Cruise boat in and you late like this?" Tubby scolded.

"Who knew?" I responded, quickly, going back behind the bar to help out.

"You the one who arranged with Myles for that fete. What you expect now? People think we put on a fete every night."

"Should we call Mike?"

"No Mike tonight. He bring his son to a football match in St. Vincent."

"Malcolm? In St. Vincent?" I was slow catching on.

"Malcolm the best at his age on the island. Mike brings him

55

to matches all over. Schools in the States and the UK want him to come to their universities. I know a school in North Carolina, Mike say, want him to come play. Offer him a scholarship. He make a decision soon."

Before I could think, I blurted, "Same with my son, Luke. The colleges are contacting him already and he's just a junior in high school." I regretted my words as soon as I said them. A father sometimes can't control his tongue when talking about the exploits of his offspring.

"This I know. You tell me so." This wasn't the first time he heard me boasting about my son's athletic abilities.

When Kathleen, my ex-wife, remarried, she moved out of the Bronx to live with her new husband, a man named Richard, on Long Island. I always wanted Luke to play baseball, but apparently on Long Island lacrosse is a bigger deal than baseball and he got hooked on the sport. "Ever watch that game?"

"We a sports bar here. I see everything even when they show the poker tournaments. People sitting around a table looking at cards. How that a sport, I'll never understand. Lacrosse? I don't understand that either."

"Yeah, you and me both, Tubby. But if lacrosse gets Luke a scholarship, let's just say that I love that game." I was joking with Tubby, but this talk wasn't making me feel good at all. I should have kept my mouth shut about my son, but I couldn't help myself, I had to let it out. Bragging on Luke's lacrosse exploits led to a bad place in my head. Mike was with his son on these outings, and here I was, thousands of miles away, tending bar, while my son's stepdad was doing my job.

Tubby could see the shift in my mood. I was relieved when a party from another newly docked cruise boat crowded the bar, asking for more alcohol.

I wasn't sure what cruise boat docked at Garrison Harbor, but it must be an even bigger one than had anchored the day before. I looked around the bar while flipping open bottle tops of Caribs and Heinekens. There was a certain uniform among the cruise-boat crowd. Men wore baggy shorts and oversized T-shirts. And the wives of these men, or groups of women on vacation, had almost identical uniforms. They all piled in, forming little groups both in the bar and out on the deck.

To help ease the flow and limit making change, Tubby and I made a deal with Harold Boothe. When the drivers picked up the cruisers, they paid a flat fee for a meal at a rotating number of island restaurants, and a beer or a rum punch at my place. That eased the flow of having to make change at the bar or deal with credit or debit cards. But sometimes a rowdy cruiser would exceed the one-drink minimum. On this day, they were in a drinking mood—one was just not enough.

While I was in the middle of opening six bottles of Caribs for a table of cruisers outside, Tubby nudged me. "I need your help on something here," he said.

Not looking up, I said, "What do you need?"

"A man…these men…they want a special drink. Something I never make here. They complain. I want to tell them off…and you know that something I don't like to do to a customer. Something bad here."

"What do you mean, bad?" I looked up now. Tubby turned in the direction of two men sitting at the bar. Right away I knew these men were not from the cruise boat. And they didn't look like they were on a leisurely sail of the Grenadines either. Both men were scowling, watching me talk with Tubby. "Let me see what they want. Take over for me."

We switched places behind the bar and Tubby went to work opening those beer bottles while I moved in front of the two men. One of the men was bald—or he shaved his head. He made up for the lack of hair on his head with the long thick black beard he sported. The other man had a buzz cut around the lower part of his dome and gelled platinum hair above. Both were pasty-skinned, as if they hadn't seen the sun in a long time, rare for visitors to the Caribbean. Earring studs pierced their earlobes, and their arms and necks were decorated with a kaleidoscope of colorful tattoos. One of them wore a black T-shirt, the other a white one. They both had prominent biceps, which I noticed they kept flexed in their tight tees. "Is there a problem here? Can I help you gentlemen?"

"No problem," White T-shirt said with a creepy smile and a thick accent I couldn't place. "I just ask your helper to make me an Americano. He stupid and don't know." He pointed to Tubby, who glared back at the man.

"See, first off you are wrong, sir. That man is not my helper, he is my partner. And don't call him stupid." I gave him a hard stare.

White T-shirt met my gaze, looked at his buddy, and then smiled. "My apology," he said. "I leave him big tip."

In New York, when things got busy at our bars, we hired security to keep an eye on the crowd to make sure there were no serious altercations. Here I never ever thought about something like that. I didn't want any trouble, so I ignored his crack. I knew now why Tubby's alarm went off. There was a dangerous hostility coming from these two men.

"You make an Americano?" White T-shirt asked.

I had made the drink many times while tending bar in New York, but never here in St. Pierre. And I could not even recall a request for it. This man's request came out as more of a command, or even a demand. And commands or demands never sat well with me, dating back to my brief tour as a Marine.

"I don't know, fellas," I said. "I'm not sure we carry the ingredients to make an Americano." We did, but I didn't want to broadcast that. Not after the way the guy insulted Tubby. He was getting no favors from me.

Black T-shirt pointed behind me. I turned. And there it was, the bottle of sweet vermouth that arrived unexpectedly a few days ago. I was almost caught, but luckily the one bottle of Campari I had, an essential in the making of an Americano, was not on display behind the bar. I had put it back on the shelf under the bar near my feet after making Tubby that Negroni the previous day.

"Yeah, I don't really know why that's there," I said. "Either way, I don't have any Campari or Italian bitters like that, so you guys are out of luck."

Both now stared at me. They didn't look happy. They had bottles of Carib in front of them that were barely touched "What's this shit?" White T-shirt said, lifting up the bottle.

"Yeah, well, it's an acquired taste," I said, laughing off their insult. Carib wasn't the best beer I ever had, but it was our beer and I had long ago learned to like it. But here I was going to act like I was with them on it. I would do whatever it took to deflect their obvious hostility, give them what they wanted and get them out of here. "The other alternative is Heineken."

Black T-shirt nodded and then smiled. "No one tell us we can have Heineken," he said, glancing at Tubby. "Give us Heineken. And please, may I see." He pointed behind me to the bottle of vermouth.

I hesitated. I really didn't want to give him anything.

"The bottle," he said, this time with a weak smile.

"This bottle?" I pointed instead to a bottle of Johnny Walker Red next to the vermouth.

"No, other one."

I had no choice but to point to the bottle of vermouth. "This?"

"Yes. I look please."

I shrugged, took the Bellezza Nera from the shelf behind me and handed it to Black T-shirt.

He showed it to his companion. I watched them as they seemed to study the bottle. They were muttering in a language I couldn't identify. I saw Black T-shirt run his fingers over the label. He looked at me and handed it back. I put the bottle where it had been behind me thinking that I should just keep it underneath the bar on the shelf below, near the Campari and ouzo, where no one would see it, but I wanted to show off that gorgeous label and its obvious St. Pierre similarities.

"Where you get this bottle?" Black T-shirt asked me.

Was I going to tell him a case of the stuff arrived unannounced at my bar the other day? I didn't think so.

"From my usual distributor. Where I get all my booze."

"Why if you can't make drink did you get from distributor?"

He had me there. Now I had to scramble for more bullshit.

"I don't know. Sometimes we buy stuff we don't need. Sometimes we get stuff by accident. And, to be honest, I like the label. It's a nice package. Reminds me of St. Pierre."

The two men smiled at each other. "Oh, you like label?"

"Yeah."

"Who your distributor?" White T-shirt asked.

I had had enough of this. There were customers lining up deep at the bar. Tubby was getting overwhelmed. I had to get back to him and others.

"Fellas, I got work to do here." I gestured to the crowd. I took away the Caribs they hardly touched and opened two Heinekens. "Enjoy," I said and then turned my attention to a group of cruisers squeezing up to the bar. But I could feel their eyes on me. I glanced at them every now and then to see them just sitting there talking to each other in their own language, sipping from the green Heineken bottles, looking me over, then glancing at the bottle of Bellezza Nera. Finally, after finishing their beers, they got up and left. My eyes followed them out the door. I wanted to go see how they got here, but I was in the middle of pouring rum punches for another group from the cruise boat. When I finished, I went to the door to see if I could catch the two men leaving, but there was no sign of them. They were gone.

The afternoon and early evening went by quickly, which was usually the case when it was busy. By later that night the bar had cleared out. The cruisers were back on their hideous boat, probably heading for Tobago. Tubby and I were starting to close up.

"Mr. Len, got a minute?" a man I recognized but whose name I did not know asked as he planted himself on a stool at the bar.

"We're just closing up," I replied.

The man had short graying hair and wore glasses. He was dressed in a blue and white striped polo shirt and beige khakis. "I understand. I'm Charles Rose. I represent Kindra Alexis."

I drew a blank on the name. "Queen Sassy. I believe you were given a cassava pone earlier today by her lovely daughter," Rose said.

I remembered now. Sassy's daughter. Teesha, had mentioned her mother's given name. "You can thank her and tell her it was delicious."

"She would like to speak with you, Mr. Len," he said with an almost shy smile.

Most on St. Pierre and other Caribbean islands would jump at the chance for an audience with the Queen of Calypso. I wasn't being blasé by not showing any enthusiasm for the meeting. I was just tired. It had been a nonstop day at the bar, and I knew that Sassy wanted something from me. That was apparent when the cassava pone arrived. Her husband was dead. According to news reports and McWilliams' public statement, he died of natural causes from a fall. But then there was McWilliams' visit, implying there was more to the man's death than he let on publicly. I just didn't know where his wife—the widow—stood on the issue. I remembered the blabber from the inebriated revelers at the fete—the gossip that she might have caused his death.

"It's late, Mr. Rose. I need to close up here. Can we do this tomorrow?" I wasn't prepared for an audience with the Queen. I had questions for her, I knew that, but hadn't written anything down or rehearsed what I would ask her.

"This won't take long. Ms. Alexis has to go abroad and won't return for almost two weeks, when her husband's funeral here is scheduled."

Tubby was listening nearby as he was also cleaning up, getting ready to close.

"That's okay...Mr. Len," Tubby said, accentuating the "Mr. Len" knowing how it bugged me. "I take care of things here. You get to meet the Queen. That a very good thing."

I glared at Tubby and tossed him the dirty dishrag I was using in wiping down the bar. I had to do this, but hadn't prepared what I would say to her, as if that was anything new.

"Okay, Mr. Rose, let's do this now," I said to him.

# 8

Rose got into his white Lexus convertible, and I followed him in my Jeep. We veered south, in the other direction from my house, to the upscale, gated community of St. Francois. Security let us into the complex. We passed condos along the way, with villas on the hills overlooking the Caribbean. Rose pulled into a driveway of a large villa at the top of the hill. The villa had an expansive front lawn and even in the dark I could see that the grass was green and manicured. It was rare to find manicured green lawns on St. Pierre. Landscaping like that was very expensive and only the very well-off could afford it. I parked behind the Lexus and got out of the Jeep.

Rose rolled down the window of his car and poked his head out. "Ms. Alexis is expecting you. There is no need for me to stay, but please let me know if there is anything you might want in regard to your conversation with Ms. Alexis. She has my contact information."

He gave me a big smile, rolled his window back up and pulled out of the driveway, leaving me alone.

I walked up some steps to the front door and the door opened before I had the chance to ring the bell. I knew what Queen Sassy looked like. Her photo often appeared in the *St. Pierre Press* and on posters around the island announcing her performances. But those were photos. Now I got a look at her in the harsh light of the front foyer of her home.

"Mr. Len Buonfiglio," she said to me as she looked me over. "Thank you for coming."

Her face was smooth and dark brown. Her full, dark Afro contained not a hint of gray, She wore flowing black slacks and a loose thin blouse. Her nails were covered in silver glitter and appeared razor-sharp. I estimated she was several years younger than I was; that would put her in her mid-to-late forties. Whatever her exact age, she was almost fifty years younger than her late husband. She held the door wide open for me as I entered.

Once inside, my hyper nose went to work, detecting the aroma of perfume, something unusual, fruity and tropical. I'm not a big fan of heavy doses of perfume on women and Queen Sassy seemed to pour it on pretty thick.

"We can talk, Ms. Alexis. But it is late, and I've got dogs to feed." I didn't know if that was rude or just my basic lack of social skills and regretted my words as soon as they left my mouth. And then realized that what I said was worse than rude. The woman lost her husband just a few days ago and I was worrying about my dogs.

"Yes, my daughter told me of your dogs. I will try to make this as brief as possible. Did you enjoy the cassava pone?"

I had also forgotten all about her gift—offering—to me. That she had to bring it up was making me look even worse. "I did, Ms. Alexis, it was delicious. And please, my deepest condolences on your loss."

She looked at me, almost surprised by my words. Maybe it wasn't just me who forgot about Ram's death. "Please call me Kindra and thank you for that. That is why you are here so late. I have to leave for Port of Spain tomorrow and then continue on to London, Toronto, and New York before returning here for his burial. There will be memorials in each of those cities that I must attend. So again, forgive me."

She gestured for me to sit. I had the choice of a plush, velvety, deep-red sofa, or two matching burnished mahogany chairs. I chose the cushioned over the mahogany. She sat on the chair closest to me, crossing her legs.

"What can I do for you, Ms...Kindra," I asked.

"As you know, the authorities have determined my husband's death an accident. The result of a fall. Yet I hear things that people suspect me of harming my husband, Mr. Len. I know what Caribbean people are like. I grew up in Brooklyn, Nostrand Avenue, but I live on St. Vincent till I was eleven. And my mother from Canouan. Do you know that small island?"

"Yeah, I know it. And you can call me Len."

"Or Mr. Buonfiglio?"

"Sure, that too."

"But everyone know Mr. Len," she said with a teasing smile. "Can I get you a drink? Some ginger beer? I can add rum if you like. You know, Dark and Stormy."

"I know what a Dark and Stormy is, but at the Sporting Place we just call it ginger beer and rum." She laughed. Her teeth and smile were as dazzling as her daughter's. "And, no, I'm fine."

My head was beginning to throb, and I thought it might be her perfume that was getting to me.

"So—Mr. Buonfiglio, my husband was not well," she said. "He suffer from dementia. His time was soon to come for sure. I know people think someone hurt him that night or morning. And many think it me who do that."

I knew the talk. That she killed him with a blow from a Dutch pot that contained a chicken fricassee...or a cook-up with goat...something ridiculous. And then I thought about my conversation with McWilliams, who also indicated that Lord Ram maybe died not from a fall, but from something else. However, he never indicated that Queen Sassy could be involved. Not even a hint. I thought it best now to keep my mouth shut and let her talk.

"The police say it was an accident. Why people cannot accept that? People here with their gossip and talk. They can be mean.

Nasty even. In New York, I'm sure you know, we don't hide our feelings. None of that phoniness with smiles at church and then the whispers and backstabbing. I want to quiet those whispers, Mr. Buonfiglio. I want them all to know I had nothing to do with my husband's demise."

"I understand that, but what do you think I can do to convince them?"

She sipped her own drink. "Lord Ram lived a long, successful life. He traveled the world. He made records that will live forever. He had fans everywhere. He also have family everywhere." She looked at me so I understood. "And I mean everywhere. But in the meantime, people point their nosy, gossipy finger at me and I don't want that. I don't like that. I still have a career. I don't want this cloud to hang over me."

I thought about what she hoped for. I wasn't so sure. These days even the truth wasn't always believed. I knew that if people saw something maybe on social media and got it into their heads that something happened contrary to the truth, they didn't easily let it go, true or not. They believed what they believed.

"I'm a bar owner," I said.

"No, no, don't try that with me. I know what you do here. What you've done for others. You think I come to you if I didn't check you out? I know where you come from, Len. We both are New Yorkers. But you left New York. I don't know why you left when you were on the top there. After what you did. You got other skills. This I know for sure. And people here know about you too. They listen to you."

Again, my past was public knowledge. Most of it. The stuff that wasn't going to change Queen Sassy's view, or anyone else's, of me. Other skills? That I wasn't so sure of.

"Okay then, Ms. Alexis," I said. "My associate at the Sporting Place, Tubby Levett, who has watched countless reruns of *Law &Order* on television, tells me that when a man is murdered in his home, the first place the police look to is the wife—same with if it is the wife that has been murdered."

"Tell me something I don't know, Mr. Buonfiglio," she said. "But the thing is, I no longer live in the house where he died. For the past several years, when I'm on the island, I live with my daughter here in this house. He live with his aides at his house in Garrison Hills. I was nowhere near his house that morning. The police know this after they indeed came to me first to ask questions."

I thought about that for a moment. I didn't want to get into any sticky personal thing between Sassy and her husband, but I guess it made sense. The man was so much older than his wife. He was known to be feeble, slightly impaired. Either way, the woman didn't want to be bothered with taking care of the man despite their vows. Again, who was I to judge?

"So then I guess your husband was not alone there."

"No, of course not. The man need full-time care. Sometimes I think he even need help to go to the bathroom. Do you think I would leave him on his own?" She was defensive about that. I'm sure she heard it from others. "And just so you don't start thinking other money-related thoughts, I hear it all the time since I marry the man. Young girl getting at the old man's money. The reality is that my income has exceeded his for the past decade. It's not even close. But people got to think their thoughts. Especially here on this place."

She had an alibi that was most likely easily confirmed. That there was no evident love there didn't matter to me. That was not a reason to murder anyone. "Who found him?"

"Jannilea Sparks," she said. "She come in for the morning shift while Lorissa Blue was upstairs in the room we have for the aides. I don't know why she was not with him at the time. She says she had personal affairs to attend to, of the hygiene nature, and was in the bathroom. She didn't even know he was up. Both were questioned by the authorities. And to be frank, Mr. Len, I don't believe they would do anything to the man. They adored him. Even senile, that man had charm like no other."

She shook her head, smiled, and then was quiet for a moment. I let her have that time even though I was very ready to get out of there. That perfume was all over me now and I had a feeling it would linger on me and overwhelm the other smells that were ingrained in my Jeep.

"So you suspect someone else might have actually done something to him?"

"No, I did not say that, Mr. Buonfiglio. I don't know for sure what happened. Maybe you will find out."

Her eyes were on me then. They were doing some talking. I just didn't know what they were saying.

"I just want people to stop pointing fingers at me. Find out the truth and maybe they will stop. Can you do that?"

I didn't want to burst her bubble on the pointing-fingers thing. And I already tried to stress my lack of investigation experience, hoping that would persuade her to find someone else who could better help her. But she seemed adamant. She wanted me to do this. McWilliams wanted me to do this. But what was I supposed to do? This one seemed more complicated than any of the others. "I can try" was the best I could offer her.

"I know you can, Mr. Buonfiglio," she said. "I've got faith in the June First Hero."

There was an awkward silence after she said that. And when she said it, she smiled. It wasn't something I publicized. But if anyone wanted to find out about me, all they had to do was Google "June 1st Hero." It was all right there. Everything but the truth.

Sensing my unease at what she said, she got up and went to her purse. "Now, what's your rate?" she asked.

I chuckled. "Hmmm, a monthly supply of cassava pone?"

And before she could respond to that, I just turned and headed outside and back to my Jeep.

# 9

It was curious to me that both McWilliams and Queen Sassy wanted the same thing. I'm not a person prone to paranoia, so I didn't think too much about it on the way back to my house. I didn't think too much of anything besides making sure the dogs got fed and brushing my teeth before I passed out on my bed, the Puppy hopping up next to me. It was the closest I had come to female companionship in a long time. The Puppy's body was warm...soft. When I turned I saw that the body was not that of my dog. I was lying next to a naked, nymph-like form. A woman was spooned into me; her long dark hair obscured her small body. I caressed her hair and she turned onto her back to stare at me with coal-black eyes. She made little cooing sounds as I stroked her hair. The sounds were familiar. They were arousing me. And then I heard other sounds—a cry for help. The woman was lying on the very edge of the bed. I wanted to pull her back into me and as I did, I peered over her shoulder and saw dark water below us. I could hear the water churning. We were on a bed with no railing. On a cliff. She started to push me away from her. I tried to hold on. She wouldn't let me. I had my hand in her long hair. One of her legs was off the bed. I gripped her hair tighter. She screamed at me to let go as she swung her other legs around. She dug her nails into my hand and scratched me until I felt warm blood on them. I couldn't hold on. I had to let her go. *Come with me*, she whispered. And then she fell off the bed, her body disappearing into the dark water. "Nura," I cried and then I heard a loud pop. I woke up—my heart pounding in my chest. The dogs were barking. I was awake now. My eyes opened wide. The dogs continued to howl; the Puppy was off the bed and whimpering.

I got up and wandered to the front room, wearing only my boxers. The dogs were circling my legs as they barked. I heard a car outside. I went to the door to see red taillights as the car screeched away down the hill. I stepped outside and the dogs followed me. I wanted to see what kind of car it was and maybe get a license plate number. But the car was gone. I had no idea what time it was. I looked around. I could hear tires screeching down the hill. Someone was driving a bit too fast on these narrow, winding roads. Once the sound of the car faded, I went back inside.

I went back into my bedroom and sat on my bed in the dark. It was two in the morning. Either someone was up late or very early. Whoever was in that car had gotten out and walked around my yard. Was the loud pop I heard part of that crazy dream? Or was it something else. A firecracker? A gunshot? I had heard neither in the decade I had lived on St. Pierre so it was too long ago for me to make the distinction. The dogs barking like that was unusual. They either heard it too or sensed something. They normally don't start up like that for a stray goat in the yard or even another mongrel wandering around. I lay back down on the bed. I should at least try to get back to sleep, I thought. But I didn't want any recurrence of that dream-nightmare. I didn't want that coming on again. There had been strangers on my lawn. Were they sending me a warning shot? If that really was a gunshot I heard. Why? I could think of no real reason. Nobody knew of my investigation of Lord Ram's death.

The Puppy hopped up against me. The other dogs went back to sleep, too. They did their duty, waking me and with their forceful barks sending whoever was around my house away, and that was enough work for them. They went and laid out on the rug in the living room. I closed my eyes and when next they opened, the sun was on me.

I staggered into the bathroom, cleaned up a bit, and made my way to the kitchen. The two bigger dogs, both of whom weighed about forty pounds, were at the front door. They weren't barking, but they were scratching at the door and whining. It was not their usual routine. Something was different. They looked back at me as I made my way to the door. The Gray One lifted up on his haunches, trying to help me open the door for him. I pushed him back so he wouldn't fall when I opened the door. I unlocked it, pulled it open, and the dogs rushed to the driveway and my Jeep. Both the Gray One and the Spotted One were barking at the Jeep. They were on their hind legs, looking into the passenger side. The Puppy came out to see what was going on, sticking close to my side.

I peered at the Jeep, moving toward it tentatively. The dogs were whining, but their barking stopped. They were protective of me. When they woke me in the middle of the night, they sensed danger. I knew that. This time their sounds were different. I glanced around, making sure there was nothing I was missing. That whoever came at night was gone. From the Jeep I heard a faint tinny sound—like a trumpet playing. I got closer and what I heard sounded now like music. I could hear a jazz trumpet riff playing, but I also heard the distinct noise of a congested nose. I heard snoring. I was close enough now to see into the Jeep. The first thing I noticed was a pale dome, a large bald spot on the back of a man's head surrounded by wiry salt-and-pepper hair. And the man—a white man—was sleeping in the back seat of my Jeep.

I stood there for a moment. My body was casting a shadow over him, and that roused him. He turned and opened his eyes. He took his earbuds off. He smiled at me—a radiant, almost contagious smile.

"Ciao, Lennie," he said to me as he slowly sat up in the back seat of my Jeep.

I stared at the man who deserted Betta when she was pregnant. The man who left her alone to care for their son. Who chose his domineering family over his young wife. I tried to scowl. I tried to frown. But I couldn't. Seeing that smile, all the rage I had for him for what he did, at least for that moment, evaporated. I found myself smiling back at him.

"Ciao, Maurizio," I said.

# 10

"I brought you beans. From the caffe you like when I bring to you last time. From Milano."

Maurizio Loffredo held up a brown bag as I opened the door of the Jeep for him. He unwound his lanky frame. He was tall and slender, with very little muscle tone. You could say his body was like one of those Gumby toys, one you could bend in multiple directions. With the exception of some gray on the sparse, wiry hair he had around the pale dome, and the sloppy stubble on his cheeks, it didn't look like he had aged much in the nearly five years he had been gone. Looking at him now made me again wonder what Betta ever saw in him. And then I saw those eyes—light blue and as expressive as blue eyes can be. I knew that was something Betta wanted to bestow on her children. But there had to be more than that. He was a kind, gentle man full of passions for so many things. It was Maurizio whose own passion for jazz was something that he passed on to me. We often talked about art—museums in Italy I never had a chance to visit, while he would pepper me about the Blue Note and Village Vanguard, jazz clubs in New York he was horrified that I had never been to. Then of course there was food and his quest to bring Italian bread to St. Pierre. I remember the days working on the oven for the bread, listening to him talk in his accented, excited voice, while jazz played in the background. Those were good times. I was happy for him and for Betta finding a man like Maurizio. Until he made the wrong choice.

He got out of the Jeep and I took the bag from him. I had a lot to say to him. I had a lot to ask. But at this moment, I couldn't speak.

"I like to see you again, Lennie." He then hugged me and kissed me on both cheeks. "I miss you. I miss everyone here."

The temporary goodwill I had in seeing him was fading. I wanted to ask him why he left. Was it that you were such a coward that you couldn't stand up to your family? So much so that you would leave your pregnant wife here, desert her because your family did not approve of your choice? How could you stay away for so long? What kind of man does that? Those were the thoughts I had, but I did not speak them aloud. I had no right, not after my own situation, not after what I had done. He might not know of my past, but admonishing him for his life decisions was something I could not do. I was many things, but a hypocrite was not one of them.

We walked into the house together, the dogs following. Maurizio still had that smile on his face. It was as if he had done nothing wrong. All was well. He was returning to his wife and son after a brief vacation. I could feel my temper rising.

"Why are you here, Maurizio?" I asked, as we went into my open kitchen.

When I turned to him, the smile was gone. He was scratching at his head. Looking for words. "I make a mess, Lennie. I'm in trouble."

"Trouble?" I thought about that for a moment. "When did you come here?"

"I come just a few days ago," he said.

"No, I mean, here. To my house."

"This morning. Very early."

I was thinking about my visitors and what I now believed was a gunshot. Strange coincidence that it happened just before Maurizio arrived. "You came here because you are in trouble, Maurizio?" The thought made me angry.

He didn't answer that. I could see his eye twitch a little. He was uncomfortable with what I asked. "No...please, Lennie. Listen to me. I live in Italy. I send money to Betta and for Paolo who I never see until yesterday. A beautiful boy I leave here and I not see. He grow up without his papa." He began to sob then. I kept quiet and put a box of tissues in front of him. He took a few, blew his nose and wiped at his eyes. While he did that— while he was composing himself—I took those precious Italian coffee beans and ran a few tablespoons through my coffee grinder. I added the fresh ground coffee to my gold filter, put in enough cold water for two cups, and turned it on.

We listened as the coffee brewed, neither of us speaking. When the coffee was ready, I poured us each a cup. Maurizio's pale blue eyes were now red-rimmed. He took the coffee, nodded and sipped.

"Betta knows you are here," I said, though I knew the answer.

He nodded again.

"How did that go?"

He looked up at me. I could tell from his expression that it probably didn't go over too well. "She a woman I never deserve. That she my wife is one of the miracles of life. It something that make me not even understand how this can be. How I given this gift and treat her like I did? Silly, stupido clown."

"Enough," I said. His self-pity was making me angrier.

He looked at me again and nodded. "Yes, yes. Enough."

"You gonna go back to Italy when your mama calls for you to come home? Are you gonna leave her again?" I know I was being cruel, but I didn't care. Showing up years after deserting his wife and now hearing him tell me she was maybe taking him back after what he did made me angry. Their relationship wasn't any of my business. I had to keep reminding myself of that. I looked at him as he slouched against the kitchen counter. I knew he didn't return just for Betta or his son. I could read it in the guilt that played across his face.

"No...I stay, Lennie. I never leave her and my son again," he mumbled, his head down. "But I must fix this mess."

I could continue berating him for his bad choices, but now I wanted to know what kind of trouble he was in. He looked at me. I nodded and took my coffee to the back porch overlooking the Atlantic, where I had two chairs with a small table between them. Maurizio followed. He looked out over the ocean and smiled. The constant breeze from the water ruffled his wiry hair.

"Ahhh, Lennie...you make a good place here."

"Sit down, Maurizio," I said. I didn't want him to charm me into feeling sorry for him. He was good at that. He used his weakness as a man to his advantage. He could be convincing in a strange way. The combination of vulnerability and curiosity was very appealing. It didn't come across as a weakness. And maybe that was what Betta originally found attractive about him. He sat down as instructed. The smile faded as quickly as it appeared. His hand shook slightly as he held his coffee mug. He turned to me.

"My life, Lennie. My life in danger. There are people...They look for me."

It was too much of a coincidence not to understand the connection between Maurizio's presence and what happened at my house just a few hours earlier. Those people looking for Maurizio had guns, I knew that now. But why they came to my house, how they knew where I lived, I did not know. "And you came here?"

"I...think it best here. But no. They find me. They know I come here."

"You are in danger, and you think it is best for you to come here? Where your wife and son live?"

"No, no. I never think they in danger. I never let that happen," he said.

"Yeah, but here you are. You tell me people are looking for you. That you think they followed you here. You know this island. It's easy to find someone here."

He took a little sip from the coffee. His head was down. "That's why I come to you, Lennie. I no stay with Betta and my son. Not now."

"You want to stay with me?"

His blue eyes were staring at me through his glasses. "Just until I settle this mess I make. This okay, Lennie?"

I didn't hesitate. "You can stay here, Maurizio, but I need to know everything. No secrets. And I need to know what kind of danger you're talking about. I just want the truth."

"Yes, of course, Lennie. I always tell you the truth. No bullshit." He downed the rest of his coffee and leaned back in his chair. "I leave you something at your Sporting Place. You get it, no?"

"What? What did you leave me?"

"I drop a box off. In that box, bottles of vermouth."

I had my suspicions about that vermouth, and now I knew. "I got it," I said.

"Good. *Diece*...bottles?"

"Yes, there were ten in there, Maurizio."

"I have a friend, he a craftsman from Torino. Did you ever visit Torino, Lennie?"

"No, Maurizio, never."

"People know how beautiful that place is. Like this island, but cold in winter. I love that place. And the food—the best in Italy I think. Vitello tonnato, bollito misto...magnificent."

I was losing patience. "What about the vermouth, Maurizio?"

He nodded. "This the best sweet vermouth you taste. You never have vermouth like this. Perfecto for the Negroni. The Americano. For aperitif."

Now he was selling me on his newest venture.

"My friend, the craftsman from Torino, he create the vermouth and I bottle in Bergamo. You try, Lennie?"

"I made a Negroni. It was very good, but Tubby didn't think so."

Maurizio chuckled. "Ahhh, Tubby, I miss him too. Vermouth sweet, not bitter. It's the Campari that is bitter. A new bar creation for Tubby. I think if he smart, Tubby can find a way to put the vermouth in a rum punch. Instead of the fruit juice."

"Maybe, but we don't need to discuss what we will do with the vermouth. I don't want gifts. I don't care if you bring me Italian coffee beans. I just want to know what kind of trouble you're in and if your wife and son will be safe."

He stared at me for a moment. "You care very much for Betta," he said. "I know this. I understand. I can say nothing what she do with her life. And if it be you she with, Lennie, I am happy."

"She's not with me, Maurizio. Stop with the drama. I need to know what's going on."

"Yes, you right. You have the bottles here? At your house?"

"I left them at the bar," I said.

"No, no. Put in a safe place please. They come for those bottles. Get them, Lennie. Do not leave at the bar, please."

He was agitated now. His face was flushed.

"We have coffee and then we go. This morning. Today, Lennie. Bring them here. Keep them safe." Spittle flew from his lips as he spoke.

"Tell me, Maurizio. What makes this vermouth so special? What makes it so valuable?"

"I tell you that when we go get them. Please. I use your bathroom now."

He got up and rushed to the half bathroom I had off the kitchen. I went inside and put on a shirt. He rushed back out of the bathroom, his face wet from splashing water on it and not bothering to dry it.

"I ready, Lennie. Let's go."

# 11

Maurizio was buckled in the passenger seat and when I started the Jeep, an opening piano riff followed by a smooth trumpet played through my speakers. Maurizio smiled. "Cantaloupe Island," he said. "Lennie, you listen to my music now?"

"Your music? Maurizio, you know I like jazz."

"But you now listen to Herbie Hancock? And the others I play for you so long ago when I here?"

I shrugged as we rolled down the hill toward Garrison.

"Perfecto," he said with a grin.

I turned to him for a moment. "What's perfect?"

"Herbie Hancock. This." He pointed to my phone and the hookup of my music to the Bluetooth in the Jeep. 'Cantaloupe Island.' For this island. Like a movie soundtrack." He grinned and looked out the window at the green around him, the bright blue sky and the even bluer sea in the distance.

I looked at him. Just a moment ago he was crying about bad guys coming after him, and now he was smiling, admiring the view. I took a deep breath. I always remembered him as quirky, that was part of his charm, but it seemed even more pronounced now.

I came to the roundabout at Garrison, avoiding cars from every direction as I headed up Windy Hill Road toward the bar. After dodging the cars, I looked at Maurizio again. "Weren't you going to tell me why those vermouth bottles were so valuable?"

"We almost there, Lennie. I show you when we there."

I pulled into a space next to Tubby's Camry. It was before eleven on a Wednesday. We rarely had any customers this early, so I was surprised to see that Tubby already opened up. He was out in the middle of the bar, sweeping up broken glass. There were shattered beer bottles all over the bar.

"See this? See what they do. They..." Tubby stopped in mid-sentence when he noticed Maurizio entering the bar behind me. I surveyed the damage.

"Who did this?"

Tubby kept staring at Maurizio, who was smiling back at him but also glancing at the shards of broken glass on the ground.

"Someone break in and do this last night," Tubby said as he continued to stare at Maurizio, trying to comprehend why he was here. "They shatter bottles of Carib only. Nothing else."

"They didn't take anything else? You checked the cash register and everything."

"Of course I did," he said. "Nothing. Just Carib bottles. Who come here to vandalize our place like this?"

Caribs only? I thought about those two men who complained about the Caribbean beer. And then I thought about the two a.m. wake-up, the gunshot, because that's now what I believed it was, and the car at my house. They had an interest in Maurizio's vermouth. I looked at him. His mouth open, also surveying the damage.

"Tubby, I happy to see you," Maurizio said, moving toward him, glass crunching under his feet, going in for a hug. Tubby hugged back, but tentatively. He had no idea what was going on.

"Italian man," Tubby said. "You come back to your family?"

"*Si*, Tubby. I come back. To my family. *Si*. Yes."

"Okay, then," he said with a grunt. I knew Tubby had much more to say about it all—he usually did—but for now he let it go and went back to sweeping up the glass.

"Did they break the lock or a window?" I asked.

"That lock, you know, is nothing. People want to get in, they get in. These people want to get in and smash up bottles of Carib. Do not ask me why."

"Lennie, the vermouth. These people. They come for it," Maurizio said. "I tell you the bottles. They valuable. They come to take them."

"What?" I was bent over, looking under the bar. I rose up and quickly looked to see if the bottle of vermouth I had on display at the bar was there. There was an empty space where the bottle had been.

I turned to Maurizio. His face sagged. "They take it, no?"

"Yeah, Maurizio, they took it."

"And the others. Nine bottles. You put them in a safe place?"

I didn't answer. I went into the back room that also served as a small office next to the bathroom. The door was wide open. The box was gone.

"No, I put them back here until I figured what I was going to do with them," I mumbled.

"They take it?"

"Yeah, Maurizio. They took it. How would I know they were valuable?"

Maurizio nodded and went back to sit on a stool at the bar. He removed his glasses and ran his hand over his face. Tubby had cleaned up the glass shards and put the broom and mop to the side. I moved back to the bar.

"They come to steal liquor? That stuff you use to make that bitter drink? Not worth much if you ask me," Tubby said to both of us.

"*Sì*, Tubby. They come for the bottles. Not so much for the liquor."

I stayed behind the bar and looked across at Maurizio.

"What's with those bottles?"

"Mimmo a genius," Maurizio said, as he sat at the bar. His elbow propped there. His face downcast. "A maestro."

"And who is Mimmo?"

"He a famous artist. You not hear of Mimmo? They have show of his work once in New York. This I know. His art—the young now—they appreciate him. He draw like a Marvel, the comic. But more style. More, how you say, depth, than comic book. He start he career in comic book in Italy and book covers, but Mimmo want more. You know Crumb?"

"Robert Crumb? Yeah. My mother threw out all my copies of *Weirdo*. She said they were sick."

"He like an Italian Crumb but with some Basquait in his work. Mimmo a serious artist, but the *critico*, they not always appreciate his style until the young, they like his work. They see on the internet. He get—you know—followers. Many many. And the *critico*, then they pay *attenzione*. He make money."

"What do you have to do with Mimmo?"

"I know him from Academy in Bologna. This the best for those study of the arts, Lennie. We study there together when we young."

Many times Maurizio talked about his life in Italy. I knew he dabbled in different pursuits. When I first met him he had just skipped out on a job in the immense kitchen of an Italian cruise line. He worked shrimp detail—deveining thousands of shrimp each day. That was it. That was his job. He hoped it would be an experience that would jump-start his career and propel him into the kitchen of a fine restaurant, but he soon realized that would never happen. When the cruise boat docked in St. Pierre, he got off. He met Betta that same day and went AWOL as the boat sailed off to Tobago. Once he moved into Betta's small room off Front Street, he knew he needed to work. He had to provide for her. He tried his hand with the local fishermen using the nets off the beach, but he was a disaster. He had to do something to keep this woman he instantly fell in love with, so he came up with the idea that St. Pierre needed good Italian bread. He asked me my opinion on the matter, and I couldn't disagree. I loved St. Pierre in many ways, but the bread would never equal what I could get back in New York. It might have been foolish, but I encouraged him to go ahead with his project. His plan was to build a wood-burning Italian-style oven where he would make his bread, or as he called it, *pane di casa*. Once it was done and in the backyard of the lot where he and Betta would live, the two of them would sell their bread to residents, tourists, and to the restaurants on the island.

The bread-baking experiment was a success, maybe the only success Maurizio had ever experienced—with the exception of his relationship, at least five years ago, with Betta. He did well enough to begin to build the house on the lot. His family in Italy soon learned of his new business and its success. The extended family—his brothers and their wives and children, along with his mother and father—planned a visit to St. Pierre. They wanted to meet the woman he married. They wanted to sample the bread he made. But on the day his family arrived, Maurizio disappeared. He didn't want to see them. He was worried that they would not approve of Betta and his choice to live on this small island making bread. He felt strongly that they would try to lure him back to Italy. I knew about Italian families. I knew of the powerful pull they had on their off-spring. His father was a very well-respected orthopedic surgeon and his two brothers, Augusto and Alfonso, followed their father in the same practice. The pull they had on him was powerful. He did not think he could resist it, so he went into hiding, hoping they would just go away and give up on their wayward son.

Betta was furious with him. She met the family. They were gracious to her. They took her to dinner. They were patient and knew of Maurizio's eccentricities and figured he would surface sooner or later. But Betta made me go find him. I finally found him in Piccadilly Caves, one of many cave networks on the island, Piccadilly being the largest and also the most visited by tourists and local teenagers who would sneak in and do what teenagers always did. He and I had a long talk over a bottle of overproof rum, with his jazz playlist of piano greats, Ahmad Jamal, Oscar Peterson, John Lewis, Bill Evans and others echoing inside the damp cave while we both got very drunk. When I left him, he promised he would stop with his foolishness and go to his family. I made him swear to me that he would. He was sobbing when I left. Unlike me, Maurizio was a very emotional man. He would cry witnessing a St. Pierre sunset. At the time, I attributed the tears to emotion as well as the influence of the large quantities of rum we had consumed. Nothing more. But I was wrong.

The next day, thanks to a very bad hangover, I slept late. When I finally got to the bar, Tubby told me the news. That morning, Maurizio's family had returned to Italy, and Maurizio went with them. I was angry. He had given me his word. I had to find out the truth and even with my head throbbing, I drove over to Betta's. She was sitting alone on a folding chair in the unfinished second bedroom of her house. I stood over her. She looked up. Her cheeks were not damp. I don't know if she had been crying or not. "I am with his child," she whispered to me and then turned away. I tried to comfort her. I awkwardly hugged her. She shrugged off my hug. She was angry at me for not keeping Maurizio on the island even though she knew it was Maurizio, not me, who failed her. There was nothing I could say, but I knew what I would do. I would finish the house for her. And when she had her baby, a son she named Paolo, I would make sure he had everything he needed. It wasn't my obligation. But it felt like it was.

"How come I'm just finding out about this art thing now, Maurizio?" I asked as we all sat at the bar.

"Because I very bad at art. I foolish to think I good. But when I young, I crazy for comic books and comic art. People say, 'What me worry?' because I look like *Mad* magazine Alfred E. Neuman. But my hair. Not so much. My...*famiglia*...they do not like this, that I care so much about comics, but I tell them I no go to university if I not study comic art. I dropout."

"Maurizio, you also never told me you were such a brat as a kid." I grinned at him, hoping to lighten the conversation.

"A brat, yes. Spoiled. Stupido. I drop out anyway, but not before I meet Mimmo and we become friends."

I tried to think if I ever heard of an artist named Mimmo. I had not really paid attention to up-and-coming contemporary artists in a long time. I was consumed with my work in New York, starting up bars and raising a family, until I met someone who was also part of that world, the art world. She was an associate professor of art history at Columbia. Maybe knowing that about her, because of my own failed youthful interest in art, was part of the attraction—an attraction that eventually overwhelmed my marriage. She and I would visit galleries, the Met, MoMA, and the Whitney, and smaller galleries in Chelsea and Brooklyn. But after that day in June when I lost her, I had no interest in ever returning to a gallery or museum. "He have a last name, this Mimmo?" I asked Maurizio.

Maurizio chuckled. "No...no Lennie. He just Mimmo. He sign his work Mimmo. The world know him only by that name."

It was still early enough in the bar that we had no customers. Tubby was listening to all of this but was strangely quiet. He usually made some sort of commentary on whatever was discussed at the bar. Maybe he was still in shock at seeing Maurizio after all these years. Or he was letting Maurizio tell his tale without interruption. Or maybe, for a change, he had nothing to say. I looked at him. He shrugged at me. Something was on his mind, and I didn't think it had anything to do with the artist named Mimmo.

"So this Mimmo—what does he have to do with the bottles of vermouth you brought here? This Bellezza Nera."

He smiled. "Oh you see? Beautiful, no?"

"A work of art. And I saw what you did there, Maurizio." Why wouldn't he just tell me he commissioned the art on the bottles of vermouth as a tribute to his wife? To his life with her on St. Pierre? Was it that he was still ashamed about deserting her and this was a shallow attempt to win her back? To show his love? I didn't know and he wasn't saying.

And then Maurizio started to sob.

"My friend—Mimmo—he die. I show him pictures of Betta. Of this beautiful place. He create from that. But now...Mimmo gone."

"What?" I expected something else. Not this.

Maurizio nodded. "The news very big in Italy when it happen. An artist. He complicated. He struggle with his mind. Depression. I know. I struggle too, but I'm no artist, Lennie. Mimmo a true maestro. But with that come difficulties. He never satisfied. He never think his work any good. The demon, he torture his mind. And Mimmo, he take his own life. That what they say in the paper."

Valuable bottles of vermouth. An artist who committed suicide. Maurizio showing up on St. Pierre saying he was in trouble. His story was a lot to take in.

"When did this happen, Maurizio?"

"At the beginning of the year, Lennie. He...he take pills. Sleeping pills. I know he have trouble sleeping. But he never say it that bad."

"And the vermouth?"

"I commission Mimmo to create the labels for special limited edition of bottles. Each label a different work of art. Mimmo sign each one of the originals. The bottles here. I bring to you to keep safe. They the originals. They worth money, Lennie."

"You paid him?" I knew Maurizio's family had money, but I also knew he would never ask them for money for any of his ventures.

"I pay him," Maurizio said. "But not so much. He do it for

me as a friend. He famous but he not rich. He have a partner. They adopt a child together. In Italy, that not an easy thing. So he and Andrea, they move to Switzerland where they can do this easier. But very expensive thing to do."

"I don't understand, Maurizio. Why would they have to move to Switzerland to adopt a baby? They can't in Italy?"

Maurizio looked at me. "Italy still—still *difficile* to do such a thing. It make me very angry and ashamed of my country that they still do this."

"How hard can it be to adopt a child?"

I heard Tubby hiss from behind the bar. "What's wrong with you? Even I know what the man talking about," he said, finally interjecting into our conversation after his long silence. "The man say he have a partner. How you not understand that, old man?"

"Yeah, so?" I was still confused.

"You know that famous Italian singer, Andrea Bocelli?" Tubby asked me.

"Yeah, sure."

"He a man, is he not?"

"Wait, are you saying Bocelli was Mimmo's partner?"

Tubby just hissed again and shook his head.

Maurizio smiled and hugged me. He was patronizing me and now I was getting angry. "Lennie, Tubby know. Andrea a man. He Mimmo's partner. But no, not Andrea Bocelli. Another man named Andrea."

"Your mind just too slow," Tubby said shaking his head. "They have vitamins, pills you can take for that."

I pointed my middle finger in Tubby's direction and then turned to Maurizio.

"I make an investment, Lennie. On Mimmo's art and on my vermouth business. I think to combine the two and sell the bottles all over the world. But only a limited edition of the bottles have Mimmo's original art and his signature."

"An investment? Where did you get all this money, Maurizio?"

He looked sheepish now. It was becoming clearer. How he got the money for the investment was the issue. I knew that now even though he still didn't answer me.

"After, Mimmo die, Andrea and the baby girl they adopt in Switzerland. The courts, they deny him the estate of Mimmo. The red tape from Italy too much. He never get the money as he deserve being the husband, partner of Mimmo. So I try to help him. I arrange with a place in Sweden. Where they sell off art a. *Asta*...You understand, Lennie?"

I was beginning to understand but I needed more. "*Asta?*"

"How you say...um..." He was looking for the word. "Auction."

"An auction house in Sweden?"

"*Si*, yes, Lennie. But I borrow this money to pay Mimmo and do this deal from some men there. In Sweden. I meet them in Torino. They know of Mimmo. They put the deal together. They help pay for the vermouth and Mimmo's art and in exchange they get to auction the special bottles with Mimmo's signature."

Before Maurizio could finish, our first customer of the day wandered in. It wasn't even noon, but Handsome Archibald would not miss his usual midday Thursday commitment to one of Tubby's rum punches. Archibald, who was in his fifties and maybe at one time earned his moniker, now was anything but, given his missing teeth and scattering of stubble on his rotund dome.

He settled his squat frame on a bar stool and smiled, showing off that sad dentistry. "Good afternoon, gentlemen," he muttered in what was still a powerful, clear voice.

Tubby glanced at his watch. "Not afternoon quite yet, Archie," he said.

Archibald shrugged. "But for me, it is time for one of your rum punches, Tubby." He turned to look at me and squinted at Maurizio. "Do I know you?" he asked.

Maurizio smiled and nodded. "*Si*, you buy my bread. My

*pane di casa*," he said.

"Your bread?" Archibald asked and then thought for a moment. "I do not buy your bread for a very long time, sir. And why is that?"

Maurizio didn't know what to say. He looked to me, but it wasn't for me to answer.

"Can I get a loaf of that delicious bread today?" Archibald inquired.

Maurizio smiled and then shook his head. "The oven...out of order. Soon we get it to work again and then you have your bread."

I marveled at Maurizio's optimism.

Tubby placed the rum punch in front of Archibald. He picked up the glass and sipped. "A pity," Handsome said. "Damn good bread. I would very much enjoy a loaf today."

We were silent now that Archibald was there. Maurizio was reticent in saying any more about his dilemma.

"You men have nothing to say today?" Handsome said after he took a sip of his rum punch.

"Handsome, since when have you known me to be talkative?" I asked.

"Not you, Mr. Len. But your partner, Tubby, will always chat me up. Today he is quiet. Why is that, Mr. Levett?" He looked at Tubby.

"What do I need to say to you, Archibald? You've heard it all," Tubby said to him.

My phone buzzed. I was getting a call from McWilliams. I walked outside to the parking lot.

"Yes, Chief?" He was calling, I was sure, to bug me about what he asked me to do the other day. I don't like being pushed into things, so I teased him a bit.

"Chief? Where you come from I may be a chief. You know what I am here."

"Yes I do...Superintendent McWilliams."

"I hear you met with the Queen yesterday," he said.

"Yes, we had a chat. It seems she wants the same thing you do."

"We do want the same thing. False rumors that poison the minds here. People do silly things when they believe lies. We need to correct that."

I was pacing around my Jeep when I saw Maurizio come outside. He was looking at me, gesturing with his hands. I wasn't sure what that gesture translated to besides impatience. Perhaps he was worried. He hadn't finished telling me about the men he borrowed money from.

"I hope you haven't forgotten what we discussed the other day, Buonfiglio."

"I have not."

"Good. Now I will text you the address of the women who work for Lord Ram that night. You go see them."

I was pacing around the parking lot with the phone to my ear. "I just show up? Will they expect me?"

"Do I have to tell you your business? You should know what to say, sir."

"My business is the Sporting Place. Serving cold drinks to happy people with a view of the harbor. Not snooping around other people's business."

I heard him laugh that deep barrel-chested laugh. "Text come now," he said and then ended the call.

A moment later I heard the buzz of his text with the address for Lorissa Blue and then one for Jannilea Sparks. Sassy had told me there were two women present when Ram died. One was just beginning her shift, the other was ending hers. I could not remember which was Lorissa Blue or Jannilea Sparks. Ms. Blue's address was closer to where I was now so I figured I'd go there first.

"Lennie, we get the bottles?" Maurizio asked with urgency.

"How would I know where they are now, Maurizio?"

"We must. They belong to Andrea and their baby. We find, okay?" He was following me into the Jeep.

Tubby came outside. "Now where you go?" he called from the bar's entrance.

"Just to see someone," I said. "I'll be back as soon as I can."

He stared at me from the doorway. He was bothered by something, I could tell. I wanted to know what he was thinking, but didn't have the time to get into it. I'd try to remember to ask when I fgot back. Maurizio climbed into the passenger seat and we pulled out onto Windy Hill Road.

# 12

From the address McWilliams texted, I recognized the neighborhood where Lorissa Blue lived as Snake Hill, a small village northeast of Garrison, and about a twenty-minute ride from the bar. I don't know why it was called Snake Hill. As far as I knew, there were no snakes on St. Pierre, and I was happy about that. I had been to Snake Hill many times. Tubby's family was from there and I had been in the parish for various birthday parties and gatherings. As I made my way down to the roundabout, Maurizio squirmed in his seat.

"How do you propose we get your bottles back, Maurizio?"

"They must be still here, Lennie. If they take yesterday can they leave off the island with customs no check?"

"Sure they can," I said. "All they need is a boat and the hope that they aren't searched. Most aren't. That's why these islands are always hot spots for smuggling. The police can't check all the yachts that come into and out of St. Pierre's waters. How did you get them here?"

"I fill out all the forms they ask and send them to Betta. She get before I come."

"She did?"

"Si."

"So she knew you were coming here?"

"Si, Lennie, I call and tell her."

I gripped the wheel tightly and turned to him. I couldn't help myself. That Betta allowed him to come back to her got to me when it should not have. I stewed a bit while I was stuck behind a line of cars waiting for the one traffic light on the island to turn green. There had been a clamoring on the island that a traffic light was needed because of congestion in and around the roundabout. There was also a history of car crashes. Funds for the light came from overseas. I had my suspicions as to who paid for it, that it was part of a political quid pro quo. St. Pierre had its bureaucracy just like any other place. I didn't have an opinion about the traffic light like so many did here, but it did help with accidents. The traffic, however, remained.

"Tell me about these men. I'd like to find them as much as you do. They broke into my bar, and there should be consequences for that."

"They too from Sweden," Maurizio said.

I visualized the two men from the bar the day before. When he said they were from Sweden, I pictured the stereotypical Swede, blond with blue eyes. These guys were definitely not that.

"They work for the auction house?"

He looked at me and shrugged. "You know what these men are, Lennie. Mafiosi. But not Italian. They have a Mafia in Sweden, I find out. Not like Italy or Russia or Albania, but these men. Gangsters too. When I meet them, I think they just businessmen who appreciate art. And I was very...ah...anxious...to do this. I think it a very good project. I love the work of Mimmo and to...how you say...partner...with him I want very much. So I make a deal they front the money for the production of the vermouth and to pay Mimmo for his work. In exchange they get ten bottles with Mimmo's original work. They all signed and authenticated. They say they give the bottle to the *casa d'aste* in Sweden and sell there."

I knew just a little about art auctions. Usually most of the proceeds would go to the artist or his or her estate and the auction house would receive either a commission or a percentage of the sale. But I guess it would depend on the deal made.

"And from the deal, Maurizio, what would Mimmo get out of the auction?"

He looked down at the black canvas Italian Chuck Taylor knockoffs he wore. "I make a bad deal, Lennie," he said. "I no think correctly. I just think, have Mimmo make the ten bottles and that help me to sell the vermouth beyond that. It good publicity for the, ah, product. These men, they offer to pay almost all my production costs. So I take it. And when he die, that make him more a celebrity. Everyone now want his work. It make more valuable. These men, they know this and pressure me, but I no can do this anymore. Not for Andrea and the baby. I no can do it."

I listened and thought about what he just said, that Mimmo's work was more valuable now that he was dead. Maybe that was the idea all along? Kill Mimmo, make it look like a suicide to raise the value of his work. My mind was going full *Law & Order*. I had to stop and just concentrate on the immediate situation.

"What was the deal you made, Maurizio?"

He wiped at his eyes again, took a breath and said, "Fifty-fifty."

I knew from what he was leading up to that it was a bad deal, but fifty/fifty was outrageously bad. An auction house should not get more than ten to fifteen percent of the sale. If they were a legitimate place, that is. We were in Snake Hill now. I passed Tubby's mother's house. Lorissa Blue's home was about a half mile up the hill from hers.

I pulled the Jeep to the curb in front of the coral-colored house. The front yard was mostly dirt. Laundry was drying on a clothesline along the side of the house. Purple scrubs hung on the line along with other items of women's and toddler's clothes.

I looked at Maurizio. "What did you do after all this happened, after Mimmo died and you realized how you fucked up the deal?"

"I try to tell them that I pay them back whatever they give me for making the first batch of vermouth. Their original investment. Everything. But I tell them I keep the bottles now. It the wish of Mimmo's partner. His famiglia. I know I have to go to my brothers for the money to pay them back, but I do that for Mimmo. But these men say no. Those bottles for them to auction now. They don't want just my money. They want interest on the investment and say the bottle theirs now. So I send them to Betta here. I want to hide them. Keep them away from those men. I don't know how they find out. I only tell Andrea that I take care of those bottles. But they find me. And now they have the bottles, and Mimmo's family do not get what they should."

I nodded. "Stay here, Maurizio. Listen to some music. I'll try not to be too long."

He looked at me as he put his earbuds on. Before I was out of the Jeep, I could hear Sonny Rollins' sax through Maurizio's tinny earbuds.

# 13

She opened the door before I got to it and looked at me curiously. "You the man who run the Sporting Place with Tubby Levett," she said as I approached. She was short and stocky with wide hips, and wearing an old housedress. She looked to be in her early sixties. She had a colorful scarf covering up most of her thick curly gray hair. There was a prominent birthmark close to her nose.

"Lorissa Blue?"

"Yes, sir?"

"Len Buonfiglio," I said.

There was an awkward pause and then she said: "Yes, I know Mr. Len. Levett family just down the road. They speak of you often."

"Why are you here?" she asked, still standing at the door. I was wondering the same thing. She looked past me to the Jeep. "Who that in your car?"

I turned. Maurizio was sitting up listening to the music. "Just a friend. It doesn't matter."

"Did Sassy send you?"

I thought about that. "No, but why are you asking? Why do you think I'm here?"

"You're not police. I talked to the police about what happened to Lord Ram. What do you have to do with it?"

I had nothing to do with it and I wasn't comfortable being

there. I wasn't comfortable with any of this. Do I tell her McWilliams sent me? Or that Queen Sassy also wanted me to clear her name? I didn't know the protocol, if there was any. "I just want to go over what happened as far as you know when Lord Ram died. There are lots of rumors. I'm just helping to clear it all up."

She studied me as I stood in her doorway. "Come in, then," she mumbled.

I followed her inside the house. The very small living room featured a brown cloth-covered couch, two matching brown chairs with pillows on them, and a glass-topped coffee table. The front window shades were drawn while the side window close to the kitchen was open and offered the only light in the house.

"Would you like sorrel? I have some chilled I made yesterday."

Sorrel was a tea made from dried hibiscus flowers. It was served either warm or on ice and usually brewed with ginger and cinnamon. The problem with sorrel, in most cases, was that it was just too sweet for me. To temper that, I liked to add rum. I didn't think I could ask Ms. Blue for that. "Sure, Ms. Blue. That would be great," I said, reluctantly accepting her offer.

I sat in one of the brown chairs on top of a pillow while she went into the kitchen to get the cold drink. She brought it over and sat opposite me. I took a sip. I did my best not to grimace. As I suspected, it was overly sweet and flavored with a heavy dose of cinnamon. "Delicious," I said, smiling brightly.

"I tell the police everything I know. The man old and feeble, but he still can walk well enough he do not need assistance. He can still take he self to the bathroom and clean he self. He do not even want me there, but Sassy insist he have round-the-clock care. The man get up so early every day. Before the sun rises. He go to the kitchen every morning and pour he self a glass of soursop juice. That what he do every morning I there. Soursop calm the nerves and better in the evening, but the man like it when he wake. Say it's good for the circulation."

I remembered Sassy telling me he needed help going to the bathroom. Now his caregiver was telling me that wasn't the case. "So he was strong enough to get up to take care of himself—bathroom and all."

"Yes of course," she said, surprised that I asked.

"And you were not there with him when he went to get his juice that morning?"

"Mr. Len, I never there when he wake. I was not hired to watch the man every moment I there. I am there to make sure he get everything he need. When he want something, he ask me. I keep his house tidy. Make sure his room and bathroom clean. I cook he dinner. Clean up the kitchen. The old man not a child like other old ones I see. He still strong enough to go on about his everyday routines."

"Did he waver at all in his walking? Did you ever know him to fall before?"

"When we get old, walking can sometimes be tricky. You'll soon find out about that too, sir."

I didn't respond to that, and she noticed.

"I mean all of us, sir. It happen to all of us. We get old. And we all eventually see Jesus."

I didn't want to get into any of that. Maurizio was waiting for me in the Jeep. I wanted to be done with this. "So you were where when he fell?"

"I was upstairs. I know he get up early and I try to be awake when he wake, but many times I sleep a bit past when he awake. But just a bit. I hear he in the kitchen and that usually wake me. The man get feisty when I hover around him. So I let him be. I give him he space."

"But on that morning you were still asleep when he fell? You didn't hear anything?"

I noticed that she was rubbing her hands together as she talked. I didn't sense that she was nervous; her voice was steady, but she was fiddling with her fingers and hands. I saw someone on television once explain how to read body language and remembered something about nervous fingers and hands meaning that person was possibly lying. I wondered about Ms. Blue as she fiddled with her fingers.

"No, I did not. When I get up, Jannilea was already here. She find the man on the ground."

I didn't know what else to ask. Just because she had a nervous habit with her hands and fingers didn't mean she was hiding anything. And I couldn't see her doing anything to hurt Lord Ram. She seemed honest to me. I forced down more of the sorrel.

"How long were you working for Lord Ram?"

She thought for a moment. "Sassy hire me about a year ago. I work before for the elderly. She check out all my references."

"What did you think when you got the job?"

"What do you mean, sir?"

"I mean Lord Ram is the most famous celebrity from St. Pierre. Were you happy? Nervous? Honored?" I really wasn't sure why I was asking her these questions. They just came to me. He wasn't just any other elderly patient. He was island royalty.

"Mr. Len, to tell you the truth, I more a fan of King Delight than Lord Ram. I believe he calypso stronger than Ram's. Ram always rhyming about pretty little girls and so on. King Delight tell the people the truth about their lives. But that's just my opinion. Lord Ram make many a wonderful Carnival song that the people love and dance to. I respect that. I know others make a rival out of the two. They form their tribes. When I am hired, yes, even though I prefer King Delight, I have no grudge."

I smiled thinking to myself, now there's a motive for murder. Whacking the man because he got more accolades than her preferred Calypsonian. I knew people here took their calypso allegiances seriously, but that was a little far-fetched even for my Clouseau-like mind. I drank enough of the sorrel to show that I was grateful for it. With that, I stood up. This was going nowhere.

"Thank you for the sorrel, Ms. Blue," I said. "And for answering my questions."

We started for the front door together. "You are welcome, Mr. Len. Tubby's mother speaks very highly of you and you working together with him has been a very good thing for his family."

"And for me too," I said, and then made my way to the Jeep. I thought about the conversation. I could only go on my impressions. She seemed credible, but, and it wasn't how she played with her hands, I sensed something was off—as if she were composed to a fault. I don't know why I felt that, but I did. But it was not enough to convince me that what she told me was not the truth.

# 14

"We go find the bottles now?" Maurizio asked, louder than he should have, speaking over the jazz pouring through his earbuds.

I put my seat belt on and started up the Jeep. "Do you really think those bottles are still on the island, Maurizio?"

"Lennie, they must be," he said. "They belong to Andrea now. Those men, I know I make a deal, but I can get out of it. I can pay them. I just need the bottles back."

I thought about what he said as I headed down toward Garrison. They took the bottles, but I didn't think they were done here.

"How much were you going to give them, Maurizio? How much do you owe them for the vermouth deal?"

He looked at me and nodded but didn't speak. That was not a good sign. He was in deeper than I thought. I turned off the music.

"How much?" I asked again.

"I borrow one hundred and twenty thousand euros, Lennie. But the deal was to give a percentage of the auction of the bottles. So they make money on that too."

"Did you give them anything yet?"

He shook his head. "I tell them I will return the one hundred and twenty thousand euros. I give them everything they invest back. Just I want to keep the bottles signed by Mimmo."

"How did they know you were here? Did you tell anyone in Italy where you were going? Your family? Friends?"

He shook his head. "No one know."

"You said you told Betta. You called her." I looked at him.

"Mannaggia..." He cursed in Italian. I knew that curse. I had heard my grandfather say the same thing many times when he was pissed off at me and my brother Pat for playing our music too loud when he and my grandmother would come over to visit. But I had never heard a word like that from Maurizio. Hearing it from him also made me want to curse, but I didn't. Who knows how they got his phone records, but they did. And that they now knew where Betta lived made me even angrier with Maurizio's sloppiness. I saw him squirming in his seat. He knew he messed up and put his wife and kid in danger. But seeing him like that—like a lost puppy—I just couldn't yell at him.

The road I was driving on was narrow and there were cars parked on curbs so if a bus or truck was coming in my direction, I had to maneuver the Jeep to the side so it could pass. But I couldn't do that safely while having this conversation. I pulled over to the side of the road.

"Maurizio, if they know you are here, if they found the bottles at my place, they know more about you than you think." I stared at him. "Meaning they know about Betta. And about Paolo."

He nodded, his face blanched white. He had been thinking the same thing I was. "We go there now. We go see Betta and my son."

I was planning on doing that whether he said so or not, but it was nice to hear it from his lips, to see the genuine concern on his face. I pulled back onto the road, such as it was, with its potholes and broken concrete. As I got closer to Garrison and out of the countryside, the road smoothed and widened. I was able to drive a bit faster. There was a knot in my stomach. Those two were Maurizio's blood, but they also felt like my own.

\* \* \*

When I pulled up to Betta's house, and even before I braked and turned off the engine, Maurizio was out the door. He speed-walked to the front door; elbows out, knees knobby and somewhat bow-legged, he burst into the house. I was happy to see that concern from him. This was a man who didn't have the guts to stand up to his mother and father and live with the woman he loved. Now, maybe, it would be different. Maybe whatever trouble he got himself into helped him see what was a part of him—that was now his own flesh and blood.

I followed behind and entered the house. Nothing seemed awry. Betta was there and so was Paolo. She wore a dark tank top and denim cut-offs, her long legs exposed. Maurizio had his hands on her arms and was speaking softly to her. Paolo ignored his father, who he just met a few days earlier, and came to me for a hug. He was almost five now. I picked him up. He was a solid, heavy kid. "How goes it, blue eyes?" I said to him.

He grinned at me. "That's my father," he said to me, turning to Maurizio.

"Yes, that's your dad. He's gonna teach you to speak Italian."

"What??" Paolo crinkled his nose.

"*Parlare Italiano*. You need to learn his language. It will help you when you go out to an Italian restaurant." I winked at him, and he laughed.

"Noooo, I speak English," he said.

"You do, and you speak it well. But there's nothing wrong with Italian. You know I'm Italian, don't you?"

He looked at me as if I were an alien from another planet.

"I am. But I'm not an Italian like your father. And I speak that language worse than he speaks English."

Paolo glanced at his father and then at me. He didn't get the joke and I understood that it was a bad one. Instead, he said, "I want to go swim again with you, Leonard." He emulated his mother in calling me by my formal name.

I was an occasional visitor at Betta's house, showing up for a dinner or taking her and Paolo on drives. When she needed me to watch the boy, which was rare, especially since her mother was usually around, I gladly obliged. A few times I took him to the beach. He loved the water and, in the calm, shallow waters of Heaven's Beach, one of the island's best, I started to teach him to swim. Like most mammals, he took to it naturally. Still, I made sure he wore those orange floaty things on his arms—at least when Betta was at the beach with us. When she wasn't there, I had him swim without them. I wanted him to feel secure in the water without any help. I would be close enough that if there any problems, I could get to him quickly. But there never were. He was a quick learner and, when he entered secondary school, he could join a swim team.

"Lennie, she and Paolo stay with you?" Maurizio asked me as I put the boy down.

I quickly shook my head. I didn't want to say anything about what I thought I heard in the middle of the night, but I suspected those men also now knew where I lived. "I don't think so, Maurizio."

"Why?" Betta asked. She didn't understand. She thought something else was preventing me from letting the two stay with me.

"I just think it might be safer if you and Paolo go to your mother's, if you can do that. And you should do it now. Get your stuff together and I'll take you over."

Betta's eyes went wide. She took a deep breath. I could tell she was angry, but not with me. Her husband was back, the father of her child. And immediately her life was upended. She knew he was in trouble, but I don't know how much she knew. She huffed away from him and went into the bedroom to pack.

"I stay with them there?" Maurizio asked.

"No, you stay with me. In fact, I want you with me all the time now. Just in case."

"*Si*, Lennie," he said.

Betta came out with a roll-on bag. She looked at me, or should I say, glared. "Ready?" I asked.

She nodded. And we all left the house together.

# 15

There was very little talk in the Jeep as I drove. Betta was fuming. What I had observed when Maurizio and Betta were together years ago, before he left, was happiness—joy—love. Now I sensed none of that. It was almost as if she didn't want him back with her. At least that was the vibe I was getting

I pulled in front of her mother's house in Vieux Castille, a village at the foot of Mount Hadali, the island's dormant volcano. I had hiked around the volcano and though it was considered dormant, I'd come across hot springs and a few bubbling mudholes, so now I always wore my oldest sneakers. The bronze mud was impossible to get off. The volcano was monitored from an observatory on St. Vincent, but still, we all wanted plenty of notice before Hadali decided to wake up.

The dark brick, two-bedroom home was on the slope of the mountain. Mrs. Baptiste lived alone. Her husband had left when Betta was an infant and never returned, so Betta never knew her father—and her mother had told her very little about him. She raised Betta alone while she worked as a cook in St. Elizabeth Hospital. And Betta was rebellious, wanting more than what her mother could give her. She left school and her house when she was sixteen, starting her own business entertaining locals, visiting dignitaries, and the tourists who could afford her. That all stopped when she met Maurizio. And if nothing else, I was grateful to him for that.

Alongside the house was an extensive garden where Mrs. Baptiste cultivated ground provisions and medicinal herbs off the rich volcanic soil. Sometimes, when Betta would invite me over for dinner, her mother, with whom she made amends soon after Paolo was born, was at her house.

Maurizio was going to get out of the car and say hello to Mrs. Baptiste, but I told him to stay put. "Please, Lennie, I should say ciao."

Betta was already out of the door and scowled back at him. He slunk back into the seat.

"I'll be right back," I said to him.

Betta took Paolo inside. Mrs. Baptiste looked at me and then peered past me to the Jeep. "Did that man bring more trouble?"

"It will be all right," I said. "Just give it a day or two."

"A day or two? Why he come back? That man weak. My daughter needs a strong man. Not one like that. What she see in him? Why she give him a boy he doesn't even know?"

I had no answers, and she knew it. I turned to go.

"Wait," she said.

I stopped as she went back into the house. I stood at the doorway, looking back at the Jeep. Mrs. Baptiste came back to the door. She held a paper bag out to me. "Shadon Beni," she said. "I just picked it."

I opened the bag and a pungent herbal aroma wafted out from the green leafy herb within. I quickly closed the bag. This was one of those times when my strong sense of smell was a curse.

"Add to a fish stew," she said. "Or when the muscles ache or a headache, it helps with inflammation, brewed in a tea with honey."

"Thank you. I could always use something for sore muscles," I said, not mentioning that a fish stew was not on my immediate menu. "It will only be a day or two, I promise," I said to her, not knowing if I should have made that assurance or not.

She nodded and closed the door.

\* \* \*

I'd been away from the bar all day. I needed to check in and maybe figure out what to do next.

"I make this all right, Lennie," Maurizio said.

"If you say so, Maurizio."

When I first saw Maurizio that morning in my Jeep, I had quickly assessed that he hadn't aged much since he left the island. Now, upon closer inspection, he looked older. I noticed wrinkles when he frowned around his eyes and forehead. Leaving his pregnant wife here had to weigh on him. I couldn't imagine that kind of guilt. Well, I could. I knew guilt. I had a dose of it when I refused to join my brother in taking over my father's landscaping business. And then more when I went against my parents by quitting college to join the Marines—a mistake I still regret. And finally—the pain I caused my wife, and then my children when I left them to come to this place. And those were just the big ones.

The phone rang as we drove back to the bar. McWilliams's name flashed on the Bluetooth monitor in the Jeep. "Superintendent," I said.

"Any news from your meeting with Ms. Blue?" McWilliams asked, his voice booming through the Jeep's speakers.

"I think she told me pretty much the same thing she told you. She was upstairs when Ram died. The other aide found the body."

"Mmhmm," McWilliams murmured on the other end of the line.

"I don't know, McWilliams. This thing seems like a dead end to me. You sure you want me to keep at it?"

"Go see the other aide and then we see."

"All right but, while I'm helping you, I need your help finding two men."

"What's this about? What men do you need to find?"

"A couple of men broke into my bar last night. They took

something of value I want back."

"Are you reporting a robbery at the Sporting Place? Is this an official request?"

"You know me better than that, McWilliams. I would like it if you could see if you can locate these two men. Off the record. I believe they are Swedish..."

"No, no, Lennie." Maurizio blurted out. "They not Swedish. They live in Sweden. Many migrant live there. Bulgarian, or Serbian. I not sure."

"Who's that?" McWilliams asked after hearing Maurizio.

"A friend."

"What friend? Did he just hear us talk about..."

"No. Don't worry about that. I'll tell you later. Anyway, one of them has bleached white hair. The other is bald with one of those ridiculous lumberjack beards. Tattoos. Earrings. The whole outfit. I have no idea how they got on the island. I don't think they were on a cruise boat, but maybe a yacht. I doubt they flew in. You can easily check that, I think. No?"

There was hesitation on the line. I was almost at the bar.

"No, Buonfiglio. Nothing is easy. I think you know that. What could be of value that they took from your bar. A bottle of our own Karime rum? A case of Carib beer? Now you have me very curious."

"Does it matter, McWilliams? I just need to get back what they took."

"Since this is unofficial business and you are not reporting a robbery, it does not matter. But if I do find these men and you get what they took back, at some point you will tell me?"

"Yes, McWilliams, you know I always keep you in the loop," I said.

I could hear his sigh as he recognized my sarcasm, even over the phone. "I will see what I can find out about these Swedish Serbian Bulgarian men."

"Thank you."

"The other aide, Jannilea Richard. Speak to her please."

I cut off the call.

Maurizio looked at me. "The police, Lennie?"

"Don't worry, he's going to do it off the books. He knows what he is doing."

"Please, these men learn that the police are involved, it get more dangerous."

"Yes, I know, Maurizio. I trust McWilliams to help us without putting anyone in danger."

Maurizio looked pained. He rubbed his face with his hands. I thought he was about to cry again. The pressure was getting to him. I needed him to hold it together. "Hang in there, Maurizio. We'll find those bottles and take care of this. It will all work out." I said it to calm him, but I knew the reality was that it might not work out at all. I just didn't say that to him.

# 16

Tubby gave me a familiar look when we returned to the Sporting Place. He always wanted to know it all, and could sense when I was keeping something from him. And I was. He didn't need to know about Maurizio's mess. I could hear chatter coming from one of the tables out on the deck. I looked through the door to the deck. I saw laughing, sunburnt faces of both men and women. The men wore baseball caps. The women had big sun hats. Neither were enough to protect their now very pink cheeks. They had already gotten too much sun.

"They from Alabama. They sailing from Bequia and Petit Martinique, they say," Tubby said.

The pained look he had just a few moments earlier was magically gone. Maurizio was now was sitting at the bar chatting, or I should say, gesticulating, with Horace Fancy.

"You go speak to Ms. Blue about Lord Ram? McWilliams say to do that?"

"Yeah, you know that. And she speaks very highly of you," I said.

"But she have nothing to do with the man's death."

"Once I speak to the other aide, it's over. I can say I did it for him and he'll owe us one. For some reason he thinks that it's bad for St. Pierre to spread false rumors when it comes to crimes."

"He right about that, but people like to believe what they

believe. Good luck trying to prove otherwise."

"Yeah, well, I'm not gonna try very hard, believe me."

"No?" Tubby was skeptical.

"No, Tubby."

"Anyway, I've got other things I have to deal with now."

Tubby looked at Maurizio. "The men who break in and take those bottles?"

I nodded but was listening in as Maurizio and Fancy chattered about the recent failures of the Italian national football team.

"Two World Cups without the Italians?" Fancy said, shaking his head.

"*Si*, a disgrace," Maurizio said. "They lose to Macedonia." He hung his head in shame.

"I do not even know where Macedonia is," Fancy said.

I looked at Fancy, remembering that Thursday was his day off from working at the airport. He was a customs officer, such as that was in St. Pierre. I moved away from Tubby and leaned over the bar.

"Horace, how's your lovely wife?" I asked with a grin.

He hissed and waved his hand derisively. "Mr. Len, it not like you to bring up Owena when I come here. Why you ruin a wonderful conversation I am having with our long-lost Italian friend?"

"I'm just teasing, Horace." I opened a fresh cold bottle of Heineken. "This one is on me."

"Well thank you, Mr. Len. And I hope you don't mind if I don't answer your question."

"I don't mind at all, Horace. But I have another question."

"As long as it doesn't concern my marital relations."

Maurizio was watching us, eyes going back and forth like he was following a tennis match.

"Never, Horace. I'm just curious. Do you check on liquor that comes from different countries and sold here? Do they have to go through customs? Is there a special department to approve that, or is it just done at the airport or the harbor at customs at either place?"

"The alcohol that comes to you, I know, Mr. Len, you get from St. Vincent. Part of Caricom so that is not an issue if that is what you are asking."

Caricom, I knew, was kind of like the European Union for the Caribbean. They pooled resources together to unify the region. Part of that was to have similar standards on tariffs and customs. "No, Horace. It's not about how I get my booze. I want to know what a person has to do to either import or export, let's say, a case of rum which, I know, is well above and beyond the allotted one liter per person."

"For that quantity, you would need a special permit and pay the import tax and duty based on the amount imported. You could not just bring it in unless you smuggled it."

Maurizio was trying to speak. I put my hand up to hold him off.

"And the same going out? Exporting?"

"The same, Mr. Len. You need to clear with customs and pay the duty and tax. But you know if you are asking if a case of rum can be exported from here, it can easily be smuggled out if you take it onto a boat. Via the airport, where I work, that cannot happen, but on the sea it is easily done."

"That's what I thought. Is that common, as far as you know?"

"These waters are known for that, Mr. Len. It has been going on forever. That is why you always hear about the drug seizures on the sea. That is what the Coast Guard of Caricom, IMPACs, and other island law enforcement concentrate on. Now if it's a few cases of rum or a lovely single malt from Scotland, they will not put the effort in to stop something like that. I'm sure you understand how it all works."

I did. That was how I got the imported cheese, San Marzano tomatoes, and other gourmet items from that boat that would show up offshore once a month—the one Tubby and I took a skiff out to meet. The authorities, I'm sure, knew about it, but like Horace said, why would they waste their time on busting a very small-time, harmless smuggler when there were big drug traffickers out there?

"Thanks, Horace. Give my best to your lovely wife."

Just the mention of Owena had him grumbling. Maurizio got off his stool and came around the bar.

"I tell you, Lennie," Maurizio said in a somewhat hushed voice. "I get a permit like he say to bring in the vermouth. I pay a duty."

"So there is a record of the bottle coming in, but, most likely, there will be none when it goes out. There is no chance they leave here by air. They'll take the bottles somewhere else where they can smuggle them onto a plane and back to Sweden."

"You think that's what they do?"

"Maurizio, I'm just guessing here. I'm no detective. I don't know. But it makes sense, no?"

"Yes. He can take off a boat? Just like that?"

"Apparently."

"Lennie, I have to get those bottles. I owe this much to Mimmo."

I looked at him. He had no idea what was coming, and I didn't know if I should tell him. Those men came a long way. They got back their precious bottles. They could just take them to that auction house in Sweden. Make the money off the dead artist's authenticated signature on each label. But they didn't get what they were owed from their initial investment. Would they just leave without doing what they do when they have to chase something or someone down? When they are shorted on a deal? I didn't like what I was thinking, and it was obvious on my face.

Someone from the group out on the deck came up to the bar, a rotund man with wire-rim glasses and a red Crimson Tide baseball cap on a head that from what I could see had very little hair on it. "You the boss, hoss?" he said in a Southern drawl.

I had heard my share of accents in the bar. With the exception of infrequent, more bohemian travelers, backpackers hiking Mt. Hadali, or the occasional elite who wanted to get away from the trendy hot spots like St. Barts or Anguilla, St. Pierre was not one of the popular destinations for American tourists. Most who visited from the States came off the cruise boats for a day tour or, like the man with the Crimson Tide sunburn in front of me, off a catamaran or yacht cruising through the Grenadines.

"I haven't been called either the boss or hoss since I left the Bronx. Are you trying to make me homesick?"

From the boozy smile on his face, helped by rounds of Caribs, and maybe a few of Tubby's strong rum punches, I didn't think he would take offense to my remarks. "Four more of those cold beers, sir," he said. "And tell me, how much did you pay to get that view?" He indicated the view of Garrison Harbor, the blue Caribbean beyond and, around six each evening year-round, one of the best sunsets you could ever imagine.

I popped open tops for four Caribs and placed them in front of him. "All it took was my priceless charm," I said.

"I don't know about your charm, fella," he said with a laugh. "But let me tell you, that view is priceless. Our friends told us about this place. Rick Benson. He's also from Birmingham. He was here, hmm, I think it was in December."

Did he think I was going to remember his friend? "You mean Rick, the Auburn fan?" I asked, giving him a sincere smile.

"Yeah, him. But besides that big fault in his character, he's a great guy. You must have met his wife, Barbara, too?"

"Yeah, sure. A lovely woman." I was in deep now. I had to get out of any more talk about Rick Benson and his lovely wife Barbara who I definitely never met. "How long are you sticking around the waters of our lovely island, Mr...?"

"Terry Liston," he said, extending his beefy palm. I took it graciously. "And we aren't sure. We have a few weeks of downtime. Contemplating retirement. The whole point of this excursion was not to rush from point A to point B."

The way he asked it and the way he looked at me, I knew he was waiting for me to introduce myself. It wasn't what I wanted to do, but again, I did have to show some business sense and keep the Sporting Place's reputation intact. "I do, Terry, and never call me 'sir,' but you can call me Len. Len Buonfiglio."

"Great to meet you, Len."

He started to pull out his wallet. I waved it away. "This round is on us, Mr. Liston," I said. I wasn't sure why I did it. I bought rounds before for customers who spent extra time drinking my booze.

"Thank you, Len." He put his wallet back in his pocket.

"Where are you moored?" I asked, inching closer to what I was remotely thinking.

"Out near the yacht club. We booked the catamaran in Martinique. Got a great crew too. They speak English, so that's no problem. Even have ourselves an unbelievable cook."

"What more could you ask for?"

"I can always ask for more," he said.

"Yeah, funny how that is. Have you seen the island? Taken the tour? Done the tourist thing?"

"Only as far as from where our boat is moored to your bar. What am I missing? I mean, you seen one island, you've seen them all. Correct?"

"Tsk tsk, Mr. Liston. I'm from the Bronx, New York, but St. Pierre is now my home, so I will take grouping this island in with all the others as an insult."

He chuckled. "Forgive me, Len. And please call me Terry."

"Terry? I was going to call you Sonny."

"Sheesh, you know, I'm old enough to hear that too often. You can call me Terry. You can call me Sonny. Just don't call me Mr. Liston. At least not here in this bar."

"I'm just teasing, Terry," I said, hoping he knew I wasn't that much of a smartass.

"I know you are, Len."

"Anyway, it sounds like you've got everything you need on that boat of yours." I felt my phone vibrate in my pocket. I was getting a call. It would be rude to pick up while chatting with a customer. And I had the glint of an idea I didn't want to lose. So I let it ring.

"Back to your question, Len. When you're retired like we are, you don't have to rush back to your empty nests. So we do have a schedule, but nothing is set in stone. Bama plays Southern Mississippi in Tuscaloosa the last Saturday in August. As long as we are back by then, all is good."

"But you can watch the game right here, Terry," I said. I wasn't sure why I was continuing this chat. But I was. There was a reason for it somewhere. I was thinking about that boat of his. Where they were moored. And wondering if they might sight others on nearby boats coming and going. Like two swarthy, tattooed Swedish-not-Swedish gangsters for example. But I couldn't come right out and ask him that.

Liston took the beers in both hands. "It was good to meet you, Len. We might be back tomorrow. We hear the sunset is something special here."

"Please do, Terry. And you are correct. The sunset here is the best you will find on the island." I wanted to make a connection. I had the ridiculous notion that maybe if I got to know the man better he would invite me out to his yacht. We could sail around the harbor. I could keep my eyes open for a boat that might be housing those men. It was a crazy idea, I knew that. But I was desperate. I realized I could easily ask Tubby to find someone with a boat and do it myself, or with him, but I sensed that could get dangerous. I wanted, needed, to find these men, get those bottles back, make sure Maurizio was cleared of all this, and then move on. Move on to what? Finding out what really happened to Lord Ram? Or to the preferred monotony of my life? Tending bar? Walking with my dogs on the craggy beach near my house?

I watched Liston go back to his group on the deck. He was laughing and pointing in my direction, most likely telling them all about the Jimmy Buffett-type character behind the bar. This one, though, was an Italian-American from the Bronx who never once in his life stepped into a place called Margaritaville.

I turned back to Maurizio. I was about to tell him the improbable plan I just hatched about getting on Liston's yacht and having him shuttle us around the harbor to find those guys. But when I turned, though Horace Fancy was still there with another Heineken in front of him, Maurizio was not. I looked around the bar for that pale dome. He was easy to spot, and the bar was not crowded. I rushed to the men's room and opened the door. I called out his name. There was no answer. I went out to the parking lot. I looked up and down Windy Hill Road. You would think a speed-walking white man would be easy to spot. But I saw no one.

He was gone.

# PLAYLIST TWO

## M's Titans of the Jazz Piano

1. You Go To My Head, Bud Powell
2. Cantaloupe Island, Herbie Hancock
3. Dat Dere, Bobby Timmons
4. Little Girl Blue, John Lewis
5. Five Spot Blues, Thelonious Monk
6. When Sonny Gets Blue, McCoy Tyner
7. My Blue Heaven, Mary Lou Williams
8. Waltz for Debby, Bill Evans
9. Excerpts From the Blues, Ahmad Jamal
10. Blue Skies, Art Tatum
11. Windows, Chick Corea
12. The Single Petal of a Rose, Duke Ellington
13. All Alone, Mal Waldron
14. You Look Good To Me, Oscar Peterson
15. Peace Piece, Bill Evans

# 17

"What did you see?" I asked Horace Fancy when I got back into the bar.

"We still talk football," Fancy said. "He tell me the Italians will never be the same again. I ask him why and before he tell me, I see he pick up his phone and put it to his ear. He getting a call. I can see he agitated. And then he just leave. He move fast. Not even saying goodbye or looking at me."

I turned to Tubby. "What about you? Did you see him go?"

"No, man, I busy back here while you chat away with the man in the red cap. I never see you so chatty with the people come here off the boats. You after something?"

"It doesn't matter now," I said. I went out the front door again and looked down Windy Hill Road, hoping I would see Maurizio in the distance, or wandering back to the bar. But as I suspected, he was nowhere. I came back in. "I've got to go. I have to find him."

Tubby made that sucking sound through his teeth and glanced around at the growing crowd. He didn't want to say that he needed some help. That sound told me all I needed to know.

"Can you get in touch with Mike? Is he back from that trip with his son?"

"He just back. Trouble come with the Italian man, I see."

"Maybe."

"I thought so. He show up like that after so many years for a reason. And he will drag you into his mess."

"You know I'd do the same for you, Tubby."

He thought about that for a moment. "Maybe so, but I don't leave an island with a woman carrying my son. What does that say about a man?"

I didn't have an answer for Tubby. It was very easy for some people to judge others. What Maurizio did was unconscionable. I knew that. Yet again, I did pretty much the same thing. Maybe that was why I cut him slack. Maybe I knew that we do things sometimes that not only hurt others, but ourselves. Why? That was a mystery that I couldn't really answer.

"Are you okay by yourself here until Mike comes? I'll try to get back as soon as I can."

"I can handle it.

"Call me if there are any problems."

"You know I will. And after I close up tonight, you can call me if you need some assistance with the Italian-man matter, which I am sure you will. So I will expect that call."


As I got into my Jeep I took my phone out of my pocket. I remembered then that I was getting a call while talking to Terry Liston. I looked at the screen. The call was from Betta, but there was no message left. I felt my stomach clench. Why did I let it ring? Why didn't I check to see who was calling? Because I was thinking about that ludicrous plan of having Liston ferry me around looking for those men on moored boats. I was an idiot.

I raced down the hill now, but you could only go so fast on St. Pierre's narrow, winding roads. Whether she called me before or after she called Maurizio didn't matter. He got the same call. And it was urgent enough for him to take off without a word to me.

It took about twenty minutes for me to get to Betta's mother's house. I rushed out of the Jeep.

Mrs. Baptiste pushed open the front door. I didn't see Betta. I didn't see Paolo. She had a strained look on her face.

And then, just as I was at the door, Paolo emerged. I felt some relief. I looked beyond him, wanting to see Betta there by her son's side. But I knew, just as I knew when I ran down those subway stairs that June day years ago, that I would not.

"Betta?" I asked. Hoping still.

Mrs. Baptiste shook her head. "They come and take her. They had a gun."

I figured they would. Just as they would smuggle the vermouth out they could possess guns on the boat and take it ashore. It was almost impossible to legally own a gun on St. Pierre, and as a result, gun violence was very rare. When it did occur, it was usually from a gun smuggled in from a boat. There were no metal detectors at the harbor or at any public facilities on the island. There was no need. Someone could easily walk around with a handgun and go undetected. But the problems that were so prevalent where I came from had not come yet to St. Pierre.

Paolo went back to watching television. I was glad for that now. I glanced at what he was watching. There were guns. Men chasing men. I didn't care. Watch all the junk you want, kid, I thought to myself. Anything to distract him from what was going on.

Mrs. Baptiste and I were at the kitchen table. "They say they take Paolo if Betta do not go with them."

"What else did they say?"

"Just that they had to go someplace. And just that my daughter had to go with them."

"You didn't call the police, did you?"

She shook her head. "Betta try to call you before they come into the house. When we see them walking around outside. We see the guns."

I had felt my phone vibrating against my thigh and I didn't even bother to check. I was too engrossed in a conversation with a man from Alabama. I would regret that for a long time, not that I could have done much to help Betta in the moment.

"Did she call Maurizio?"

Mrs. Baptiste's face was pained. She nodded. Her eyes had seen so much. She had Betta with a man who left before her daughter was born. And then her daughter, when she was old enough, left as well. Betta was all she had.

I sat there at the small, plastic-covered kitchen table. I could hear the guns again from the show Paolo was watching. I looked at my phone, hoping I'd get something. But there was nothing. Maurizio knew where his wife was. They took her to get to him. A pale Italian with wiry tufts of hair rushing around the island would be noticeable. Someone had to have seen him. I wasn't about to canvas door to door. I thought about McWilliams. He had the resources. He would immediately step in as soon as I mentioned that Betta was abducted at gunpoint. But that might be a huge mistake. That might put her in greater danger, make those men panic and do something they didn't want to do. I had to keep McWilliams out of this. I needed to find Maurizio and Betta, and I had to do it fast.

"They said nothing about where they were taking her?"

"No, Mr. Len."

Paolo got up from the couch. He leaned against my hip. I knew he sensed the trouble around him. I looked at him and smiled. "My son is sending me that baseball cap I told you about," I said to the boy. "It's the original. Not a knockoff or cheap multi-colored version. This one is navy blue with white stitching and the interlocking 'NY.'"

"The one you say everyone very smart wears?" Paolo said.

I smiled that he remembered. I was kidding, of course, brainwashing him into being a Yankee fan even though gravitating to baseball would be a very long shot here on St. Pierre. "That's right. And you are smart, so you need the hat. It's the most famous hat in the world. Once you put it on your head, kid, you will feel the magic from it."

He smiled and I was glad to see that. My childhood home in the Bronx was about a fifteen-minute drive to the stadium. My brother Pat and I spent many an afternoon and evening in that place back in the glory days. I was a Yankee fan, but Pat was a fanatic.

"More magic than Harry Potter?"

"Who?"

He laughed, knowing I was teasing him, and went back to the television smiling.

I felt Mrs. Baptiste's eyes on me as Paolo and I chatted. I stood up. I needed to figure this out. I had to get to Betta. I had to find Maurizio. I was doing my best to show calm. I wanted them both to see that I was in control of the situation even though I had no idea where to start.

"I'm gonna go find her now and bring her home," I said with false confidence. "She'll be fine, Mrs. Baptiste. Those men won't hurt her."

When I said that, Paolo turned from the television to me. We looked at each other. And then he turned back to the television as if he was confident that what I just said to his grandmother was true. That they wouldn't hurt his mother. I wish I had that same confidence.

# 18

On a hunch, I drove up to the entrance of the national park. The park was a protected rainforest with typically very muddy trails leading up Mt. Hadali. The hike was not for everyone. One of the few times I did the hike, I watched as a tourist from the UK slipped and fell off the side of the trail and down into a gully. I was right behind him and helped pull him back up to the trail. He was around my age, wearing tan-colored khakis and flat-bottomed tennis shoes. He thanked me in a very British way, polite, with an embarrassed smile. He then brushed off some of the mud and resumed his hike up the mountain. When I reached the summit and the panoramic view of St. Pierre, the surrounding Caribbean and Atlantic, and in the distance some of the nearby islands, he was already there, sitting and eating an orange. He saw me as I took in the view and offered me one of his oranges. I took it, and after eating it, made my way back down.

At the entrance to the park were the famous Piccadilly Caves. It was where I found Maurizio hiding from his family, and my hunch was that he might be here again. But would he hide while his wife was in danger? Maybe my hunch was way off. To get into the caves during the day, you had to hire one of the Rastas who lived around the park to guide you in. The entrance fee was nominal. I paid my way and followed a barefoot man wearing only shorts, his dreadlocks swaying, into the dark caves. I called out for Maurizio.

"Who you call for?" the Rasta asked.

"A guy I know," I said. "He probably came in here maybe a few hours ago."

"No, no one come today. You could ask me that before you pay me."

"You sure?"

"Yes I sure, man. You the only one visit today."

I felt foolish now. I had to start thinking more clearly. Of course, I should have asked him first. I thanked him and went back to my Jeep.


I had another idea. I hoped this one would pay off, but it was a long shot. I drove to the Harbor, but first stopped at Uncle Harvey's Delightful Roti Shoppe, a few blocks from the Harbor. I picked up a chicken roti, an Indian flatbread stuffed with curry chicken, peas and potatoes. It was a staple on St. Pierre, an island favorite, and a substitute for the encroachment of fast food like Burger King and Kentucky Fried Chicken that had made their way to other islands, but not yet to St. Pierre. I knew it was a lost cause and that they would come here soon enough, but for now, we would enjoy Uncle Harvey's delightful rotis, and I always did.

But this chicken roti was not for me. I put the paper bag on the front seat of my Jeep. The grease from the roti was starting to dampen the bag. It wouldn't be the first time the vinyl seat covers would get roti grease on them. I didn't care. I had other things to worry about.

I drove down to the harbor not far from the cruise-boat port. No cruise boats were docked, and I was glad of that. I got out of the Jeep and walked close to the water. I looked both ways. He was usually here, a local mainstay, but because there was no cruise boat anchored, I couldn't be sure. I didn't know where else he would go. And then I saw him, closer to where the

Brian Silverman

harbor connected to the lagoon. There was an old wall made out of stone—the remnants of an eighteenth-century fortification. He was sitting on top of the wall, his chalky bare legs dangling. He was rocking on the wall.

I headed his way. He saw me coming now and laughed. It was more of a cackle, actually. The closer I got, the more he laughed, shaking his head. He had long dreadlocks, or just overgrown hair matted together until they formed ropes from lack of care. The locks were copper-brown and speckled with a good amount of gray. There was gray in his matted, knotted beard as well. When he laughed, his few teeth looked like animal incisors jutting from his jaw.

"Fuck you!" the man said, but he said it while laughing. "Devil man fuck with me. Fuck you. Bastard? Hero?"

Despite the hostility coming from him I kept moving toward him until I heard those last words from him. He looked back at me and seeing my shocked expression he laughed and then he noticed the brown paper bag in my hand. *"Steak au poivre, s'ilvous plait?"* His voice became steady when he spoke that little bit of French. His tone was now almost elegant.

I walked up to him and handed him the bag. He grabbed it and opened it. Sniffed. Looked inside. Shook his head. "Fuck you!"

"I know, it's not a steak, Fincey," I said. "But it's one of Uncle Harvey's rotis. Chicken. It's the best I could do."

He put a dirty hand into the bag and grabbed a piece of the roti and shoved it into his mouth. Crumbs from the flatbread spilled onto his matted beard.

"Pepper sauce?"

"Didn't they put it on?"

"Where the spice?" he asked as he consumed the food rapidly, crumbs spilling from his mouth.

Fincey Pierce was better known on the island of St. Pierre as Filthy Man. He was a constant presence at the harbor. There had been complaints about him over the years. In addition to his unkempt appearance and the accompanying odor that emanated from him, Fincey could be downright hostile. He had a foul mouth and used it on pretty much anyone who came into his sights. He was one of the first Peteys the Cruisers would see when they arrived on the island. He hissed and howled at them, his words mostly unintelligible, but the anger was clear. The authorities, embarrassed that he was the unlikely initial ambassador for St. Pierre, tried to relocate him but he always returned to the harbor area. He saw everything that went on in and around the harbor. And that was why I was there, roti in hand. I knew it was a long shot, but I was going on my instincts, whatever they were worth. I was hoping he saw something that could help me locate Betta and Maurizio.

I sat on the stone wall bravely close to Fincey, waiting while he ate the roti. He paid me no mind as I sat there. I noticed underneath all that hair and dirt that he had light, almost green eyes. They were clear. Alert. I said nothing. I let him eat, hoping a decent meal would soften his mood and that he might actually cooperate with me.

When he was finished, he wiped his hands clean on the flimsy napkins provided by Uncle Harvey. They didn't do much good on the mess caused by the greasy roti. The paper started to fall apart in Fincey's hands. He shook his head. "Shit they make," he mumbled.

My arms were crossed over my chest. I was trying to figure the best way to talk to him. So many spoke to him like he was an idiot—they assumed he was mentally challenged. I knew he was not.

"How much money you take from this island," he said in a serious voice. He didn't look at me as he said it. I was caught off guard by the question.

"What do you mean, Fincey?"

"This island you come to. You open a business here though you are not from here. Others do. You are not the first. I just want to know how much you make off of my people here."

I shrugged. "Enough to make it work," I said.

He snickered. "To make it work?"

I knew what he was getting at. I didn't want to get into it with him on how foreigners come to these islands and take advantage for their own profit. It was true, but I hoped the Sporting Place provided something to the island besides making me rich, which it certainly wasn't.

"You should come by some day. Tubby Levett will make you one of his special rum punches." After I said that I tried to picture Filthy Man in his tattered clothes, unwashed, probably barefoot, and staggering in for a drink.

He stared at me like I was the crazy one. And maybe I was. "Tubby Levett know nothing, And I don't drink poison," he muttered.

"Well, if you ever feel the need to see the bar and judge for yourself, you are welcome." Coward that I am, I knew that he rarely left the harbor area so I was pretty confident that would never happen.

"I would be welcome? Oh yes, sir, I'm sure. Now why are you here? Why?" He focused those intense green eyes on me.

I nodded. Small talk was over. That was good. "Do you remember the Italian man who made the bread?"

"*Pane di casa.*" He pronounced it with a near-perfect Italian accent. He cackled after he saw my surprised reaction. "I study languages at the University of the West Indies. I speak many foreign tongues. French. German. Japanese."

He waited for me to doubt him. I did not.

"*Pane di casa,*" he said again. "That's what they call that bread. The bread of the home. Don't you know that?"

I came down to the harbor thinking I would be struggling to communicate with a madman. Instead, the madman was making me feel stupid. "Yeah, well, I do, but…"

"You not a real Italian," he said with a snicker.

"Buonfiglio is not real Italian?"

"Not like the real Italian," he said. "The man who make the

bread. He bring me that bread all the time. Day-old, he said. But still, better than that soggy roti you bring me. That Italian man take that girl who I see with men around the harbor. That skinny girl. But then she stop and help him with his bread. She is a dark, skinny girl. Some white men like dark girls. Do you like dark skinny girls?"

I ignored his question and got to why I was there. "Have you seen her? Or the Italian?" I asked. He had given me the opening I needed.

"I know that's why you are here and bring me that roti. I see you with that girl."

Betta had her room not far from here—back when I first arrived on St. Pierre. When I would take her for steak dinners. "Fincey..."

"I know. I see you."

I wanted to get back to why I came to see him. I wasn't going to talk to him about Betta and me. "Did you see them?"

He scratched at his chalky thigh. He got off the wall and turned his back to me as he peed against it. He reached down to wipe his hands with sand and then turned back to me. "The girl go with the two men," he said, pointing out to the sea.

"Where?"

"Out there," he said. "They take her out to a boat."

I looked out at the sea. "What boat?"

"That bad boy from Lavantville. He take them on he little boat, but they go out too far for me to see. Why would that dark skinny girl go with those men? With the bad boy. I know she don't go with men like that anymore. But I see it with my own eyes." He pointed to his eyes as he said that.

I clenched and cracked my fingers as he told me this. I knew I had to do my best to remain under control. But that could never happen. And Fincey noticed. "You didn't see them do anything—to her?" I asked as calmly as I could.

"No," he replied. "She just go with them. Peaceful."

I looked out to where he pointed. She was out there on a

boat with two, maybe more men.

"Your face get red, man." He laughed. "Girl too young for you."

"And the Italian? Did you see him?" I asked, ignoring his remark. If they took Betta, they did it to get to Maurizio. I knew it was he they really wanted.

Fincey shook his head. "If I see the Italian, I ask him for more bread. *Pane di casa.* I like the Italian man. He different than other white men. I like him."

I wasn't sure what he meant by that and didn't have the time to press him on it. I just needed to find the two of them. "So you didn't see him?"

"The bad boy from Lavantville know where he take them."

"What's his name? This bad boy?"

Fincey just looked at me. He picked at his matted beard and then lay across the stone wall. That was his way of saying he didn't know. Or that he was just done with me. He stared up at the darkening sky. His light green eyes opened wide. "Now I wait for the stars to come."

Wait for the stars to come? I knew then I'd get nothing more from him. He was considered the island madman. How reliable could what he told me be? I had heard that he once was brilliant. That he taught at the University of the West Indies in Barbados. What made him go mad, I wasn't sure. Some family matter, I think, and that made sense. Family matters can often make lunatics out of us. Still, how would he know Betta was escorted to a boat commandeered by the "bad boy from Lavantville?" Did he dream it in his muddled mind? I didn't think so. I went to him for a reason. If I didn't think he had information that could be helpful, why did I bother? I was now making myself crazy, going in circles. I had made plenty of mistakes in the past by doing bits of investigative work since I came to St. Pierre. But I also got some results. I had to calm down. I needed to continue to trust my instincts.

My hands were damp as I gripped the steering wheel of my

Jeep. I was headed back to the bar. I punched Tubby's number into my phone. He picked up immediately. "I'm not gonna say I told you so, Mr. Len. Just tell me what you need from me. What I do to help."

His words calmed me at least for the moment. My breathing slowed. He knew me well enough to cut through the bullshit and get right to it. I was grateful for that and very lucky to have a friend like Tubby. "I'm almost at the bar. I'll tell you when I get there."

# 19

"You went to see Filthy Man for information?" Tubby said from behind the bar as I started to explain where I had been and what I learned. There was a contingent from the Bougainvillea Inn, one of St. Pierre's more exclusive hotels, at a table, and a few of our regulars at the bar. Mike was leaning back against the bar listening to us. Otherwise the place was empty.

Mike nodded. "Fincey act crazy, but the man a genius, I hear. Teach physics or something like that in Barbados."

"And he sees everything that goes on around the harbor," I said, defending my move.

"The man see everything through a cloud, Mr. Len," Tubby said, shaking his head.

"Yeah, well, cloud or not, he mentioned someone from Lavantville. The bad boy."

With that, Tubby stopped what he was doing, which was mindlessly wiping down the otherwise dry, clean counter of the bar. "He said that?"

"He said he took Betta and those two men out on a skiff. I assume he ferried them to a bigger boat. You know who this bad boy is?"

"The bad boy from Lavantville Filthy Man talking about is Johnny Too Bad."

"Johnny Too Bad? What kind of name is that?"

"That the name everyone call him here, they think he a bad

boy like Tosh in that movie."

"I don't know what you're talking about, Tubby." And I didn't.

"The man earn that bad-boy reputation. He an outlaw. He get into all sort of trouble here. Drugs. Fights. I know he go to jail for a stretch for a chopping and for possessing a firearm."

"A chopping?"

Tubby took out a machete, known as a cutlass on St. Pierre and other islands, from under the bar. We used it to slice open pineapples, mangos, oranges and limes for bar drinks. He made a chopping motion with the sharp instrument.

"What did he chop?"

"From what I recall, Johnny Too Bad chop a few fingers off a man he say owe him money. They put him in Fort Philippe down in the prison there for a year or two. He come out and I know he still bad news."

"We need to go talk to him now," I said. "What's his real name? I'm not gonna go there and ask, 'Are you Johnny Too Bad?'"

Tubby chuckled. "Why not? He proud of being Johnny Too Bad. And with a name like John John, I take Johnny Too Bad too."

"His name is John...John?"

"That's what I just say to you."

It took me a moment but I finally got it. "Okay, let's go."

Tubby looked around the bar. "Now?"

"Yeah, now. Tubby, we're wasting time."

I knew I sounded dramatic, but Betta was out there on a boat with thugs. Killers maybe. I tried not to think of what they might have done to her. I knew they were using her to get to Maurizio and whatever he owed them. I didn't want my mind to go to a bad place when I needed to concentrate on finding her, getting her out of there safely, finding Maurizio, and then dealing with these men and Maurizio's problem. But it was hard if not impossible, and now I was angry at myself for spending even a few moments jabbering with Tubby.

"You got this, Mike?" I asked him.

"All good here, Mr. Len. Everything under control." Mike said.

I checked my phone again to see if Maurizio had tried get in touch with me. I was hoping I would find him, bring him to those men and negotiate some sort of settlement on what he owed them. Unless they had Maurizio already. I hoped not. I needed to get to him first. If I had to, I would get them enough money to hold them off until the full amount Maurizio owed was repaid. But the phone had nothing for me.

"I'm ready," Tubby said.

"All right, we're out." I grabbed my keys, headed to the door and then stopped.

"What?" Tubby looked at me.

"Bring the cutlass." I told him.

He looked at me, grinned, and grabbed the machete from under the bar.


Mary Lou Williams' "My Blue Heaven" came on when I started the engine. I knew that it was one of Maurizio's favorites. He made sure to put it on my playlist. The great pianist who arranged many of Duke Ellington's masterpieces ripped through the standard. It was a happy, cheerful song. I quickly shut it down. I wasn't cheerful and I wanted silence.

After the roundabout in Garrison, I took the West Road north. Lavantville was on the western slopes of Mount Hadali. The village was one of only a few in what was considered a rainforest. Soon I could see the white of the cedar trees reflected from my headlights. Though it hadn't rained anywhere near the bar or the harbor where I had been earlier, I was driving through puddles and heard water splashing against my wheels.

"Do you have a plan?" Tubby asked after giving me some time without talk.

"No plan," I said.

He took a breath. No plan was something he had gotten used to with me.

"So we just knock on the man's door and ask to see him, carrying this cutlass?"

"Maybe," I said, still thinking about how I would get this Johnny Too Bad to cooperate with us. Bribery or buying him off was my first idea. I could match whatever the men on that boat were paying him, but that was too easy. I knew it wouldn't go that way.

"This the street," Tubby said.

Near Lavantville's center was the St. Pierre mini-equivalent of a convenience store, a provisions shop where you could get milk, water, beer and light snacks. Next door to that were a few small ramshackle homes.

I maneuvered the Jeep over the drainage ditch on the curb, straddling it precariously, then cutting the engine and lights. Tubby looked over at me.

"You know what house is his?"

He pointed to the last house on the right side of the road. The road was a dead end. I would have to do a broken U-turn to get back out to the west road. I got out of the car and looked down the street to the house. There was a light on inside. I heard music coming from one of the houses, what sounded like old country-and-western. Tubby stayed inside the car and then grudgingly got out.

I leaned against the Jeep.

"Is this what they call surveillance?" Tubby asked.

"I don't know," I said. "But I don't think I have the patience for it. Do you?"

He shook his head. Then we both started to make our way to the house at the end of the road. Tubby carried the cutlass.

We came to the door. The music playing was country, as I suspected. Old country music, not the stuff they play on those television awards shows today. I never understood or bothered to ask why country music was so popular on St. Pierre. I often heard it coming from idling cars and taxis. I looked at Tubby and then banged on the door. We waited. The music still played. I banged again, louder this time, making the flimsy screen door rattle. The music stopped. A head emerged from what must have been a reclining position inside. The man was wearing a white tank top over his slender but muscular frame. His arms and shoulders were defined. His hair was a combination of dyed red and bronze braided locks that fell to his shoulders.

"Who there?" he mumbled.

"John," Tubby called, using the man's last name. Or maybe he was using his first name? In John's case it could be either.

The man approached the screen door. His eyes were wary and bloodshot. He glanced through the door. He was surprised to see me and then even more surprised to see what Tubby was holding. "You gonna do some chopping, Levett?" He knew Tubby. It should have surprised me but it didn't.

"That not the first option," Tubby said, with some menace in his tone.

"We need to talk to you, Mr. John," I said, hoping to ease the initial tension. I sniffed and smelled perfume from inside the house. It was a fragrance that was familiar, but I couldn't quite place it.

"Anyone in there with you?"

He didn't respond but kept his eyes on the cutlass.

"Can we come in?"

He hesitated and then said, "I come, just wait."

I peered over the door to see that he was wearing very high-cut briefs. He grabbed a pair of shorts that were lying on a couch and slipped them on. His back was turned from us as he bent over the couch giving us a view of the crack of his ass. And when he stood up and turned around, he not only had shorts on, but he also held a gun in his hand.

"Come to my house like this? You two go before it get ugly

here." He waved the gun as if he were going to use it. The gesture, to me, meant he was just trying to scare us. Nothing more. When we didn't move he said, "Who send you here?"

"No one. We just want to ask you something," I said, raising my hands in surrender. He glanced quickly at me, but his eyes were mostly on Tubby and the cutlass.

I looked at Tubby. He looked back at me and then let the cutlass fall to the ground. It would be of no use if the man was serious about using his gun.

"You took a woman out to a boat with two other men," I said, still talking through the screen door. "I need to find her and get her off that boat. Tell us where the boat is anchored and if anyone else is on that boat besides the three of them."

He snickered. "And why I tell you this?"

"Why not?" I asked.

"Because they pay me to do this and tell me no one need to know where they are."

"I can pay you to tell me," I said with some hope. The only hope, really. "I can pay you more than they paid."

He just shook his head. "Maybe so, but then these men learn I the one who tell you. They say if I tell anyone they come back, find me, and they say they flay me. There a man on that boat. An ugly man. They tell me he do it."

"What? Do what?"

"Take the skin slowly off my body. They say they make it hurt like nothing else."

"You believe that? Two men can't do that to a tough guy like you. You're Johnny Too Bad."

He laughed through the screen at me. "This not in your league, old man," he said.

Tubby took a step forward and John raised the gun, pointing it in his direction and glaring at him.

"These men not from here. They from those places where they do that thing. Where they hurt and not care who. Women. Children."

Listening to him talk about the men who took Betta had me clenching my fists. He couldn't see what I was doing, but maybe he could hear the sound of the joints in my fingers cracking. The older I got, the more they cracked. I stood there, trying my best to control myself.

"I need to get that woman off that boat. I need your help."

He laughed again, a snort came from his nose, and he shook his head.

"What you owe them? Nothing. They not from here. They not one of us," Tubby said. "They take a woman. She is one of us. A Petey." He was hoping to appeal to the man's St. Pierre pride.

"That woman? I know that woman," John said. "What does it matter what they do to she? You know what she is? She just a whore, that one."

I listened to what he said while I studied the screen door. My fists, I realized, were no longer clenched. The hinges of the door looked weak, old and rusted. It was a flimsy enough door.

"Why you care about a woman like that? What she to you?" he said with scorn, his tone derisive. I knew then that negotiating between the door wasn't going to work. Without another thought, I swiped my foot up and with a loud grunt, drove it through the door, crushing the metal below the screen and sending it off its hinges. The door flew back and knocked John down, the gun flying out of his hand.

My reaction didn't come out of nowhere. It was brewing. He just didn't know it. I had practiced the calm flow state for years in my Muay Thai training. With the exception of those damn loud joints I was cracking, he thought I was just a tall older man from the wealthy United States ready to use money to get what he wanted. He had no idea. I was on him before he could grab his gun. My forearm was tight on his neck, my knee against his solar plexus. Tubby had the cutlass in his hand again. He kicked the gun away. I lay on top of John while Tubby stood over us. "This your plan?" Tubby said to me.

I was breathing hard. "I guess it was."

Tubby shook his head. "You go to prison for this already," he said to John, his foot on the gun's handle. "Johnny Too Bad is Johnny too stupid."

He struggled to push me off, but despite his wiry muscles, there was no way he could move me. "Now, my offer still stands," I said. "I will pay you to tell us where that boat is and take us to it."

I applied a bit more pressure to his throat and to his solar plexus. I studied him as I held him tight. I tried to gauge his age, but it wasn't easy. He had a youthful body, but his face had some lines. I figured he was late thirties to early forties.

"They kill me," he murmured, his voice weak, my forearm choking him.

"No, they won't. They won't see you. Take us to them in your skiff."

"They see me for sure, I do that," he cried. "Your guarantee is shit."

"Take us just close enough so we know the boat and location. That's all we want. Tell me what they paid you. I'll top it. I turned around but kept him tight under me. "I'll even make sure you get a new screen door. Deal?"

"Pay me now," he said.

"You'll get money." I kept the pressure on his lower chest.

"They kill you too. And you," he said turning to Tubby. "The woman. She dead already."

I didn't believe him. She was there to get to Maurizio. Once they had him, what did they need her for? But would they just release her after what she witnessed? After what they might have already done to her?

"How do you know?"

"They killers. That I know."

"Do you know she is dead?" I moved my hand to his throat. Gripped it tight.

He shook his head.

141

I slowly released my grip on the man's throat and removed my knee from his gut. I even pulled him up so he could stand.

"We're going out there now," I said. "Come on. Get whatever shit you need and let's go."

He looked at the gun.

"No gun," I said.

"They kill us all then," he said with a shrug of his shoulders.

# 20

The skiff was moored in Garrison Harbor. It was late and the only sounds were the gentle lapping of tiny waves against the many boats, the buzzing of insects and high-pitched whistling of tree frogs. Still, I wondered if Fincey Pierce was sitting on that stone wall, awake and watching us.

Tubby had the cutlass in his hand and kept it on his lap as John started up the motor.

"Go slow and get just close enough so we can see the boat," I said.

"This I know," he said. After the motor revved to life, he quieted it as we slowly made our way out toward the sea. I looked back at what lights were on back on the island. I thought about what John said. The dread I felt about what they might do to Betta was churning in my belly. I could only hope that Maurizio was still on land. That he hadn't gone to her aid even though that was probably his first instinct. What they would do to him if I wasn't there to help would be much worse. Or to her if he ran away again. I couldn't imagine that. And then I worried that the boat would be gone, that we wouldn't find it. What would I do then?

John swerved the skiff north up the coast, adjacent to the west road. We remained about two hundred yards from the shore. There were a number of boats anchored off Heaven's Beach, far enough away that their presence would not intrude on what was one of St. Pierre's best swimming and snorkeling beaches. He maneuvered the skiff around some of the yachts, catamarans, and sailboats, and kept well away from them all. The boat was quietly, slowly drifting us through the calm waters without calling attention to our presence there. He turned off the motor. We rocked there for a bit while I looked at the array of expensive boats.

"Is it here?" I asked John. I held my breath as he looked around in the darkness. He focused out toward the sea and pointed to a mid-size yacht, maybe forty-two feet. "That's it?"

He nodded. I let out a breath, relieved, and then stood up and the skiff wobbled. I kept my feet planted firmly as I looked in the direction of the yacht. It was white with dark-colored siding. The yacht was the farthest from the shore and far away from any of the other boats. I noticed lights were on below deck. I didn't bring a Maglite or flashlight and even if I did, it would be risky to shine it in the direction of the yacht. I had to do the best I could in the dark.

Seeing those lights and knowing Betta was on that boat, I just wanted to go to her now. To get her out of there. I wanted to end this and make a deal with those men to release her. I wanted her safe at home with her son. And I also wanted Maurizio's self-inflicted ordeal to be over. I wanted to make it all right, to be the peacekeeper. I also knew it would not be that easy.

"No worries, Mr. Len. Unless it move from here, we come back and take care of this," Tubby said, sensing my apprehension.

"Have they been going to different locations?" I asked John.

"No, they stay there."

"Just the two men?"

"They have someone take care of the boat," he said.

"Anyone you know?"

He shook his head. "He not from this island," John said. "That one the worst of them. This I can tell."

"How can you tell?"

"I know. I just look and I know."

So I had to deal with three men. I knew the first two would be enough of a problem, and I had to assume that whoever was manning the boat was loyal to those men. I looked at Tubby. He was again reading my thoughts. "You know I don't let you do this alone, Superman," he said. "You know you need me with you."

I should have protested. I should have told him no, reminding him of his wife and four children. But I couldn't. And that I didn't have to ask just reaffirmed what I pretty much knew about Tubby soon after I met him for the first time.


John ferried us back to the harbor. I drove him back to his house. "You pay me now," he said when I let him out.

"How much did they pay you to do this?" I asked.

He looked at me and Tubby. "Five hundred," he said, and I knew he was lying. Tubby knew too and started to tell him so, but I put a hand on his shoulder to stop him. We had the man's gun. I broke his screen door. He delivered us to the yacht, showing us where they were. I didn't have the time or patience to go around and around on this. I took out my wallet and saw that I had a little over two hundred dollars in it. I gave it all to him. Tubby hissed.

"I'll get you the rest later," I said.

He took the money without an argument. "Those men bad. They kill you both," he said.

"Well then, Johnny Too Bad, you won't get the rest of your money." I wasn't in the mood for kidding, but I forced a smile. "And that screen door will remain broken. That is unless you agree to bring us out there again."

Tubby glared at me. "What you say? No, we get someone else do that. We don't need this man." Tubby turned his glare to John.

I didn't want anyone else involved in this. Tubby and I were taking enough of a risk. By taking us out there and working for them, John was already part of it. I had a feeling he really didn't like those men. I was pretty sure the threat of having his skin flayed was not a sign of a good business relationship.

"Give me your number," I said to John. "I'll text you. We'll need you to take us there again. Maybe tomorrow night."

He snickered. "You think I stupid. I go out there again, they kill me for sure. I tell you they take my skin."

"What did you say your number was?" I asked with my phone out, looking at him, ignoring his protests.

He just shook his head and then his snicker turned into a laugh. He blurted out his number and I punched it into my phone.

Tubby was muttering to himself. I knew I would hear it from him as soon as we pulled away from John's house. I didn't care. We needed the man.

"You can no trust a man like that," Tubby lectured as I headed back to the bar. "I get my friend Mosiah to take us. He fish near there. Or Rondo. They not betray us like that man will."

"I don't know Mosiah, Tubby, and if he is your friend, why would we want to involve him in this? Same with Rondo. If it goes bad, then they will suffer. I know you don't want that."

"It won't go bad. They make it work for us too. You worry too much. You think we can't handle danger like this. So you trust a thug instead. A man who do bad things all he life?"

I turned to look at Tubby as I drove. I was tired. It was just an hour or so from sunrise. I didn't want to argue with him. I wanted to sleep, but I knew that most likely wasn't going to happen today, or in the near future. "Speaking of trust, Tubby, just trust me on this."

That got an elongated, dramatic, tooth-sucking response from Tubby, indicating his displeasure with me.

The bar was closed and locked tight when I pulled up. Tubby got out of the Jeep and before heading to his car, turned to put his hands on the open window of the passenger side of my Jeep where he had been sitting. "Any plan yet, Pink Panther, on how we get on that boat?" he said to me.

I ignored the sarcasm. "Plan? I don't know, Tubby. I do know that you need to make sure your dive equipment is up to speed. We're going to need it tomorrow."

I learned to dive when I was in the Marines. I took to it with pleasure—one of the few pleasures I got during my tour. But once I started my life back in New York, diving was a very rare occurrence. On the few island vacations my wife and I took, I tried to sneak in a dive. She wasn't happy about being left alone for half a day, so I gave it up. When I relocated here, I took it up again, going to sites recommended by the St. Pierre Dive Center. One of Tubby's many occupations before he came in with me on the Sporting Place was to take tourists on diving expeditions, working part-time at the Dive Center off the Lime Tree Hotel's beach during the busy season. He'd do a dive during the day and then hustle over to the Yacht Club to bartend. Or referee a youth cricket match. Or drive one of Harold Boothe's taxi vans. Tubby was nothing if not industrious. Lucky for me, he now spent all his energy on the bar and making it go. Every once in a while, when Mike could run the bar, we'd go check out a wreck he heard about outside the island's waters, sometimes traveling as far as Petit Martinique. But those occurrences seemed rarer and rarer lately.

"Dive equipment?" He shook his head. "That's your plan? We now Navy SEALs? If what I think you planning, Mr. Len, you better not trust Johnny Too Bad. He leave us out in that sea with tanks that run out of oxygen, we end up sleeping with the fishes."

I looked at him with my mouth open. "You did not just say that, Tubby."

"Yes, Mr. Len, I did. Is that a problem?"

I shook my head and despite the situation we were in, I smiled. "Nope, none at all."

# 21

When I got back home, the dogs were up and acting as if it was morning and feeding time for them. A glance at my wall clock showed that they were off by just a half hour. Through the back window, I could see a quarter orb of the sun rising up over the Atlantic. I had been out pretty much all day and night. They scurried around my legs, especially the Puppy. She was even whining a little. Going through the morning motions, I dumped dry kibble into the two bowls for the older dogs. The Puppy tried to get to the bowls, but they wouldn't let her in. I took the bag of food to the other side of the kitchen and she followed me. She knew the routine. I gave her the allotted morning amount, standing nearby to swat her brothers away if they got too greedy.

I emptied my pockets of some loose change and the bulky phone, which always seemed to weigh me down. I glanced at it. There was a voicemail waiting for me. I didn't get many of those unless it was one of my kids calling from New York, or my ex, Kathleen. On St. Pierre, it was brief texts mostly or whoever wanted to reach me would come to the bar to say "I've been waiting to talk to you all day." My response was always, "Then why didn't you call?" That person usually had no answer and would look at me as if it was ridiculous to ask such a question.

I didn't recognize the number. It wasn't a local number. I got spam calls from all over the world. I would see a strange number and not answer. Most of the time, there was no voicemail attached to it. The voicemail hooked me in, thinking it must be someone who actually wanted to speak to me. But often the message was blank, or a recording about the warranty expiring on a vehicle I didn't own, or something in Cantonese— or Mandarin, as if I could distinguish the difference. I was about to delete the voicemail but stopped myself. I looked at the number again. The message wasn't just a couple of seconds. It was over three minutes long. That was unusual. I put the phone to my ear and pressed play.

I expected just dead air or a robocall, but instead I heard music. I was about to delete it when I listened a bit longer, recognizing the tune. It was something familiar. Something I even had on one of my playlists, usually compiled by a friend who wanted to educate me on his own tastes. The music I was listening to was jazz. Maurizio's jazz.

I barked Maurizio's name into the phone. I forgot that I was just listening to a voicemail. The song that was playing was "Pretty Eyes," from Horace Silver's *Cape Verdean Blues*. "If Silver create this song—this song about pretty eyes—he create about Betta. This the song I listen to and think of my woman. I think of her pretty eyes." Maurizio, when he said this, was slurring his words. At the time, we were in Piccadilly Caves and both of us were drunk on overproof rum. The next day Maurizio would desert his woman with the pretty eyes.

The voicemail recording abruptly stopped just when Joe Henderson's solo was about to begin. Was this Maurizio's way of getting in touch? I didn't know what to make of it.


I went down to the beach with the dogs. The wind was fierce near the water, which was even more choppy than usual. The Atlantic Ocean side of St. Pierre, where I live, has beautiful black sand beaches similar to what you might find in Ireland,

Scotland or Wales. The waves can get high and there are large rock formations jutting from the water that make it a no-go for surfers who would usually seek out those waves. I rarely did more than stick my feet into the water, which always remained warm. With the exception of a few beaches on the island's south Atlantic coast, swimming was off-limits. Why fight the relentless surf when you could swim in pool-like waters on the island's west coast?

The wind was ruffling my hair and the dogs were chasing the invisible breeze that swirled around them instead of the tennis ball I had brought to toss to them. I needed to think about what to do and I hoped that being on the secluded beach with the dogs would clear my mind.

After I heard that voicemail, I called the number. All I got was a recording in a language I did not recognize. I waited for a tone, a beep, anything that would indicate I could leave a message, but there was nothing.

As I approached the water, wanting to feel it on my bare feet, I felt my phone buzz in my pocket. I quickly picked it up. It was the number I had just called.

"Shit phone you have don't let me leave real message," a voice barked. The wind was making it hard to hear. I started walking back up to my house.

"Who is this?"

"You know who this is, Mr. Bartender. What that sound I hear?"

"The wind. I'm outside."

"You hear me good though?"

"Good enough."

"We have girl," the man said. I wasn't sure if it was Black T-shirt or White T-shirt on the phone now, but it was one of the two who were at the bar the other day complaining about my beer selection.

"Let me talk to her."

He just laughed.

"Do not touch her."

"Why we touch black skinny bitch?"

"Maurizio? Where is he?"

I thought I heard more derisive laughter in response to my question. That was all I got. "You come here. Bring money. Empty bank. Then you leave with the girl."

"Maurizio?" I asked again.

I was up in front of my house now and heading inside when I could hear the click of another call coming in. This one was a local number.

"What that sound?" whoever was on the line asked. He had heard the click.

"Nothing."

"Fuck you then," he said and cut off the call.

I pressed the other call that was waiting, hoping it was Maurizio.

"Buonfiglio," said a deep, echoing voice I recognized.

"Yeah? McWilliams?"

"You need to come," he said.

"Why? Where?" I was inside now, pacing. I was hoping the kidnappers would call back. I needed more from them.

"To Massacre. Just off Doctor's Road. You'll see my vehicle. Come now. I need you here."

Massacre? It took a moment, but I realized he was referring to one of St. Pierre's several lagoons. I knew which one was Massacre but rarely, if ever, heard it referred to as such. The lagoon was located just north of Garrison and was most often just called Garrison Lagoon. Why McWilliams called it by its other name, I wasn't sure, and it didn't really matter.

"Why do you need me there? I have a thing I need to do, McWilliams." I figured he wanted to talk to me about the Lord Ram thing, but with Maurizio and Betta out there, what happened to Lord Ram was the last thing on my mind.

"Just off Doctor's Road. Near Massacre. The lagoon," McWilliams repeated, making sure I understood where he meant. "Come."

"I'm busy, McWilliams."

"Now, Buonfiglio, or I send someone to get you."

# 22

When I first visited St. Pierre, before deciding to move here, I toured the island, eager to know its history. It was on this same tour where I was introduced to Lord Ram's birthplace. I learned that the Garrison Lagoon was the sight of a slave revolt. The lagoon was close to the island's mid-eighteenth-century slave market. The enslaved were kept in huts in the shallow waters of the lagoon until they were paraded out and sold. One night, with the help of others who had been in hiding from their owners, they were freed from the huts. The freed, knowing that fleeing was useless—where would they go and hide on such a small island—instead went on the attack, hacking at the French, who occupied the island at the time. But they had no chance. They were eventually slaughtered. Massacred by bullets.

Rawle "Big Tree" Johns, the guide of that tour, was a large man befitting his nickname. He had a melodic, high-pitched voice that contrasted with his bulk. His knowledge of island history made him one of the most sought-after guides and he had accumulated numerous five-star TripAdvisor reviews for his tours. I thought about Big Tree and that tour as I drove to meet McWilliams. I remembered imagining floating bodies in blood-red water when he described what happened there. It was a place not to celebrate, but to mourn. Big Tree was an enthusiastic ambassador for St. Pierre. He loved his island even when recounting some of its brutally tragic past. I maneuvered through the very narrow Doctor's Road, with its unpaved, stone road and centuries-old, white-washed brick and mortar structures, close on either side, and thought about another of St. Pierre's landmarks. It was a place called Freedom Drop, a cliff overlooking the ocean where many of the enslaved sacrificed themselves by jumping off the steep cliff into the water below rather than endure the indignity of being another man's chattel. These were not happy thoughts I was having. Considering what was going on around me, happy had no business in my thoughts.

I spotted McWilliams' police cruiser parked on an embankment just at the foot of the lagoon. I pulled in behind his vehicle and got out. He was almost standing in the water.

Massacre Lagoon was really just a small murky inlet with a narrow channel that led out to the Caribbean. There were mangroves around the perimeter of the lagoon. The water was mostly still and smelled of rotting fish and dead crabs. Seagrass was visible and grew from the shallow waters. St. Pierre had many beautiful, dramatic natural offerings. Massacre Lagoon was not one of them.

When I got close enough to McWilliams, my nose went to work, detecting something rotten and decaying. I stood next to him and saw something tangled in some of that seagrass just a few feet from where he stood. I hesitated before proceeding further. I didn't want to move. I didn't want to see what was there. I wanted to turn around and get in my Jeep and go home. I wanted to believe this wasn't real, that McWilliams had me come here for something else. But I knew that was just a wild hope. I had to go. I had to see.

My eyes were on that thing at his feet. I was closer, but I still couldn't make out what it was. There were arms, though they weren't protected by flesh. Cartilage and bone were visible. The same on what was once a face. The flesh was gone, empty sockets where there were once eyes and a nose.

I stood next to McWilliams and could feel myself shivering. I was in the Marines but I never saw active duty. I didn't serve in a war zone. Living in New York for as long as I had, you see things, some very bad. I had seen dead bodies in New York, usually homeless, surrounded by police and paramedics. And I had seen mutilated bodies, like in that subway station, on that day many years ago. The day that catapulted me to where I was now. Yet what I saw on that day in June could not prepare me for what I was staring at now. What once was human had been reduced to something beyond recognition. But not to me. The face was gone, the flesh on the arms flayed, yet I knew. I knew who this once was.

I worked my fingers into my fist. I kept looking at what lay before me. I knew I shouldn't, but I had to. I didn't realize until later that I had bruised my own palms with the pressure I put on them.

"This is the man who make the bread?" McWilliams asked me. "The Italian man who took up with that girl who have the place on Front Street?"

I nodded and looked at McWilliams. I knew he wasn't trying to judge Betta or Maurizio when he mentioned how they met. He was just stating what he knew. He didn't know them like I did. He was going on what he heard about them, those nasty rumors that circulated on the island. The same type of rumors he was hoping I would quench about Lord Ram's death.

I couldn't look away from what was left of Maurizio. The baggy khaki pants were the same pair he wore last time I saw him. And the black sneakers he always wore—the Italian knockoffs of the Converse Chuck Taylors. They were intact.

"You know for sure this is the Italian?" McWilliams asked. "You make this positive identification?"

"Yes. Yes." I wished that I wasn't sure, but there was no doubt. I could almost feel Maurizio's aura coming from the dead thing in front of me.

"I recall someone telling me that the man leave her with child." He shook his head and made a tsking sound, judging now. "But he come back. Did you know he was here?"

I closed my eyes for a moment. I pictured Maurizio. I tried to summon up his engaging, contagious smile and that almost girlish laugh. The passion in his voice when he talked about things he loved. Jazz. Food. Betta. I hated him for leaving. I thought he did a bad, selfish thing. And now this? Why did he come back? He should have stayed away.

I felt McWilliams grip my arm. He could see that I was teetering. There was a mix of sorrow and rage doing combat inside me now. I wanted to roar. I wanted to cry. I couldn't do either.

"Where is his woman?"

I lifted my head to look at him. I knew where she was, but I didn't answer. I wasn't going to tell him. I didn't want him to do what I had to do now—what had to be done.

"Mr. Len?" His bloodhound eyes were on mine, his grip tight on my arm. He knew what I was thinking. He saw how I was clenching my fists. "You tell me what you know. This here is very bad. This a serious thing. Whoever do this thing, let me handle it. I take care of it."

His words meant nothing to me. I started away from him and headed back to my Jeep.

"Don't be foolish, Buonfiglio," he called to me.

"Give me twenty-four hours and then it's yours," I said, not looking back.

He said something back to me, but I started the Jeep and skidded out of the mud and onto the road. It didn't matter what he said. I needed to erase what I saw here. There was a way—but only one way. McWilliams knew this. He also knew he couldn't stop me from doing what I had to do.

# 23

My phone was connected to my Jeep's sound system through Bluetooth. That's how I listened to music and the playlists I had accumulated. And if I needed to make a call, I could do it without having to hold the phone to my ear. I didn't want music now. I wanted no sounds. I needed to think. But thinking was bringing me to very bad places. Did Betta witness what they did to Maurizio? Did they make her watch as they flayed him? Or did they do it here, on land? I hoped to hell they did. I couldn't imagine Betta seeing Maurizio endure what had to have been pain beyond belief. I thought John was just exaggerating the evil of those men.

I was driving faster than I should to get home. And what would I do when I got there? There was no time for strategizing. I knew where the boat was. I had to contact Tubby and we had to go. I was about to press his number on my phone when I heard the ring over the Jeep's speakers. A number flashed on the screen. Not St. Pierre's area code. And different from the last call.

I pressed the green button. "Who is this?" I quickly pulled over into the driveway of the Lazy Boy Rum Shop, a small establishment where rum, beer, and other cheap beverages were sold. There were a few men playing dominoes at a small wooden table in front. They peered at me for a moment and then went back to their game.

"Did you get money?"

"Let me speak to the woman," I said. "You get nothing if you touch her."

There was a pause and that worried me. And then there was laughter.

"I know you know what we do to that fool," the man on the phone said. "I know you see what we do and what we will do to her. Do you think we care? Man. Woman. Child. It does not matter to us. We make it painful. You know we do. So, Mr. Len, yes I hear they call you Mr. Len, you are not the one to make demand."

I didn't want to admit anything they said was right, but they had Betta. I saw what they did to Maurizio. I did not doubt them.

"You have those bottles. That isn't enough?"

Again there was laughter. I had the feeling I on was on speaker phone.

"We travel a long way. We pay for big boat. We put out money to come get what is ours. And now we on this island. You from New York, man. Why come to a place like this? There's action in New York. People. Beautiful women. Music. Food. Fun. Everything. And you come here? This island got nothing. Food shit. Even your bar serve shit beer. So for this, to have to come here, we must be paid. Not just what is ours. But more. We don't go back without more. The fool say he have money, but he talk too much. He all talk. No more. Now this woman. You want her? What that Italian see in her? At least the African bitches where we from have big ass, big tits. This one? Nothing. There no white women on that island for a man like you?"

I listened to all this. They wanted to get a reaction from me. Maybe they would have if they could see me, if they could see my face and how I was struggling to hold back.

"I need to hear her voice to know she is alive. And that you haven't hurt her. Otherwise you get nothing from me."

There was more laughter. They were enjoying this.

"Speak," I heard one say away from the phone.

"Betta?"

I could hear her breathing.

"Speak to your boyfriend," one said with a snicker.

I waited.

"Leonard." It was a whisper.

"Have they hurt you, Betta?"

"Maurizio?" she asked, her voice breaking. She was asking me. So she didn't know. She didn't see what they did. I was grateful for that at least.

"Are you okay? Have they touched you?"

"Maurizio?" she whispered again.

"No, no, Maurizio," I heard one of them say to her. "He gone. He weak. He not a man to save you. But maybe hero come for you? He smart. He take care of things. Right, hero?"

I heard what he said but I wasn't listening. All I could really hear was Betta's crying. I had to focus on that, not their taunts.

"She know that fool gone. We tell her she never see him again. So that's it. You hear her. She still breathe. You get money and come get her."

"I want to know that you haven't touched her."

I heard more laughter. This was a joke to them. "Why we touch her? Only Migos want her, but we tell him she make him sick, his dick fall off. You want her safe. You want her back. Come tonight. Bring the money. Anything less than two hundred thousand, we kill her."

I tried to compose myself. Hearing Betta crying like that made me fearful of what they had put her through.

"Do you think I have that much?"

"Maybe. We hope. But you get it. Today. Or she die like the Italian die."

"I don't know where you are," I said. "How am I supposed to get it to you?"

"We have someone take you to us," one of the men said.

"He call you. Tonight you come. He tell you where to meet."

"You gonna kill me and her after I give you the money?"

"Why we do that? That make problem for us. The fool, he not from anywhere near here. No one miss him or care for him except this African bitch. Think. We kill you for no reason, it different. People know you. The hero. In New York. We know. We check. But we have reason if you don't bring the money. We deal with problem if we have to and if you try stupid things. The woman die first. And we not nice this time. We don't make the woman watch her man die, but this time we make you watch what Migos do to her. Think about that, Mr. Len."

I still didn't believe them. Anyone who would do what they did to Maurizio would not care about consequences.

"I'll get you the money" was all I could say.

"Yes. Good. We see you tonight. Have a beer when it all over. Heineken. Not that pee-water shit they drink here. We celebrate."

I pushed the red button on my phone, ending the call. I had been gripping the steering wheel the whole time. It was wet from my sweaty palm. I rubbed my hand against my jeans and pulled out of the driveway. The domino players again looked me over. They knew me. Everyone on the island knew me. They thought I was a hero. They believed the hype. The bought into it as so many had. But they had no idea what was going on now in my mind.

# 24

I was closer to the bar than home, so I headed there and was grateful to see Tubby's car in the lot. What I was going to ask of him was more than I should ask of anyone. I wanted to handle this alone, but there were two of them and whoever was manning the boat, the one John said was the most dangerous. I needed better odds. They would be armed, no doubt—guns and other things I didn't want to think about. I needed Tubby.

The bar was quiet. It was still early in the day. Terrance McFarlane was the only pre-noon customer. He was sipping white rum out of a small glass. He worked nights at St. Elizabeth Hospital as a technician, making sure the power stayed on. As far as I knew, he was single and often would come to the bar after his shift. Tubby was arranging bottles of liquor to display against the burnished mahogany backsplash of the bar. He turned when I entered and just stared. I knew I hadn't slept in over twenty-four hours. That tropical glow I thought I attained after years living in the Caribbean was gone, replaced by a ghostly pallor. Whatever I was feeling usually could be seen on my face and was a good excuse to bow out of any poker invitations. Tubby was used to my usual grumpy visage, but what he was looking at now was grief he'd never seen from me before.

"We're going to need Mike again," I said as I moved behind the bar.

"I text him already. I tell him to come regardless."

We both kept our voices low. We didn't want Terrance to overhear our conversation. To make sure, I raised the volume of the sound system just a bit. Tubby had a calypso playlist going. Mighty Sparrow, Growling Tiger, Calypso Rose, and of course, Lord Ram, singing his cover of the Roger Miller hit "King of the Road," retitled "Lord of the Road." Over the course of the last day, I had forgotten all about Ram's demise and my part in trying to find out the truth of how he died. It was the least of my worries now.

"Your scuba gear all set and your tank full?" I asked Tubby.

"You tell me to do so, and I do. It ready."

"I'm going to call John. We need him tonight."

"You a mess, Mr. Len," Tubby said. "What happen?"

I looked at Tubby. I was tall but he was taller, though not by much. Our eyes were almost at the same level. I turned to see Terrance looking at his cell phone. He still had a bit of white rum in his glass. "McWilliams had me identify a body this morning. The only thing I recognized were the black sneakers he wore."

"Those shoes...?" It took a moment to sink in before, Tubby said, "He?"

I nodded. I didn't need to say his name. Tubby knew.

I went into the back room and shut the door. I had John's phone number and called him.

"I was just about to call you, man," he said as soon as he picked up.

"You were gonna call me?"

"They call me. They say they need me to take a man to their boat. I ask who. They tell me your name."

I was surprised. I thought they would rely on someone else, someone professional, reliable, not a local thug, to transport me and the money to their boat. They were getting cocky and careless. Or maybe they just were lazy and hooked up with the first connection they found—in this case, a small-time, small-island criminal. It gave me some hope. "And you told them you would."

"Yes. I tell them that. I not fuck with those men."

"I told you I'd pay you whatever they paid you and more. Are you going to work for me or them?"

I could almost hear him considering that. "I guess I work for both of you," he said. "I bring you there like they ask. But you need something else from me, I work for you too."

"You might have to pick a side here. Am I going to be able to trust you, Johnny Too Bad?"

"You trust me, man. Yes. Fuck those two. Give me my gun back and I help you more, you want me to."

I didn't know him beyond what Tubby had told me. His reputation was not a good one. But if he was anything, he was an opportunist, that much was obvious. "Where did they tell you to pick me up?"

"At the harbor. Out near the yacht club. Late. When it quiet."

"What time?"

"They say come to them by midnight. I tell you to meet me before then."

Tubby peered into the room. I looked at him. "Do you want your gun back?" I said into the phone.

"You fucking with me, man?" The belligerent tone had returned, not that it ever left his voice.

"No, John. I'm not. I'll give you back your gun. And I'll give you a job. If you work for me tonight. Not them. I need you and that skiff."

I heard a hiss, not unlike Tubby's. "You get me killed."

"No."

"What I have to do?"

"I'll tell you tonight. And you'll get your money up front. You good with that?"

"We see," he muttered.

164

# 25

After I was captured on video carrying men and women out of a smoky subway tunnel and proclaimed a hero, the mayor, in a bullshit ceremony, presented me with the key to the city. I had the keys, but I could no longer live in that city. I could no longer live the constant lie of who I was to myself and to my family. I had to go and before I did, I sold my shares of the bars I owned in Brooklyn to my partners. At the time our business was booming. With each new bar came more success. We always seemed to be in the right place at the right time, opening in neighborhoods that were on the cusp of gentrification, starting in Williamsburg and on into Bushwick, Greenpoint, Bedford-Stuyvesant, and Gowanus. Just before I left, we were considering moving into Chinatown next—east of the Bowery, near the Manhattan Bridge. When I sold out, we were at our peak and I profited in a big way. Before leaving, I put my finances in order. I set up a trust fund for my two children. I had my bank direct-deposit monthly alimony checks and child support for my ex, Kathleen. The alimony and child support stopped, however, when she remarried a man whose finances were in even better order than mine. But I did make sure that Kasie and Luke would have money for their education beyond high school, whatever they choose to do and without the help of Kathleen's new husband. What was left, and it was still sizable, I let an investment bank handle, and opened savings accounts in

New York and at Windward Savings here on St. Pierre. My computer was at home. I needed to get to it and go online to my investment account. From there, I could instantly transfer the funds I needed to Windward Savings and make the withdrawal before they closed later in the afternoon.

I came out of the back room. One of Harold Boothe's drivers, Lennox Godwin, had brought three Dutch tourists to the bar. Tubby was pouring them rum punches. Their smiles were constant before and after a sip of Tubby's strong concoction. And then Godwin led them out to the deck so they could admire our view of Garrison and the harbor.

"When Mike comes, go home and try to sleep," I said to Tubby. "This could be a long night."

"You have a plan?"

There was that question again. "I'm working on it," I said.

He shook his head. "You rest too, Mr. Len. No sleep and the plan worthless, whatever the plan be."

"Yeah, Tubby, tell me something I don't know." What I did know was that there was little chance I would be sleeping anytime soon.


Once I got back to my house, I got on my laptop and made the online transactions. The money was immediately transferred to Windward Savings. I drove to the bank located on Front Street in Garrison, close to souvenir shops and a few harborside restaurants.

Despite how professional they might be at the bank and claiming to respect every client's privacy, the fact that I was making such a significant withdrawal would not go unnoticed at Windward Savings. It was no one else's business what I choose to do with my money, but it didn't work that way here. I was very happy with the choice I made moving to the quieter life on St. Pierre, but a downside was the small-town gossip. Even though the bank had no right to ask me why I needed

$200,000 in cash, I knew it would be best if I just volunteered an explanation for the withdrawal, preempting the gossip. It would be a business expense, I would say. A needed bit of construction to fortify the bar from any potential hurricane damage, even though St. Pierre was south of the hurricane belt, and big storms were rare. After what happened recently in Puerto Rico, I couldn't take a chance.

Franklyn Worthington, a long-time clerk, slender, dressed impeccably in a dark blue suit, had my money ready for me when I got to the bank. His smile was broad as he counted out the cash while I sat at his desk. "Yes, what happened in Puerto Rico was tragic," he said. "You are wise to protect your investment like that. So many people lose so much. Their homes. Their livelihood. And insurance cannot be counted on."

Alma Modeste, Worthington's colleague, also dressed in a dark blue suit with a white blouse under her jacket, the skirt hugging her curvy hips, entered the cubicle. She leaned over Worthington, whispered something to him, and left a paper on his desk. He smiled at her and thanked her. And then she departed. Worthington gave me a sheepish smile and resumed counting my money. He was a married man, yet on alternate Thursday nights at the Sporting Place, Slow Jam nights, when old-school R&B and reggae played by a local DJ, Worthington and Alma, who was single, would commingle openly. Their affair was common knowledge despite how they acted professionally. I didn't care. I liked them both and noticed that they were very happy on those Slow Jam Thursdays. I was getting anxious, and Worthington was counting slowly. Sitting at that desk was making my heart race. I had to calm down. I needed to prepare mentally.

He finally finished counting and put the cash in a sealed envelope along with a copy of the printout of the withdrawal. I thanked him, trying to act as normally as I could, hoping my anxiety was not so obvious. I grabbed the envelope and got out of there, noticing Alma Modeste's eyes on me as I hustled out.

\* \* \*

The Puppy was on me as soon as I got out of the Jeep. I took her into my arms. The other two dogs let her have the affection. They were not jealous of it. As long as I filled their bowls daily and tossed them a tennis ball now and then, they were happy and loyal.

I felt my eyes get heavy. I lay down on the couch and closed my eyes but as soon as I did, the image of what I saw at the lagoon came up.

I got up and made coffee. I drank it staring out at the Atlantic. My eyes looked north and I thought of my family there, almost 2,000 miles away. They were my blood. My children lived not far from this same ocean. And my ex-wife, who I put through so much for my own selfish needs, what was she doing now? I picked up my phone and looked at it. And then I hit the familiar contact number and held the phone to my ear. A deep, husky voice answered. One that I knew had changed not too long ago.

"Luke?"

"Hi Dad," he said. "What's up?"

What's up? My son assumed that I was calling because something was up. Why else would I call? Maybe just to hear his voice? To say hi and how much I missed and loved him and his sister? "Just checking in," I said, hoping the anxiety I was feeling wasn't obvious in my voice. "What's going on up there?"

"Mom is out," he said.

"Where is she?" I asked as if it was any of my business.

"I have no idea," he said.

"And Kasie?"

"She went to the beach with Austin."

"Austin...oh yeah." He was the kid I was told took Kasie to the prom. Another major event in my daughter's life I missed. She hadn't mentioned that they were girlfriend/boyfriend, just her date for the prom. I wanted to gauge his worthiness for my daughter. Would I ever get that opportunity?

"What are you doing, Dad? Aren't you working?"

I hesitated. "No, I'm home this afternoon." I knew after I said it that it was a mistake.

"Are you okay?"

"Yeah, I'm fine. Why?"

"I don't know. You just sound different."

There it was. My voice was as much of a tell as my face.

"No, all good," I said. "I just wanted to say hi to you and the others. We haven't talked in a while."

"Oh...okay. Imma 'bout to go to work, Dad."

I remembered that Luke had a summer job at an ice cream place near the water—the water being the Long Island Sound. "Oh, right. You go. I just wanted to see how you guys are doing. Say hi. You know."

"Yeah. Well, call again, okay?"

"Yeah, I will. Give my love to your mom and to Kasie. Love you, buddy."

"Yeah, you too, Dad," he said and then abruptly disconnected the call. I stared down at the blank phone. That's what it had come to. And I had no one to blame but myself.

The phone buzzed soon after I put it down. It was Tubby.

"I'm ready with the scuba gear. You got a plan now?"

"Yeah...well, I don't think you need the scuba stuff."

"What you mean by that?"

"It's not part of the plan."

"I don't even know what plan you got, Mr. Len. You tell me earlier get my scuba stuff ready for tonight. It ready. I'm ready. When we go?"

"Change of plan," I said. I realized that I could not involve Tubby in this. I couldn't risk him. This was my battle. I was friends with Maurizio—and with Betta. Nothing going on here concerned him. "I'm going out there with John. I've got the money they want. I'll give it to them and get Betta and come back. That's all I can do, Tubby."

I waited for his response, hearing only dead air until: "They just take your money, give you her, and let you go?"

"Yeah, that's the deal."

"After what they do to the Italian?"

"What can I do, Tubby?" I did know what I could do, but I wasn't going to tell him. I waited for him to speak. He was angry. He thought I was doing this because I didn't need him. I needed him, but not enough to risk his life. He was right to ask that question. That was the risk. I give them the money and then what? It seemed nonsensical that they would just let us go. But if something happened to me and Betta, McWilliams would not let it pass. She was a Petey. I was a white man from the States who owned a business on the island. And whose own history could be found on Google. There would be some blowback. He was the superintendent of police for St. Pierre. He would do whatever he could to bring them down. I knew that. And maybe they did too. "Tubby?" There was dead air— silence. He had hung up on me.

The sun was beginning its descent over the Caribbean. My front lawn was darkening. I went outside in what little light was left and went through a few kicks and punches. I needed to move. I struggled with knuckle pushups and rapid high kicks. I was breathing hard. I liked to challenge myself physically, but it seemed more and more that whenever I tried, something would halt my progress—a stiff back, inflammation in my knee, an already arthritic big toe—anything. This time it was my lack of rest. I could feel the weight of that on me. Was I that old now that I couldn't get through a few tough nights? There were all those years working behind the bar until four in the morning, trying to catch up on my sleep during the day, but never really feeling tired, weary, like I was feeling now. I couldn't use lack of sleep as an excuse. I couldn't afford excuses.

I cut the workout short and went inside to gulp down water. I showered and dressed, wearing loose sweatpants and a T-shirt.

I kept checking my phone to see if anything changed, if, by some miracle, Betta was released and home with Paolo. Yet I knew that was never going to happen. There was no way out of what I had to do.

I made sure I ate even though I wasn't hungry. There was some leftover of that cassava pone from Queen Sassy. I also had a couple of pieces of barbecued chicken I brought home from the fete for Lord Ram. I still had to deal with that if I survived this.

After eating, I sat back on my couch. I had one of those small speaker systems that also connected to my phone. I stared at my many playlists. I shuffled to one of my jazz playlists and closed my eyes, listening to the music Maurizio loved, remembering his enthusiasm for it, for everything really. But it wasn't delivering the calm I wanted. Thinking about him and what I saw was left of him this morning had me breathing heavily. I couldn't hear his music now. I turned off the music and sat in silence until it was time to go.

# 26

"You go out there with him too?" I could hear the voice, but I wasn't sure where it was coming from. I was at the harbor, in the spot John designated, where he would meet me with the skiff. I wore jeans, a black T-shirt, and running shoes. I carried an old Nike athletic bag with the cash. I also had my phone and keys to my Jeep. But that was it. I looked around in the darkness for the source of that voice. It was almost midnight.

"I know you go out there," I heard again. "I hear the screams. They far away, but I hear them. And I know now you must go."

There was rustling from the overgrown manchineel trees that bordered the southern end of the harbor, opposite where the yachts, catamarans, and cruise boats docked. I pulled out my phone and turned on the flashlight. Within the cover of the manchineel trees, I could see the copper-and-gray beard of Fincey Pierce. I could see he was staring at the bag I carried.

"Very bad out there," Fincey said.

"I have to go there, Fincey. This is no concern of yours," I said.

"Everything here my concern," he said, stretching out his arms as if he was embracing all of St. Pierre. "And now no more *pane di casa*. Will the hero be a bastard?"

I looked at Fincey, who everyone called Filthy Man. How did he know? What did he know? His words were shaking me.

"Or will the bastard be a hero," he whispered with those intense green eyes on me.

I could hear an outboard motor in the distance. I looked away from Fincey's gaze to stare out to the sea. In the distance and in the dark I could make out the approaching skiff.

"Fincey, I got to go," I mumbled, not knowing how to respond to what he just said to me.

He smiled at me and nodded. He put his finger to his lips and went "Shhhhhhhhh."

The skiff was just fifty yards from where I stood. I could see John working the motor. I looked back once more at Fincey and then headed to the skiff.


"You talk to someone? Who over there?" John was wearing the only outfit I had ever seen him in: a tank top and shorts, but this time the tank was black. He looked past me toward where Fincey had been.

"Fincey..." I said, forgetting his last name.

"Filthy Man?" John sucked his teeth and shook his head. "You tell him what you do?"

"No, but he can see. He knows I'm going out there."

"How he know this?"

"This is his territory. He knows everything that's going on around here. He's the one who led me to you, John. He might be unkempt, but he's no dummy."

"Shit, man, you give me my gun back, I come back here and shoot him. He get us both killed. Filthy Man disgrace us all."

"He'll say nothing. Leave him be."

"We see," John said, glaring toward the manchineel trees. I hopped onto the skiff, and he fired up the motor and turned the skiff around as we headed north along the coast.

Maybe it was the still water and the absolute quiet as we slowly made our way to the cove off Heaven's Beach, but I felt calmer than I had all day. This thing was in motion now. I would soon see Betta and try to get her out of there.

We passed the anchored crafts closer to shore and drifted quietly out to the yacht John showed us the previous day. I noticed that it had anchored farther from the shore than where it had been. There was a light on in the chamber below the deck. As we got closer, I noticed a man emerge onto the deck. He stood watching us. John kept the skiff moving, angling it so it was parallel to the yacht. I looked at the man. His skin was burnt orange, long stringy hair flowing from a baseball cap. He stared down at me with rounded, close-lidded eyes; eyes whose emptiness scared me. This was the man John told me about. The one he thought was most dangerous of the three. The man was glaring and gestured with a guttural sound for me to come aboard. I held onto the Nike bag with one hand and gripped the ladder with my other, pulling myself up. John pulled the skiff away from the boat. I looked at him and then the man in the baseball cap. He was maybe half a foot shorter than me, but stocky, and upon a closer look, I noticed he had tattoos all over his neck.

He put his hands out. "Search," he muttered and started to pat me down, making sure I carried no weapon. And then he took the bag and squeezed it, feeling for anything hard or sharp. He nodded, keeping his eyes on me, and handed me back the bag. He had me move in front of him. His hand was on my back, pushing me forward and around the walkway of the yacht. I looked back at John as the skiff bobbed in the water. I had told him to wait for me. I needed him to take Betta and me back to shore. The man in the baseball cap pushed at my back, urging me forward. I ducked inside the boat and down the stairs with him right behind me.

We entered a saloon with a wraparound couch, dining table, a kitchenette off the helm, a bar, television, and a music system. The man pointed to the couch. I sat, holding the bag with the money. I studied the boat as I sat there, my eyes taking in the entrance to the saloon and then up to see a sunroof open to the night sky. In the galley's bar area I saw a familiar box, and sticking out of it were the bottles of vermouth that had found their way to the Sporting Place, back when this mess all started. Maurizio's dream of making handcrafted vermouth with signature labels from his famous artist friend had led to this. Now Mimmo was dead. Maurizio was dead. A suicide and a murder, all for what?

While I stared at that box, I saw the platinum head of one of the men I remembered from the bar. As he emerged from below, he saw me and smiled. Then the other one, the skinhead with the beard, emerged as well. I glared at both as they circled around me. These men tortured and killed my friend. And here they were still living, breathing, smiling.

"So we do this," Platinum Head said.

"Where's Betta?"

"What kind of name is Betta? African?"

I just looked at him. I wasn't going to play this game with him. "I want to see her now." I gripped the bag with the money.

Platinum Head laughed. "Old man want to see her now," he said, turning to his buddy. "So concerned with African bitch. She skin and bone. No meat I see. You fuck her? You and the crazy Italian?"

I didn't think he was trying to taunt me. He asked it as if it was just a normal question that interested him. There was no malice in his delivery. He was talking matter-of-factly. And that, to me, made him even more malevolent. I stood up. I went to the staircase to the lower state rooms. I started down the steps when I felt a very firm grip on my biceps, stopping me. The man who I had followed into the yacht held my arm tight. I knew I could have gotten out of it quickly; his face was exposed, I'd easily break his nose with a strike from my elbow, but that wouldn't help the situation. I couldn't do anything but let him pull me back from the stairs.

"Migos, go get her," Platinum Head said. Migos, the man wearing the baseball cap, released his grip and brushed past me down the steps.

"Now sit, hero. You bring us money, there no need for any trouble. Right? We settle this soon."

"I just want the girl and to get out of here," I said.

"We want too. We have enough of this place. I see no wild girls in bikinis, only skinny or fat bitches. Penko, he like the fat ones with the big ass. Right, Penko?" He said it to the other man, the skinhead with the lumberjack beard, who had been silent.

"Fat ass good to fuck and spank," the other man—Penko—said.

They both snickered at that. While he was laughing, Penko reached over and grabbed the bag from me. Again, the temptation was to strike with a quick jab. It would have been more than enough to break his jaw, but I needed to see Betta. I would not do anything that might jeopardize her safety. That was motivation enough to hold back. I focused on my breathing instead—slow quiet intakes of the sea air around me. It wasn't easy, but I was able to do it and stay composed.

"Holding the money like that make no sense, man. You know it is ours now." He glanced over at Penko, who took the bag and zipped it open. He put his hand inside and felt the bills. He brought some out and showed Platinum Head, who smiled. "See, this no problem for a man like you. We know you no Musk or Bezos, so we make the price fair for you. We know no man can get millions in cash immediate in a place like this. We don't get greedy. Greed give problems. I know this. We come here for what the Italian man owe us and the shit liquor he say so special. We know what special and the people we work for, they do too. They pay us to get this back for them. To take care of this business. They make investment in the bottles. They worth big money for those who hire us. See? We make it happen for them."

My eyes were on the stairs to the state rooms below. "Where is she?"

"She come now." He called out. "Migos! Bring her."

Finally I saw her head emerge. Her eyes chilled me. They were sunk deep into her sockets, almost ghostly. The clothes she wore were wrinkled and dirty, and her jeans hung low on her slim hips. I noticed a slight reddish hue under her right eye. One of them hit her. I had to remain calm, but it was as hard a thing as I ever had to do. I stood up when she stepped up into the saloon. She stared at me, doing her best to keep from crying. Whatever composure I had just a few moments ago was gone. I reached for her, bringing her into my arms, glaring at the men around me. I didn't care about my actions. They would not touch her again.

"Relax, hero. We not treat her so bad," the dark-haired one, Penko, said. "Migos like her. But we make sure he go easy on her. He don't do what you think he do, but maybe she not happy about that. Maybe she like Migos. Right, Borka?" He turned to his partner.

"The man angry with us. We don't want that," Platinum Head, whose name I now knew was Borka, said. "Don't start trouble."

Penko laughed at that. "What he do? He tell police? He send island army after us?" He laughed again and shook his head.

"Enough talk like that now, Penko," Borka, who seemed to be in charge, said. He looked at me. "You take care of her. She heal up, forget all this, and be just like new very soon. Old white man can enjoy."

I ignored his dig at me and what he was implying. I took Betta's hand in mine and started out of the saloon and up a few steps to the outside walkway. Migos blocked my path. Betta clung to me as his stout body blocked us. Those round, close-lidded eyes were glaring into mine. He then grinned at Betta and started to move his hand to her cheek and the bruise there. Before he could touch her, I swatted his hand away. And before I could do anything else, he waved something very sharp in front of my nose. He swayed the sharp instrument in front of my face like he was conducting an orchestra. He said something in a language I could not recognize. I could feel Betta push closer into me.

"Let them go, Migos. I tell you no trouble," Borka called to him, a stern look on his face. "He like to use that thing. His people good with reindeer. You know reindeer? They eat it like steak. But the skin tough. You have to take fur and flesh off to get to the meat. Migos know how to take the flesh off with knife."

Borka smiled, waiting for that to sink in. I knew what he was getting at. And I also knew what I had to do.

At Borka's command, Migos stepped aside. With Betta in my grasp, I moved past him.

"And hero, don't be a stupid man. Be glad it end like this. Easy peasy."

I heard him but made no response. I walked Betta around the cockpit and toward John and the skiff. I helped her down the ladder onto the small boat, following her. John saw right away the shell-shocked look on Betta's face. He said nothing but just started up the motor and quickly turned the skiff toward shore.

She leaned against me as we traveled the short distance to the harbor. She was shaking. I could feel her bones—she hadn't been on that yacht long, but she had lost a substantial amount of weight in the few days she'd been there. I tried to comfort her, my arm around her. I kept her to my chest, her head buried there. I didn't know what to say. I didn't know what to do other than hold her.

John eased the skiff to the dock. I helped Betta out. "Don't go anywhere," I said to John. At my words, Betta pulled away and stared angrily at me. She knew.

John shook his head. "Not unless you bring me my gun, man," he said.

"You'll get your gun," I said and then led Betta, who clung to me, to my Jeep.

We were silent in the Jeep. I was going to take her to her mother's house, where she could reunite with Paolo. And where her mom could take care of her. Feed her. Clean her up. I pulled up to the house and before I even opened the door for her, her mother was out the door, coming to us. I could hear her sobbing.

Betta looked at me before going to her mother. "Please don't," she said softly, her hands on my chest. I tried to turn away from her eyes. Her mother put her arms around her daughter. Betta pushed her away. "Please don't," she said again, but this time her voice was now louder, angry.

I turned away from her.

"Don't...please...don't." Her pleas to me grew louder and louder until she broke into a sob and gave up as her mother guided her into the house.

I got into the Jeep and drove away quickly.

Please don't?

I knew that was impossible.

# 27

I left food in the bowls for the dogs. I didn't know when or if I was going to be back. I didn't know much about anything, but I did want to at least make sure they had enough to last them the day. I put my scuba mask, snorkel, diving fins, dive vest, and dive tank into the back of the Jeep. There was a dive knife in one of the vest pockets. I patted it again just to make sure it hadn't fallen out. I went back into the house and looked around. I was already wearing my rash shorts and top, a T-shirt over my top, and baggy shorts over the rash shorts. I didn't want to, but I knew I had to bring John the gun we confiscated from him. I had to let him defend himself if things got bad out there.

I had everything I needed. It was still very early in the morning; daylight would not come for at least a few more hours. I had to get going.


John was where I left him. I could see the glow from a cigarette, but when I got closer I smelled that it was cannabis he was smoking. I pulled out my equipment and brought it to the skiff. He just stared at what I was doing but said nothing and made no effort to help me.

I started into the skiff. "You forget something, man," he said.

And I did. Why was I so resistant? Why was I so stubborn about putting a gun in my hands? It never felt right to me, not even in the Marines. In my early years in bartending, I remember taking a mandatory course taught by an off-duty cop on how to handle a gun in various situations. My employer at the time, the owner of the bar where I worked in Brooklyn, insisted that his bartenders learn to handle the gun he had bought and licensed as protection for us. This was back when things were still rough in the Brooklyn neighborhoods. The owner didn't want any accidents if the time ever came to use it. The Marines taught me how to handle a gun, but I had no use for them, and had no interest in learning more. I went to the course just once and never returned. Had I not been the most popular and trustworthy bartender he had, he probably would have dumped me. But I was both and he couldn't afford to let me go despite my resistance to the gun experiment. Now I was being stubborn again, and it probably was not a wise move. A gun would give me a much better chance at succeeding in what I planned to do. But I couldn't change what I felt. And it was John's gun. I wasn't the one who was going to use it. I went back to the Jeep to get it.

"About a hundred yards from their boat, turn off the motor. That's where I'll get in the water with all this," I said, gesturing to the scuba gear I brought along.

John looked at what I brought aboard and shook his head with a snicker.

"You think this a good idea, man?"

I didn't think it was a good idea, but it was the only idea I had. The only advantage I had over them would be surprise. If they knew I was coming, I was doomed.

"And you think they don't hear you come on that boat with your tank and all this stuff?"

I shrugged. "I got to hope they're sleeping by now. I'll do it quietly."

"Vengeance, man." He shook his head again.

I knew what he was implying. "You know what they did," I said.

He nodded. "I know, I do the same as you, my woman treated like that, or they kill a friend."

I wanted to tell him that Betta wasn't my woman. But I didn't.

"I get in trouble. Go to the Fort for two years because I act on vengeance. A boy cheat me and I go after him without thinking. I just want to cut him bad. Make him suffer for doing me like that. And I think about that all the time I in there."

The Fort he was referring to was Fort Philippe. Built in the late seventeenth century by the French to hold off the invading British, the Fort was an historical attraction, an essential stop for cruisers in their limited time on St. Pierre. It was also where St. Pierre's police station was housed, and its dank basement was the site of the island's only prison.

I knew he was right. Acting on impulse, on my raw emotions, was something that was always a mistake. I was taught that in my Muay Thai training. Control was essential for success. I was out of control now. But if I let them just sail away, how could I live with that?

John knew what I was thinking, and he smiled at me. "If we smart, we know there are other ways for revenge. Is vengeance worth it? Was it worth two years of my life? Maybe not for some. For me, man, I would do it again just like that. But that's because I'm not smart."

We were out past Garrison Harbor, closing in on the boats settled around Heaven's Beach. The big yacht was still out there, keeping its distance from the others. I didn't think they would start out until daybreak, and I was right.

I heard a motor, similar to ours, coming upon us. I turned in the dark and could see another skiff gliding our way. I didn't want any traffic out here. I knew fishermen went out early, but I didn't think this early.

John was slowing down the motor. I looked at him. "What

are you doing?"

He didn't answer. The other boat was approaching. I picked up my scuba diving flashlight and aimed it in the direction of the oncoming skiff. I saw two men inside the boat. As it got closer one of the men stood up. "Goddammit," I muttered.

The boat was slowing as it came to us. Tubby was sitting in the front of the oncoming skiff. He saw the dive equipment in the skiff and shook his head. "Now you think you double-oh-seven?"

I peered to see who was with him, working the motor. Shining the flashlight on his face, I saw that it was Tubby's friend, Rondo. He had helped us out once before—taking care of other bad men. Rondo's head was clean-shaven, and he had bulging muscles under his black T-shirt. He had a prominent beard to compensate for the lack of hair on his head, and made sure it was intricately braided and adorned with colorful shells. He was stocky, but short—so short that some might have mistaken him for a midget or dwarf. He was neither. He was a small man, but only as it applied to his height. And I would never forget how reliable he was when we needed him once before.

I turned to John. His lack of surprise at Tubby's arrival said it all. He just shrugged. "I agree. You no James Bond, man," John said. "You need help on this."

"Help? Do you understand who we're dealing with? And do you know what has to be done?"

The two boats were rocking close to each other. "Mr. Len, we do know. They hurt one of us. They do something very, very bad to your friend. I know what they do. I know what kind of men they are," Tubby said, trying to justify his presence.

"Yeah, then you know they won't hesitate doing the same to the two of you. I will take care of it. I don't need your help."

Ignoring that, Tubby said, "Well, that not possible anymore. We here. We do this together."

"And McWilliams? If he finds out, do you think it won't come back to you? You think he will just let it slide?"

Tubby smiled. "Oh yeah, Mr. Len. He the one tell me to come out here to help you. Not that he had to. I know what you do."

"What?"

"Uh-huh."

I took a deep breath. "They have guns. I saw them. These men are killers."

"You think they start shooting at us here? You think they want IMPACs on them? They create a firestorm, it not go unnoticed," Tubby said.

IMPACs was a law enforcement agency that worked in coalition with most of the Caribbean countries, St. Pierre included. They had a naval patrol, like a coast guard, but their resources were limited. I didn't think they would respond to a firefight in the middle of the Caribbean Sea in a very timely fashion.

"What do you think you are going to do, Tubby? Do you have a plan, a way to take them on?"

"Besides what you taught me?" He was joking even now about our informal martial arts workouts. Muay Thai didn't give out belts as recognition of rank but based on my fighting record—and it had been over fifteen years since my last competition—I would have been considered the equivalent of a black belt. Tubby was strong and a quick learner, but I wasn't sure he could do what was needed with just his fists and feet. He kept grinning at me and then, almost in unison, both he and Rondo lifted up what looked like spear guns.

Did they expect me to be happy about that? This wasn't what I had planned. But really, what had I planned except going at them and getting my revenge? And now others were involved. I didn't know what to make of it all. I just knew we didn't have much time. I stared at the yacht in the distance. There was a light on in the sleeping cabin, but otherwise it was dark.

I started to put on my diving vest. The others were watching me. I slipped the knife, long and serrated, into the vest. I looked at the tank. What was I thinking? They were right. I was no

James Bond. I left the tank where it was in the boat. "I'm gonna swim over. Let me get started before you come closer. I don't want your boat to spook them or wake them," I said to Tubby. "I need to do this. Just hang back. John, now that these clowns are here, you should just go back. No reason for you to get further into this. I'll get the tank and other stuff from you later."

John gave me a hard look, as if he was pondering what I just said. Then he nodded and turned the skiff toward the shore.

"Don't worry Mr. Len, we got your back," Rondo said with a gleeful smile, like this was a game to him.

I shook my head. I took the mask and snorkel off, but kept the fins on. Knowing that they had my back made me feel a little better, but that they were soon to be involved also kept me on edge.

I lowered into the warm water and looked at the yacht. I reached down and took the fins off, tossing them into Rondo's skiff, keeping only the vest on now with the dive knife buttoned into its pocket. The yacht wasn't that far away, and fins would be cumbersome getting onto the boat. If I could find the time— and I usually made sure I did—I would swim every day; leisurely laps in the calm, pool-like water off either Heaven's Beach, near the Bougainvillea Inn, or the more remote, secluded Coral Beach, my two favorites on the island. The hundred yards to the yacht I knew I could do easily. But then again, I hadn't slept in almost two days. I was going purely on adrenaline. Adrenaline fumes.

I was close enough now to see a light on in one of the lower staterooms. What did that mean? Maybe someone was up. It didn't matter anymore. I made my way around to the starboard side of the yacht where I knew the ladder was. I gripped it as I started up.

With water dripping down my body, I walked slowly around the deck to the companionway. As I stepped down, I sensed something. Before I could react—before I could get to the knife in my dive vest, I felt a hard blow smash into my back, sending me down the steps. I turned to see Migos, with his narrowed eyes and weathered, tattooed skin, looking down at me as I sprawled there. He grinned at my prone position there and gripped the railings leading down to the saloon. That blow, I knew, was just the beginning.

I scrambled up as quickly as I could as he headed down, aware of the knife he flashed at me earlier, the same knife I knew he used on Maurizio. I had been taught to fight in competitions, to study my opponent and defeat him with both intelligence and skill. But I also knew, and learned, that I wouldn't always be in a controlled fight. Muay Thai was a form of self-defense, not just a sport that gave out trophies. That knowledge was ingrained in me deep enough for me to react to situations. But for this I knew I had to go on the attack. Now I had to resort to pure fighting instincts. Without hesitation, I swung my leg around and knocked him back, my foot jabbing solidly at his head. While he was falling back, he raised up the hand that held his knife, the thing he used on Maurizio. Before he could slash it at me, I peppered his midsection with blows from my knees, ramming him over and over into his solar plexus and ribs. I could hear the air whoosh from him before he dropped the knife. I didn't stop. He was back against the steps when I went harder at his ribs. I could hear the cracking of bones as he screamed. The more I hit him, the more I wanted to hit him. This is the one, I thought. This is the one who hurt Maurizio. Who tortured him. This was the one who touched Betta. I kept that in my mind as I watched his eyes roll back. I moved on top of him, and taking him by his hair, I bent his head back. I felt the heft of the dive knife that was still latched in my vest. I could have taken it out and used it, but I didn't want to. I needed to do it my way. With my own hands. No knife. No gun. His Adam's apple was bulging. That was my target. The blow there would end it. It would be quick. He wouldn't suffer. Not like he made my friends suffer. I would get my revenge for what he did to them. The thought and the word itself—revenge—made me hesitate for just a moment before striking that final blow. And it was in that moment of hesitation that I felt the hard barrel of a gun press against the skin just below the hairline on the back of my head.

"We know you come back," I heard Borka say. "A man like you, we know, need to come back. Settle this. We would be surprised otherwise."

I turned my head slowly. As I turned, the gun remained tight against me. I released my grip on Migos's hair. He was having trouble breathing and groaned from the pain in his ribs, but I hadn't finished him. I made a move for the knife now, but Penko slashed at my hand with his gun. "No, no, hero. Take it off."

I pulled off the vest. Penko patted it and felt the knife in the pocket. He tossed vest and knife into the water. Borka kept the gun at my neck.

Migos continued to groan and Penko bent over him. He put his hand on his shattered ribs. Migos screamed from the pain. He was wheezing and gasping for breath. "What we do now with Migos? We take him to hospital? We let him suffer with broken rib against lung?" Borka asked me while keeping the gun tight to the back of my head. I knew he didn't expect an answer. He and Penko conversed in their language, and from their tone, they seemed to be talking matter-of-factly about Migos's situation.

They stopped talking for a moment. Penko stood up, holding a handgun. Without any hesitation, he raised it and fired, the bullet going clean through Migos's forehead. I grimaced as the man's narrow eyes fluttered for just a moment but did not close.

"Poor Migos," Borka said after the smoke cleared. "He wanted to make filet out of you. Like he do to the other. But you, hero. You make him useless to us. Now what we do with you?"

My knees ached from battering Migos with them. I was

kneeling and holding that position was excruciating. Who was I kidding? There was no way I could have taken on the three of them.

Borka gestured with the gun for me to stand up, as if he could see the pain I was in. I heard creaking coming from my body as I stood and I'm sure he did too because he smiled. It wasn't so much a sadistic smile as one of wonderment.

"You have very hard day. You need nap, I think. You need sleep. We have pill that make sure you stay awake. You know boat?"

"What do you mean?"

"To work boat like this. Migos know. He, how you say, drive boat here. Now how we get back? Penko and I don't drive boat. You know how to drive boat?"

"Not much," I said. But I was lying. Though I was no expert, I had piloted boats like this a few times. One of my partners in the bars I owned had a yacht and took my family out for trips along the north shore of Long Island, on the Sound. He even let me borrow it once when I asked to take my father on a fishing trip a few years before he passed away. So I knew the basics well enough to get it in and out of dock.

He laughed, my face again a giveaway. "You lie to me. No, hero, we need you to take us back to Venezuela where we pick up boat. Margarita Island. You know this place?"

I did but just shrugged.

"We have someone there we meet."

I looked at the two men. There was a dead body close to my feet. They wanted me to stay with them, pilot the yacht, on what was close to a five-hundred-mile trip. And then what? We would go our own separate ways? Doubtful.

Borka could tell what I was thinking. Who wouldn't? "We let you go then. How you get back, that your problem. But get us there, and we don't care that you make Migos useless. You come back to this shit island and little bar you have. Live your life. I know you don't chase us down."

The more he talked, the more I knew that once we were out of St. Pierre waters and out onto the Caribbean away from other islands, I would not get back. There wasn't a chance that they would let me go. I had to think of some way to stay here. To stop this before we got too far. I didn't have my phone. I didn't even have dry clothes, and the trip would take a couple of days.

"I hope you at least have coffee on this boat," I said. "Or let me get some sleep first."

The two men laughed at that. "Sleep? No, old man don't need sleep. But we have coffee and pill keep you up and alert." Penko said. "We have plenty food. We have steak. Migos cook for us but now what? Who cook? So, hero drive us and make us steak. Eggs. Okay?"

I didn't answer.

Penko whispered something to Borka. "We see what you do to Migos," Penko said. "Migos try to use knife. We not stupid. We have gun. You stop gun with knee? With foot?"

Again I didn't answer.

"No, just drive boat to Margarita Island. Course chart up in cockpit. Go. Now."

Penko was behind me with the gun to my upper back. He was pushing me to the cockpit. I moved toward it and looked at the controls. I knew just enough to get the thing going, but I wasn't concerned. We weren't going far, at least not with me at the helm. On this state-of-the-art yacht, there was a control switch for the anchor winch. Penko was watching what I was doing. My knees throbbed and my back was stiff and sore. I contemplated going at him right there and worrying about Borka after, but I still needed some recovery time. I flipped the switch and could hear the grinding of the winch as it drew in the multiple anchors.

"What you do?" Penko asked.

"Just getting the anchors up so we can go," I said. "I guess this is how it works, but let me go check."

"Check what?"

"You want out of here or not? I need to make sure the anchors are in."

He looked at me suspiciously. He waved the gun at me as I headed out onto the deck toward the bow. I walked around the deck to where I figured the anchor locker was. I could hear the winch pulling the heavy anchors up. Penko followed me. I stood there over the locker. The winch stopped. The anchors were up, and we began to sway and drift in the choppy water. I took a deep breath. My whole body was sore. I didn't have a lot left. They were right; I was an old man trying to do youthful shit. Who was I kidding? But I remembered my friend and what I saw they did to him. I would never forget that. I felt the boat drift more and heard the sound of an engine closing in on us. No more, I thought. He was right behind me with that gun, as the boat rocked. I balanced myself and, ignoring the pain, I swung my leg in a wide, quick arc, slashing it across Penko's head, sending him onto his back. How he held onto the gun I had no idea, but he did and fired from his back and into the air. He tried to scramble up from where he fell, but before he could, I quickly drove my foot hard down into his chest. I heard a sound I never wanted to hear as I crushed his ribs. But he fired again. The sound of my next blow—the one to his neck—was even more horrific. It was that blow that ended it.

"I fucking kill you now," I heard Borka yell from behind me. I turned to see him coming at me with his gun. He fired, but the boat was rocking from the fighting now that the anchors were up; his aim was off, sending the shots wide. He made his way closer. There would be no wide shots now. His legs were set apart to steady himself. The gun was up. And then two spears flew past him...and me. The spears sailed over the boat and back into the sea. They missed. Tubby and Rondo missed.

The spears surprised him and Borka turned with the gun up in his hand. He saw Tubby and Rondo standing up in their skiff. He was going to shoot my friends. I was scrambling to rise up, but my legs were not working, and the boat was rocking wildly. I needed to get to him before he fired that gun. "Down," I heard a loud voice yell from behind me. I instinctively ducked and then heard a gunshot. I watched as Borka's arms fell to his sides. He sunk to his knees facing away from me, and then he pitched over. I could see dark liquid flowing from a hole in the back of his head just above his neck.

I was shaking. Breathing hard. There were dead bodies on either side of me. One I killed, the sound of broken bones—the sound of death—still loud in my brain. I turned to look behind me. I saw a skiff alongside the yacht. John was standing up in it...holding his gun. I finally got to my feet. I looked behind me. Tubby and Rondo were also standing up in their skiff. They held the spear guns and then dropped them. I turned back to John.

"We done now," John said. Holding the gun, he reared back and threw it as far as he could into the water. And then he started up the skiff and turned it around, heading back to St. Pierre.

# 28

But we weren't done yet. I couldn't leave the yacht there with three dead bodies in it. McWilliams would have no choice but to investigate this. There would be no cover-up. There would be questions. These were foreign nationals, meaning other entities would want to know what happened. Even though I was really just functioning on fumes, I had work to do. Tubby knew without me telling him what had to be done. He moved from the skiff to the yacht. I helped him up and on board.

"Can you follow us out about five miles?" I asked Rondo, not sure the small boat could withstand the rougher waters.

Rondo grinned. I had seen that confident look on his face before. It was as if he welcomed the challenge. "Easy. You go. I follow."

As we traversed the deck, we sidestepped Penko's dead body. Tubby glanced at him. He could see the angle of his head and neck and what was done to him. He looked at me, and I turned away from him. What did he think of me now? I didn't want to know. I went back into the cockpit and started the yacht. We slowly headed west, toward the channel between the islands and out of St. Pierre waters. "He with us?" I asked Tubby, looking back at the skiff and wondering if it could keep up with the yacht.

"Don't worry about Rondo. He coming."

When we hit the channel, the yacht started to bounce in the

waves of the rough sea. Water was splashing up from the side of the boat. "Far enough?"

"This good," he said.

I turned off the engine. We were now just bouncing and swaying. It was hard to stand without holding on to something. The channel between islands was known for its ferocious turbulence. If I wasn't so tired and in so much pain, I would probably have my head hanging over the side of the boat, vomiting my guts out. But I was distracted from all that.

"See if you can find where they keep the emergency equipment."

"What we need?"

"Look for a flare gun. There's got to be one on a boat like this."

Tubby searched while I went to the back of the boat where the fuel feed was. I opened the fuel fill. I needed to get gasoline out of the tank. I peered into the engine and noticed a few hoses. I needed a knife but mine had been tossed into the sea. I went to where Migos still lay. I saw the knife. I hesitated, not wanting to touch the deadly thing knowing how it was used, but I had to. I went back to the fuel feed and, using the knife, cut off a long piece of hose. I had what I needed and then, like John did with his gun, threw that knife as far as I could into the sea.

Tubby was waving the flare gun at me. He had found it.

"Help me with them," I said as I started to drag Migos's body, still splayed out in the saloon, to the back of the boat.

Tubby saw the bullet hole in his forehead. "You do this?"

"Later, Tubby, we have to do this first," I said.

He stopped to look at me, realizing what I had just been through.

We dragged the other two bodies from the deck to the back of the boat. Piling them on top of each other.

"Now what?" Tubby asked.

I showed him the hose as I lowered it into the fuel tank. I started to inhale, pulling the gas from the tank. I had done it before—siphoned gas from other cars as a stupid kid trick. Now as a supposedly mature man, that stunt was finally useful.

"You learn that in the Bronx?"

I nodded but didn't look up.

"You a bad man," Tubby said, shaking his head.

Yeah, I am. I'm a killer. I thought to myself as I sucked into the hose again. Soon I could feel the gas rushing up. Just as it touched my mouth, I pulled it away, spitting out whatever hit my lips. I doused the bodies with the gasoline, careful to step out of the way. The gas was flowing freely onto the deck. That was also what I wanted. I hosed down the deck near the bodies with the gasoline.

"Okay, let's go."

Tubby started to the side of the yacht. The skiff was there. The water was so choppy, Rondo's body seemed to be bouncing up and down.

Once Tubby was in the skiff, I went back to the yacht's saloon. I grabbed the box with the bottles of vermouth. I carefully handed them down to Tubby and then went to get the bag with my money. I gripped it tightly as I maneuvered myself into the skiff, trying not to get tossed from it as it swayed. I was moving slowly, my back and knees not cooperating. Both Rondo and Tubby held my arms to steady me as I lowered to the skiff's bench. Tubby held the flare gun.

"Pull away, Rondo." I said.

Rondo started up the motor and moved away from the yacht. When we were about thirty yards from it, I told Rondo to stop. I reached for the flare gun. Tubby pulled it away from me. "No, no, you miss. You don't know how to shoot a gun," he said.

"I was in the Marines," I reminded him.

"I wasn't even born when you one of the few and the proud," he said, shaking his head at me.

"Who are you to talk after that pitiful display with the spear gun?"

"The boat rock too much…"

"*Big ship sailing on the ocean…we don't need no commotion,*" Rondo was singing an old reggae tune so we would understand the urgency—that we had to get out of here or lose the skiff.

"What are you waiting for?" I said to Tubby. "Do it."

Tubby nodded, raised up his arm, with his hand gripping the flare gun, pulled the trigger. The flaming flare shot up into the air in an arc. We all watched in the darkness as it slowly fell down onto the boat. And then we waited for something—but nothing happened.

"Try again?"

"Why?" Tubby said.

I was about to take the flare gun from him. I was impatient. I wanted to get this done, but before I could, I heard a whoosh and saw flames burst up from the back of the yacht. It was done.

Rondo started to pull us away, heading back to the island. I watched the flames grow and then there was an explosion. The yacht was breaking apart while the skiff we were in was bouncing and rocking in turbulence, slapping the boat down onto the water. I held on to whatever I could so as not to get tossed from the boat. I turned from the wreckage of the yacht to see St. Pierre in the distance in the opposite direction. There was just the faintest glow of light on the eastern horizon, barely visible over Mt. Hadali. It was morning now. If I were home, I might be up after a good night's sleep, holding a cup of coffee and at my window watching the sun rise up over the Atlantic. It was where I wanted to be, but we were on the water. The skiff was straining, seemingly heading right into the waves. I was now very worried the wooden boat might break apart.

"Are we gonna get out of this, Rondo?" I asked. He didn't answer me. I wasn't sure if that was a bad sign. I watched the man as he worked the motor and guided the skiff through the waves. "Rondo?" Finally he pulled his head up and looked at me and smiled. And then he laughed. While he was laughing at me, I could feel the skiff break through the rough water. We were out of the channel and into the now calm waters closer to shore.

To home.

# PLAYLIST THREE

## Nura's Island

1. Dreamland, Marcia Griffiths
2. Rollin' Down, Dennis Brown
3. Coming In From the Cold, Bob Marley & the Wailers
4. Nice Time, Phyllis Dillon
5. Sun is Shining, Winston Matthews
6. Cool Down the Pace, Gregory Isaacs
7. My Time, Barrington Levy
8. Young Lover, Cocoa Tea
9. Small Axe, The Wailers
10. Don't Let Me Down, Marcia Griffiths
11. Shine Eye Gal, Barrington Levy
12. Greetings, Half Pint
13. Hurt So Good, Susan Cadogen
14. Promise Land, Majek Fashek
15. Calypso Blues, Calypso Rose

# 29

The espresso was so good at Moka, one of the many cafés in Milan Malpensa International Airport, I ended up drinking two. But they were small shots—you sucked them down in one gulp. It took just about twenty-four hours, minus the time difference and with layovers, to travel from St. Pierre to Barbados, Barbados to London, and then London to Milan. I had cleared customs and immigration, and was waiting to meet Augusto Loffredo, Maurizio's older brother. After getting the approval from the Loffredo family, McWilliams released Maurizio's body to me. I accompanied his remains from St. Pierre, along with the bottles of vermouth, minus the one that I had already opened, which I kept. I paid the customs tax to clear the vermouth and now carried the heavy box with me. Maurizio's body was in a temporary coffin in another area of the airport. When Augusto arrived, I would go with him to receive the coffin, if he so wished. Or I would just pay my respects and get on a later plane to London and trace my steps back to St. Pierre. Either way, I would be in my home within the next twenty-four to thirty-six hours. I wasn't in Milan on a sightseeing trip, but I could enjoy the espresso.

"Lennie," I heard someone call as I was contemplating an-other espresso. For a brief moment, I felt a chill at the back of my neck. The voice was Maurizio's—or just like his. I looked and saw Augusto waving to me. I only met him once, the one time the family visited St. Pierre.

Augusto was an orthopedic surgeon in Bergamo, like his father and younger brother, Alfonso. Besides his voice, the wire-rim glasses and the blue eyes were the only similarities to Maurizio. Augusto had a full head of salt-and-pepper hair. He was robust, where Maurizio was slight. He was fashionably dressed, as many northern Italians are, especially compared to the mostly slovenly Italian-Americans I grew up with in the Bronx.

As he approached, I could see he was crying. He came to me and hugged me, kissing me on both cheeks, his tears now marking my face. "I'm so sorry, Augusto," I said as we embraced.

"Augie...Augie...please," he said, wanting me to call him by his less formal name.

"Augie," I repeated.

"Lennie. You a good friend to my brother."

I just nodded. I didn't know what to say.

"Why this happen, Lennie? What my brother do for this to happen?"

We sat at one of the café's small high-top tables. I got us both espressos. Augusto took off his glasses and wiped at his eyes again. I pushed the box to him. "This is for you." I was avoiding his question.

He opened it and took out a bottle, examining it. "They are beautiful," he said. "Mimmo was a maestro. I know my brother study with him. They friends. Poor Mimmo. Now my brother."

He started to sob. I sipped the espresso instead of sucking it down. I was waiting, giving him time to grieve.

"Because of this? This bottle?" he asked once he composed himself. "They kill him over a bottle of vermouth?"

It was his right to know the truth. He was his brother—and what did it matter now? "He borrowed some money to finance it," I said. "From some bad people. And then he changed his mind. After Mimmo's death, he wanted to return the bottles to

Mimmo's partner. He didn't want them auctioned off, as I guess was originally planned. And with the interest they charged, he could not pay off his debt. They wanted these bottles back."

"My brother. Why he not come to us? Why? We love him no matter what he think. Alfonso and I give him anything he need. He not even have to ask. He can come just to us. We take care of him. We always take care of him."

I knew his relationship with his family was complicated. And maybe that was why he didn't go to them.

"These men. Tell me who they are. I find them and...I find them and take care of them. What they do to my brother."

I gripped his shoulder and shook my head. "No need," I said.

He stared at me. He hadn't touched the coffee, but now he did, sucking it down as I had the previous two. He practically slammed the cup down.

"You?"

I didn't answer.

"But, Lennie. This my family. My blood. Alfonso and I should do it. Not you. It is our job."

"There's nothing more to do."

He was breathing hard, his face red. "You make them suffer, Lennie? Like they do to Maurizio. Please. Tell me this." He spat that out with malice. Where was that rage in Maurizio? I never saw it.

I didn't want to think about what I did on that boat. I didn't want to think about suffering. "Like I said there's nothing more to do," I said. He looked at me and then pounded the table with his fist. I waited for him to work through his anger and his tears. He blew his nose with a loud honk. When the sobs subsided, I nudged the box with the vermouth bottles. "You can get these bottles back to Mimmo's partner."

"Partner?" He pondered that and then nodded.

"Yes, they...he has a daughter. Maurizio wanted whatever the bottles with Mimmo's signed art was worth to go to his family."

"I get it to him, Lennie." He looked again at the bottle. He studied the one with the illustration of the dark-skinned Afro-Caribbean woman. "His wife. Betta?"

I nodded.

"How she now? She does not deserve this."

"She will be okay."

When I left for Milan, Betta was still ensconced in her mother's house—her mother caring for her as she recovered from the trauma on the boat. We talked briefly. I told her what I was going to do, that I was going to Italy to bring the body to his family. It was then I learned how she really felt about Maurizio. And it surprised me. Though it shouldn't have. At first I thought it was her grief talking, but the almost cold way she confessed her feelings so soon after his death convinced me. She told me she would never forgive him for leaving her as he did. That he abandoned her with child and no man she could truly love would ever do that to her. They were husband and wife only on paper. She knew this despite taking him in when he needed her—when he needed to come back to her because he had no other place to go. He was the father of her child and she was his widow. But that was all it was. The affection for Maurizio remained, but not the love. She did not protest when I told her I was going and she would not.

"My nephew." Augusto almost whispered the words. "We take care of him. I talk to my brother and we make sure he get everything he need."

He was tearing up again. He took his handkerchief and wiped his eyes.

"Don't worry about Paolo," I said. 'He's in good hands."

He looked at me. I didn't have to explain anything else.

"We go get my brother now," he said as he moved off the high-top stool.

* * *

The temporary coffin was in a lot about a mile and a half from the main terminal. Augusto had hired a van and a driver. I rode with him to the lot; we were silent during the short drive. The temporary coffin containing Maurizio's remains was waiting there as we pulled up. I got out of the van with Augusto. The back doors were opened and we watched as two of the lot's workers lifted the coffin and placed in the back of the van. There wasn't anything for us to do but watch. We got back into the van and Augusto had the driver take me back to the airport terminal. On our way back he invited me to come to Bergamo, to be with his family for Maurizio's service and burial. I declined as politely as I could. At the terminal, we embraced again. "He have few good friends," Augusto said as he looked at me through the thick lenses of his glasses. "You his good friend. Grazie." I thought about that for a moment. I wondered why I was his good friend. Maybe I saw just a little of him in me. I didn't know and if so, wasn't sure that was a good thing. I had no words for Augusto. I could only nod. I stayed there for a moment and watched the van pull away, and then went back into the terminal and got on the security line. I had slept much of the trip over, but I was weary still, so very tired. I looked forward to sleeping on the long trip home.

# 30

But after those multiple espressos, the sleep I hoped for on the flight to Barbados was fleeting. The flight from Milan to London was less than two hours and I didn't bother to shut my eyes. I wanted to hold off for the long flight to Barbados. I had a three-hour layover before my connecting flight. I wandered around Heathrow Airport. I had no bags to check for the flight back home and carried only a backpack that I slung over my shoulder. I glanced out the windows of the terminal. The sky was gray. I wasn't sure what time it was. I would get back on some sort of schedule soon enough. Until then, day or night, it didn't matter. I just wanted to get home.

I was wide awake for the first two hours of the almost nine-hour flight to Barbados. I scanned the movies, hoping to find something that would help me off that caffeine buzz. I started watching a documentary about the different pizzas available in an Italian neighborhood in New Haven, Connecticut. I was enjoying it, but the shots of the coal-dusted pizzas and bubbling hot fresh tomato sauce were making me hungry. If I was hungry, I definitely wouldn't sleep, so I turned it off.

I put in my earbuds and scanned the playlists on my phone. I paused as I looked at some of the names I had for them. There was "Boogie Woogie Blues," something I put together after listening to a local St. Pierre station every Saturday morning that played from a feed from an NPR station out of Chicago.

Another was titled "Uncle Ciccio's Doo Wops," named after my Uncle Frank (my grandmother called him by his Italian name, Ciccio) who returned from Vietnam mentally scarred. In his diminished state, he would wander the Bronx streets where we lived, listening to his beloved doo wops on a portable reel-to-reel tape deck he carried with him everywhere. Uncle Frank died in 1987 but in his honor, I made my own version of what I thought would be his playlist. Tubby hooked me on Calypso and Soca and helped me put together a playlist I called "Tubby's Calypso Jams, Soca and Such." I needed something that might turn my brain off and calypso wasn't it. I settled on "M's Titans of the Jazz Piano, the "M" being for Maurizio, who introduced me to all those titans.

It didn't happen immediately, but I think I lost consciousness soon after Bill Evans' "Peace Piece" began to play. While Evans' piano played, I found myself in the Bronx with my mother, father, and brother, Pat. I was trying out for my high school's baseball team. I was up at the plate, a bat in my hands. The pitcher wound up and let loose. I could see the ball clearly. I swung and missed. My mother, who didn't know a baseball bat from a rolling pin, was telling me I needed to choke up on the bat. I did what she said but kept swinging and missing. My father, who never watched a baseball game in his life, said to use a lighter bat. And my brother, who was a star outfielder in high school, was telling me to keep my head down, but mostly he was just laughing at me. Each time the ball was pitched, I saw it clearly, but I couldn't hit it. I was huffing. Grunting. And missing each pitch no matter what the pitcher threw me. I swung harder and harder hoping that would help, but it just frustrated me more. Why couldn't I hit the ball? The frustration and the taunts from my brother and parents made me cry like a baby.

I woke up suddenly, my head bouncing up from my chest. My face was wet. I touched my forehead. It was sweat, but I wasn't hot. I was cold. There was an empty seat between me and a man who had the window seat. He looked at me with some concern. I tried to smile to indicate I was okay. I still had the earbuds in. I looked at my phone. Oscar Peterson's "Meditation" was playing. I paused the music, unclasped my seat belt, and stood up. I swayed, and had to grip my seat to keep my balance. I was dizzy. I waited a moment to regain my balance and then headed to the restroom. I squeezed into the tiny space. I looked into the mirror. My face was flushed and damp. I splashed cold water on it hoping that would revive me and cool me off.

The plane was dark, with just laptop and movie monitors lighting the aisle. As I made my way back to my seat, there was some turbulence. I moved unsteadily through the aisle until I practically collapsed into my seat. Something wasn't right. I didn't want to make too much of it. I closed my eyes and it wasn't long before I was dreaming again.

My daughter Kasie had returned to the island, she visited once before, and this time she brought the boyfriend, Austin. I was anxious to get a look at him, but he was hidden from my sight. I strained to see him. "Daddy, this is Austin," she said. And then I saw him. "No, honey. No. Not him." She held his hand and was smiling at me. "Yes, Daddy. I love him. He takes care of me." I saw Migos—grinning. "I take care of your honey," he said.

A bright light flashed over my face, and I opened my eyes. I could feel the pressure in my ears as we were descending, making our way to Grantley Adams Airport in Barbados. My body was damp, but I was cold—almost shivering. I knew then that I had a fever.

I bought a small packet of aspirin at the airport while waiting to board the prop plane to St. Pierre. I gulped down two and then, still unsteady, boarded the small plane. The flight was just forty minutes and by the time we landed, the aspirin had knocked down the fever enough to give me the strength to get off the plane.

Tubby was waiting for me outside the tiny terminal. The sun was out, but the slight breeze was making me shiver. I could see his concern as soon as he saw me come through the airport's doors.

"What happen to you?"

"Nothing. I'm just sick. The flu or something," I said, not wanting to make a big deal of it. But I hadn't felt like this in many years. This wasn't just sick. This was really sick, and I didn't need a doctor to tell me that.

"You stay home. We take care of everything," he said as he dropped me off and went inside the house with me. He had fed the dogs while I was gone, but you wouldn't know it. They were on me as soon as I stepped out of Tubby's car. The Puppy, who seemed to have grown considerably in the two days I was gone, was whining happily. I bent to pick her up but as I did, I felt shaky, like I was going to collapse, so I lowered her back down.

"I'm gonna go lie down, Tubby," I said.

"You rest. I check in on you later."

Once Tubby was gone, I filled up a glass with cold water, took it to my bedroom, kicked off my jeans, but kept my T-shirt on. I never wore a shirt to bed, but I had that chill. I pulled the window shade down and got under the covers. My body hurt as if I had just been in a fight. It wasn't from what happened on the boat, though that didn't help. I just had a few bruises from that and my knees and back were working again. No, it was something else. Aches I never felt before. I picked up a virus or flu somewhere. Maybe in the Milan airport? Or on the multiple planes I had just been on? People always got sick on planes. I could hear the congestion in my lungs as I breathed. But soon I heard nothing.

It was dark when I got up, so I pulled up the shades. Again my body was wet, soaked with sweat, but I was freezing. I wasn't sure if I fed the dogs. My head was spinning as I tried to stand. I wrapped my bed cover around me and went into the kitchen. I bent over to pour kibble into the three bowls and almost fell. I held on to the kitchen counter and righted myself. I went to the bathroom, my eyes fluttering, my body aching. And then I got back into bed.

I stayed in bed, in and out of sleep. There were dreams, but these were just quick blurs—almost like snapshots. There was my ex, Kathleen, a flirtatious smile on her face as she cashed one of my checks from behind the Chase bank counter where she worked before we were married, and another where I was sitting on a bench watching my young children romp in a playground near the elementary school they went to in the Bronx. Then I was in one of the bars I ran in Brooklyn. I was observing—no, judging—one of my partners, Carl, who was openly groping one of our female servers while she pretended to enjoy it. And I did nothing to stop it. There was darkness, a blank space in between some of these brief, vivid dreams. I was turning from one side to the other on the bed, trying to find comfort there, but it wasn't coming. My eyes would open and close in the dark. And when they closed next, I was desperately searching through the heavy smoke that filled the subway station. I was tripping over bodies, pulling them up and out so I could get to Nura. But in that thick smoke, I couldn't find her. Just moments before, I walked her to that subway station, kissed her goodbye, watched her descend down the subway steps, and then left her to go home to my wife, and to finally confess what I could no longer hide from her. That was the plan. Nura insisted I tell her; we could no longer keep our affair a secret, and I agreed. But then I heard the explosion and felt the ground under me shake and it all went to shit. When the smoke cleared, I could see the island of St. Pierre from the air. I was looking down at the rainforest green that surrounded Mt. Hadali, the white-and-black sand beaches around the coast, and the impossible blue of the waters off the many reefs. The land of promise. Dreamland. I wondered if it was delirium from the fever that brought on this unconscious slide show of my life? All through it I was aware of my own heavy breathing. I felt the bright sun as it splashed over my body. I didn't want the sun. I wanted the dark. I was sick. I was old. And I was alone. This was the choice I made. Was I prepared for it?

I fell asleep again but for how long, I didn't know. I did know that now there was something cool on my forehead. It felt good. My breathing wasn't as loud. I lifted fingers to my forehead. I touched something cool and wet. I opened my eyes.

"No, Leonard, keep it on," Betta said to me as she sat on my bed, her fingers on mine as I touched the cold compress she had put on my forehead.

"Betta?" My voice was raspy. My throat hurt.

"Yes, it's me. I'm here," she said. "Don't talk. Rest."

Through my barely open eyes, I noticed her hair was in a series of braids that fell below her shoulders. The braids were adorned with colorful beads. I wanted to reach out and touch them. I wanted to touch her cheek. Her lips. But I didn't. I wasn't alone and that was satisfaction enough for me. I turned to see that there was a glass of water with a straw in it and a coffee cup on the side table next to my bed. She picked up the glass of water and held it for me. I didn't hesitate. I sucked through the straw. I wanted more, but she pulled the glass away.

"A little at a time, Leonard." She put the glass down and picked up the coffee mug. "And I want you to drink this. It will make you better."

"Coffee?"

She shook her head. "Sip please."

She held the mug up to my lips. My hands were over hers as I steadied it and sipped. It wasn't coffee. Or tea. I could taste chocolate without much sugar, but with ginger and lime. I looked at her.

"Cocoa tea," she said. "It help you heal."

She watched me as I took a few more sips and then I handed her the mug.

The Puppy jumped up on the bed. "No, no," Betta said and lifted her off.

"It's okay. She can come up," I said with a smile.

"I want you to sleep more. You are getting better. I know this. But you still sick. You need more rest."

I thought about what she said. "How long have you been here?"

"I come yesterday morning," she said, looking at me. "Your fever is coming down now."

"Betta...you didn't have to. Where is Paolo?"

"Paolo with his grandma. I say for you to hush now. No talk. Rest."

She was right, the talk was tiring me. My eyes were heavy and I closed them again. This time when I slept, there were no dreams.

I woke up in the middle of the night. The chills were gone, but I had a pounding headache, and I felt weak as I made my way to the bathroom. The house was dark and before getting back into bed I peered into the living room. I saw Betta, asleep on my couch, a blanket pulled over her. I wanted to wake her and send her into the second bedroom where there was a comfortable full-sized bed, but I figured I should just let her sleep. I looked at her there on my couch until my legs started to give way. I got back into bed and drifted off again.

When I got up, the headache was gone, and I could smell something good coming from the kitchen. I got up and padded to the kitchen. Betta was over the stove, stirring something. "You didn't have to sleep on my couch," I said to her. She was startled and turned to look at me. "You could have slept on the bed in the other bedroom."

"You think you are well, but not yet. Stay in bed," she said, ignoring what I just told her.

"I'm okay. Whatever it was I had, is gone. I'm sure of it."

She shook her head. "One more day, Leonard. Please."

"What is that you're cooking?" I asked, changing the subject. I didn't want her babying me. Even though whatever it was that knocked me on my ass and made me think of things we do when...well, we are on our ass and can't get up. Dark, gloomy things. "Get back into bed and I bring it to you."

I was hungry but still tired. Maybe she was right. Maybe I did need one more day.

I got back into bed and sat up. She came into the bedroom with a bowl on a tray, along with a coffee mug and a spoon. She sat on the bed and placed the tray on my lap. Her presence here was doing more to heal me than she could ever have imagined. I looked at her as she held the tray and for a moment there I even forgot that I had been sick. Betta was with me. In my home. My thoughts were going to other places. I had to dash those thoughts. She was a friend, nothing more. She was here to just take care of me. She was nursing me back to health. Maybe she was doing it out of a sense of obligation, because I helped get her off that boat and back home to her child. Or because of all the other things I did for her and Paolo while Maurizio was gone. Now it was her turn; payback for my assistance. That was all it was.

"What have you brought me?" I asked, looking down into the bowl—an orange-yellow soup with pieces of carrots and other root vegetables, and chunks of what looked like beef, bones and even beef cartilage.

"Cow foot soup," she said.

I knew about cow foot soup. Men on the island believed it enhanced virility. But men on St. Pierre and around the Caribbean thought many things enhanced virility. "Are you trying to get me in trouble," I said.

"This for you to make you strong after being sick. My mother make this for me all the time whenever I sick. This not just for men, Leonard."

"True, but it couldn't hurt, I mean, if, you know, what they say about this soup is true."

She slapped my arm and got off the bed quickly, embarrassed at what I implied. It felt good to smile. And to see her smile after what she had been through was even better. "I have to leave for a few hours to take Paolo to school and change my clothes. Will you be okay?"

"I'm fine now. And after I have this soup, who knows how good I'll be." I was still teasing her.

"Stop," she said and shook her head. "I come back later this afternoon."

"You don't have to. I appreciate what you've done. I might go to the bar later to check up on things."

"No. I say one more day. Listen to me. The bar you know is in good hands. You don't need to go there. You get your strength today and tomorrow you go."

"Who am I to argue with you, Betta. You're in charge."

It had been a whirlwind few days since I got her off that boat. Before leaving for Italy she had confessed to me her true feelings for Maurizio, but we never talked about what happened on the boat. What they did to her. Maybe she would talk to me about it when she was ready. Or never.

"I'll stay home."

She touched my forearm. "Eat. I come back later."

# 31

I heard the generic ringtone blare from my phone. I was getting fewer and fewer real, legitimate phone calls and more and more texts. I wasn't sure how I felt about that. On the one hand, fewer calls meant I didn't have to talk, and that was a good thing. But with texts I struggled to say what I wanted to say, and it seemed like what I did say just came out wrong. I was grumpy in general, I knew that. My words reflected that even more than my gruff tone. When I saw that it was Tubby who was calling, I was glad it was not a text.

"You all good now?" Tubby asked.

"Yeah, I'm all good now, Tubby. Still a little tired but much better. No problems where you are?"

"Everything run smoothly without you. No rush for you to come back. Stay away. The longer the better." I heard him snicker.

"You just don't want me there so you can do nothing but watch cricket and suck on a toothpick."

"When you ever see me suck on a toothpick?"

"Never, but I have a feeling you would if I wasn't there to bust your balls about sucking on a toothpick."

I heard him hiss at that. "No, nothing to worry about here, Mr. Len. Come back when you ready. Mike and I have it all under control."

I knew they did. Still, after the few days away, I actually

missed being there. It was my purpose, I thought, never a burden. Unlike what I experienced in New York, the Sporting Place was a pleasure.

I finished the cow foot soup and took a shower. That cocoa tea that Betta had made for me was delicious, but now I wanted a cup of coffee. After my shower I made a pot and took the cup to the chair facing the big window overlooking the Atlantic. The Puppy was more than happy to see me out of the bedroom and back in my familiar spot. She hopped up onto my lap and curled against my hip. I stroked her copper coat as I looked out at the ocean. The windows in the kitchen were open. I could hear the rough surf down below the cliffs. It was a noise I realized I could not live without.

I hadn't been outside in a couple of days. I wanted fresh air. I went out and walked down the steep incline to the beach. I carried the Puppy while the other dogs followed happily. The wind was blowing as it usually did on this side of the island. It was a constant. My hair seemed to be persistently massaged by that wind. I felt the sun on my back. It was getting late in the day. I walked down to the beach, but soon my legs were dragging in the sand. They felt heavy. Betta was right; I needed this extra day. Whatever this bug was had really wiped me out. I walked back up to the house just as the sun was setting. I had a bit more of that soup and then got into bed and closed my eyes.

I felt her slide into my bed and at first I thought it was another one of the dreams I had been having, but when her arm wrapped around my chest from behind, I knew I was not sleeping. "Leonard," she whispered. I could feel her warm body through the clothes she wore. I turned to her and knew that she had come to me for comfort—nothing more. "I was worried.

You were very sick."

"I'm here, I'm okay now," I said.

"Yes. you are here. You are always here."

I didn't know what to make of her words. I didn't know what to make of her presence in my bed, but though it could have been something much more under different circumstances, on this night it was just soothing to me. And I think to her as well. She held me like that until we both fell asleep.

It was very early in the morning, still dark when I heard her whisper again. "Are you awake, Leonard?"

I thought I was awake. I wasn't sure. My eyes were half-lidded. I could barely open them. I was in a dream-like state. I know I was on my back and she was leaning over me. I think I mumbled a yes.

"I know you should sleep, but I want to tell you something."

I heard her, but I didn't.

"Please listen, Leonard," she said. "I want to bake bread again. I want to fix the oven and bake bread for people like before. I know how to do this. I can do this."

I tried to get myself up to turn. I wanted to listen—at least that was what I told myself. But I was so tired—weary even. I just wanted to go back to sleep. Later, I would kick myself thinking about that. I would tell myself it was the virus. That it was not that I didn't want to hear what she had to say, I just couldn't. That's what I would tell myself. My eyes were closing.

"Will you help me? Will you bake bread with me, Leonard? We make pizza too. I learn to make real Italian pizza. We can do it together. Will you?" That was the last I remembered of what I think she said. Or maybe what I dreamed.


Just before sunrise I felt her leave the bed. I was still sleepy, but weakly tried to pull her back to bed in a faint hope of some-thing more. "No, Leonard," she said. "I must go home."

"Huh?" I mumbled, half awake. She was looking at me

laying there. And then she turned and left.

When I heard the front door slam shut, I sat up in bed. Was she angry? I wasn't sure and, if so, wondered why she would be. I didn't know. I knew nothing. And that was what cluttered my mind in the days and weeks that followed.

I fell back asleep until the sound of a car engine idling outside my house woke me up. The sun was streaming into my room. I looked at my phone. It was after eight, much later than my usual wakeup. I got up and put my jeans and a T-shirt on quickly. I peered out the window to see a police cruiser in front of my house. I heard the doorbell and checked to see who it was before opening it; a New York habit that never left me. Through the peephole, I saw the bulky figure of Superintendent McWilliams, in uniform, standing there waiting.

I opened the door. He stared at me. "I hear you sick," he said, taking his hat off. I opened the door wide for him to enter.

"Yeah, a nasty virus or something. I think I caught it on the plane or in Italy."

"Many get sick over there these days, I hear."

"Oh yeah?"

He just shrugged. "But you feel better now?"

"Yeah, much," I said.

He was peering around the living room. My bedroom door was open. I saw him glance that way. I thought I heard him sniffing, wondering if he could detect Betta's unique fragrance, the one that still lingered in my home. If I didn't know any better I would say he was snooping.

"I'm fine now. In fact, I was getting ready to go to work."

He turned to me. "IMPACs find the wreck of the boat," he said.

What he said wasn't registering.

"They contact me, but I tell them I know nothing about it."

I gestured to my couch. "Coffee?" I understood what he was

saying now.

"Certainly, sir," he said. "Cream and sugar."

I put coffee and water into the machine and flicked it on. "Did they find anything else?"

"Not that I know of," he said.

The coffee was ready. I prepared his cup with cream and sugar as requested while I took mine black. I brought both cups over to where he was sitting.

"The boat was found in waters closer to St. Vincent. They have more of those kinds of problems over there. Drugs. Gangsters. Smuggling. I highly doubt I'll hear from IMPACs again. You make a very splendid cup of coffee," he said with a smile.

"It's the beans," I mumbled and thought about where I got those beans. I took a breath. The news about IMPACs, I knew, was just an excuse. I was waiting to hear why McWilliams was really here.

He put his cup down. "Lord Ram funeral on Friday," he said.

It had been almost two weeks since his death. McWilliams had come to remind me of my obligation to him. Despite what I had just been through, he hadn't forgotten his request for help in finding out the truth of how the man died. "As you know, McWilliams, I've been preoccupied with other matters."

"Yes, I know, but you seem fit now and those matters are taken care of. They no longer concern you."

"From my discussion with Ms. Blue, I am leaning heavily toward believing it was indeed an accident."

"Mmmhmm," he muttered, his hands clasped at his waist. "You go talk to Jannilea Sparks and if that is your conclusion, I will thank you for your efforts."

He glanced around the house again, taking time to peer into my bedroom, that hound dog investigator's nose sniffing as he surveyed the scene.

"I'll go see her later today," I said.

"Thank you, Buonfiglio, for the coffee. I'm very glad you are feeling better."

On my way to the Sporting Place, I took a little detour that took me past Betta's house. It was a nice house that Tubby and I helped finish for her after Maurizio left. I slowed down in front, hoping to get a glimpse of her, but I didn't stop. I drove away and headed to the bar. I didn't think stalker would be a good look on me.

# 32

"You look like you were sick," Tubby said as I entered the bar.

"Good observation, Tubby," I said as he and Mike, both behind the bar, looked me over. "Especially considering you knew I was sick."

"When I leave you from the airport I know you were not well, but now you look like you were sick. You are whiter than usual. There's a difference."

"I'm good now. Don't you worry, partner, it won't be long before I get my sexy glow back."

"What was it make you so sick?" Mike asked. "And you lose too much weight, I see."

"Just some bug I caught traveling," I said with a shrug. "All I've eaten was some homemade cow foot soup."

"Where you get that soup? I never know you to make cow foot soup or have it anytime I know you."

"Betta made some for me."

"She make you cow foot soup?"

"She said it's good for when you are sick."

"Betta?"

"Yeah."

He was trying to interpret that. "You know, cow foot soup good for other things."

"So I've heard."

Mike laughed and said, "Now, now, Tubby. I do know some

believe cow foot soup also a remedy for illness."

Tubby studied me as I started to make my way to the bar. "Betta make you cow foot soup?"

"I think I just said that, but to be honest, I'm still very hungry. And since you are concerned about my eating habits, I hope you have breakfast for me."

"No breakfast. It's lunchtime," Tubby said. "And Elfera's just open for lunch. Hurry though, you know she run out cow foot soup early. But if you are lucky she will still have baked macaroni and ham."

"Baked macaroni and ham? I don't think so, Tubby." I looked around. The bar was empty. "You two drive all the customers away?"

"A cruise boat just arrive. We have plenty of people soon come." Mike said.

I wasn't sure how I felt about that. I wasn't sure I was up to working a crowd. And after McWilliams' visit, I wanted to end the Lord Ram business. I just wanted things to get back to normal.

"Can you work this afternoon if it does get busy, Mike?" I asked.

"No problem, Mr. Len," Mike said.

"You know we lose Mike to North Carolina soon," Tubby said.

"North Carolina? What's this all about?" I asked looking at both of them.

"His boy, Malcolm, get a football scholarship to that school there," Tubby said.

"Football?" and then I realized Tubby was referring to soccer and remembered Mike had been away with his son Malcom on those recruiting trips. "That's great, Mike. Congratulations to Malcolm. But what does that have to do with you?"

"My wife, we chat about it. We want to be close to our boy and North Carolina has opportunities with many urgent-care medical centers and hospitals for Sheila to work. I find work there, I'm sure."

Mike started as mainly a fill-in at the bar. I know he used the work to supplement his job working construction. As we got busier the past couple of years, he helped out on a much more consistent basis. He was a good balance between Tubby and me. When we had our petty disagreements about anything, Mike would always be the voice of reason and sway us in the right direction.

"Mike, don't you know you are irreplaceable," I said.

"You replace me or not, Mr. Len. I sure everything go very smoothly here without me. And thank you."

I wasn't so sure of that. We would miss Mike in many ways. "This isn't for a while, correct? Next year?"

"No, Mr. Len. Malcolm graduate secondary school. The school in North Carolina have an opening when another drop out. Football start soon there. Malcolm leave here in a week. We think we move in late September."

That was much sooner than I thought. We would have to find someone to replace him, but we did have a little time, and it was the least of my worries at the moment.

On my way to Jannilea Sparks' home, I did stop in at Elfera's Home Cooking, a tiny restaurant at the bottom of Windy Hill Road. I passed on the baked macaroni and ham, but devoured her delicious Tuesday lunch special, fish blaff: sea bass poached in a hot marinade of lime, garlic, onion, vinegar, white wine, and hot peppers. I ordered a side of dumplings made from island-grown arrowroot.

My hunger temporarily satiated, I got into my Jeep and made my way to Rawlins Hill, a small parish south of Garrison and the Sporting Place. I turned down Egg Road to number sixteen, a single-story house with a driveway and carport, both unusual for St. Pierre. I pulled into the driveway and slowly made my way to the front door.

I hadn't made an appointment, nor had I checked to see if

Ms. Sparks would be home. The trip could be a complete waste of time if no one was home. I searched for a doorbell but didn't see one. I was about to knock when the door opened.

"Yes, sir," a woman said as she stayed behind the flimsy glass door.

"Jannilea Sparks?"

"This is me," the woman said.

She was older than Lorissa Blue, the other caregiver, and she moved slowly as she let me inside. I explained to her that I was just following up on some questions regarding what happened on the morning of Lord Ram's death.

"I speak to the officer when they come to talk to me after I find him dead," Jannilea Sparks said. "I don't know what I tell you different than what I tell them?"

"His widow asked me to just check on a few things to make sure it was all official. That Lord Ram's death was definitively an accident."

"Sassy?" Ms. Sparks grinned and shook her head. "She worry about her reputation. She really believe island gossip hurt her career?"

"Well, I don't know if it's that, Ms. Sparks. Maybe it has something to do with his estate. I just don't know." I made that up, not wanting to steer the woman in any particular direction. I just wanted her account of what happened.

"No, I know that woman. She can be mean to that poor old man. I see it sometime, how she talk to him. He cannot even fight back to her wicked tongue. Everyone know it. That is why people here talk and spread the nonsense that the woman kill her own husband."

"Can you please tell me what you told the other officers? What happened when you came to work that morning?

She sighed. "You the man who own the bar on Windy Hill?"

"Yeah, the Sporting Place."

"Then why she have you asking these questions? You not police."

"No, I'm not. I'm just double-checking, making sure nothing out of the ordinary happened."

"Nothing did! I come in that morning. The man on the ground in the kitchen. I know he dead when I see him. He had a gash in his forehead...from the fall. I call out to Ms. Blue who was upstairs. She come and see the dead body and then we call for an ambulance and they notify the police."

I could have wrapped it up right there. Case closed. But for some reason I felt I should put in a little more effort. I owed McWilliams at least that. He knew what I did out on that boat and he gave me the time I needed to take care of it. So I pressed Ms. Sparks a bit. "And Ms. Blue was upstairs when you arrived?"

"Yes she was."

"Did she have any problems with Lord Ram or Queen Sassy?"

"Not that I'm aware of, sir. Sassy can be a diva, if you know what I mean."

"I do, but was that a problem?"

"Not for me and I don't think for Ms. Blue either. At least she never really complained about it. I work for the man for many years. Ms. Blue come on after Ms. Moseley retire. Just a year ago, I think. For me, it was an honor to work for the great man. We all grow up listening to his music and so proud that he from our little island."

"I would think so," I said, "but Ms. Blue told me she like the other Calypso guy better...Delight."

"Yes I know, King Delight. Ms. Blue not a Petey...well I guess she is now. Her husband was. I believe she was born in Dominica and then go to New York and meet her husband. Her daughters move with her here over twenty years ago. After her husband pass, poor man. Then she marry Marlow Blue, but he also pass. And the older girl, she also pass and so young. It's the poison that kill her. Some people have so much tragedy in their life."

At first I was barely paying attention to what Ms. Sparks was saying. I didn't know why, but I was making small talk which led to this island drama—gossip I didn't need to know about. But then Ms. Sparks mentioned New York, a dead husband, and that one of Ms. Blue's daughters died, and my interest in all this suddenly was sparked. I wanted to know more.

"Poison?"

"Drugs," Ms. Sparks said. "She struggle for a long time with that and finally it kill her. Ms. Blue strong in the church and try to teach them the ways of faith, prayer, and God. But some things even God cannot control. And she try with that boy too."

I was getting confused. When I talked to Ms. Blue her family never came up. I just stuck to the investigation of Lord Ram. Now I was getting the history of her extended family—who passed, who didn't. "What boy?"

"The stepson. Before he move to New York the father have this child with another, Cecily John. But that woman die a long time ago, when the child was very young. When he go to New York he start another family and the boy live with Ms. Blue's family and the younger girls here, but he vex them so. He go the wrong way," she said.

"You mean the boy? He had a drug problem too?"

"No, not drugs. Without a real father, that boy, he become bad, and I know Ms. Blue worry about him very much. Poor woman work hard all day and come home to a daughter who sick with drugs and a boy who get into mischief and crime."

"What's his name?"

She looked at me for a moment. Something came over her and her face tightened. "You do not need to know more about poor Ms. Blue's family. That's not why you are here. I think I am talking too much."

Why she stopped so suddenly had me wondering. Now I needed to know more. "When I spoke to her, she never mentioned a stepson," I said.

She shook her head and rose from where she was sitting. "Then, sir, you should ask her about that. That her business, not mine," she said. She started walking to the front door as I remained seated. She opened the door for me.

I got up and made my way to the door. I got the message. We were done here. But after what she just revealed, I wasn't done, and I was not happy about that.

# 33

"Leonard? I tell you not to do much today," was the recorded message from Betta on my phone. She had called while I was at Ms. Blue's house. That is where I went right after my talk with Jannilea Sparks. I needed to ask her a few follow-up questions. I listened to the voice message again. Betta's voice was terse. Hearing it, I vaguely remembered that in-and-out-of-sleep conversation we had in bed. It wasn't really a conversation—she did the talking, what little there was of it. I was barely listening. It was about baking bread. She was telling me something important to her and I just wanted to go back to sleep. I didn't want to listen. I had to remember to follow up with that. To ask her what she meant—or what she was asking me. She was right—I should have been home in bed. I hadn't planned for this to be a long day. Things were just happening. I would call her back later. We would talk about everything. At least that's what I told myself.

I was now in my Jeep, on that dead-end road in Lavantville, parked outside that last house on the right—the one Tubby and I visited less than a week ago. There were lights on in the house. He was home.

The few follow-up questions I'd planned for Ms. Blue evolved into almost an hour and a half with her. At first she was wary to let me in, as if she knew why I had returned. But when I told her I just spoke with Ms. Sparks, she opened the door for me. There was more fresh sorrel, and I didn't refuse. I was thirsty. And I was getting hungry again even after that lunch of blaff. She sensed that and offered me spice cake. More sugar was not what I wanted, but I did not refuse.

"You didn't tell me you had a stepson," I said to her.

"What does it matter about him? He not part of my life anymore, sir," she said. "I want nothing to do with him. He my late husband's son with another. He not my blood."

"When the police talked to you, did they ask about him?"

"No, and why should they, sir? Lord Ram fall, hit his head and die. They know this. You are wasting your time now."

I probably was. I wasted too much time in my life, but that's something I didn't want to think about. I took a bite of that spice cake. "You are an excellent cook, Ms. Blue," I said. "This is delicious." I washed down the dry cake with the sugary sorrel. I wouldn't have minded a nice shot of Karime rum to temper the sugar in that drink and maybe to clear my head. Something to help me make sense of everything I was slowly putting together.

"Thank you," she said. My compliment seemed to soften her.

"I'm sorry to come here and ask these questions again," I said. "I know you've not had it easy. Ms. Sparks told me what happened to your daughter. And that you lost your husband, their father, and Mr. Moseley as well. That's tough."

She started to wipe at her eyes now. "You have no idea. I see so much. So many die," she said. "My husband was a good man. Both my husbands were. But if my first were still here none of this would have happened. I am sure of that. If he returned to his home, everything would have been so much different."

"Returned from where?"

She lifted her head up to look at me. And then she told me

about him. And her daughters. And then she told me about her stepson.

I could hear music thumping from inside the house. Soca? Dancehall? Reggaetón? I had no idea, only that it was loud—the heavy bass vibrating all the way to my Jeep. I wasn't sure if I preferred it to the twangy old country I heard the last time, or not. Whatever, his taste in music was definitely eclectic.

I got out of the Jeep and headed to the front door. As I made my way to his door, the distinctive aroma of weed wafted from his house triggering my overactive sense of smell. In St. Pierre, cannabis was still illegal but rarely prosecuted unless the quantities were enormous and it was smuggled from other countries. I had noticed the few times I would get a whiff on the street that island weed had a distinct smell. Not that I was an expert—I very rarely smoked, preferring the more dangerous high that came from overindulging in alcohol. But the scent of New York cannabis, I recalled, was sharper than what I sniffed occasionally on St. Pierre. Maybe it had to do with the rich volcanic soil that gave it a fragrant, almost flavored aroma. I got to the door. The screen door that I had destroyed was still there, dangling from the hinges, reminding me I needed to get him a replacement. The heavy wooden door was shut. I knocked. Because the music was loud, I didn't just knock. I banged. The music stopped and the door opened. He stood there in shorts and a white tank top, his familiar attire.

"Hello John Saint John," I said, peering at him through the door. He just stood there looking at me when I said that.

"So you know my name," he said, still not inviting me in.

"I guess I do, but, well what is it? Tubby said it was John John. But then I found out it was really John Saint John Jr. Which is it?"

He shrugged. "Nobody be a saint."

I wasn't sure about that but it didn't really matter what he chose to call himself. John John. John Saint John Jr., Johnny Too Bad. He was Ms. Blue's stepson. And he was the man who saved my life less than a week earlier. "Can we talk?"

He opened the door to let me in. When we got inside he offered me what he was smoking. I was going to refuse but then thought, why not. He laughed when I coughed after sucking the smoke into my lungs. He got up and went to his refrigerator and got me a cold Carib, knowing that was preferable to what I just inhaled. After I cleared my lungs, I noticed, within the whiffs I had of weed, there was a fragrant scent of perfume I detected somewhere else. I couldn't place it, but I knew it was something I smelled before. I didn't know and it didn't matter. That wasn't why I was there.

"I never thanked you for what you did out there," I said. "You came back when you didn't have to. Why did you do that?"

He laughed after taking a long puff. "You pay me more than they," he said. "Simple as that."

I sipped from the bottle of beer. "Simple as that? I don't think so, John. You could have just taken off. Something made you come back. I'm curious about what that was."

"You curious?" He laughed again. "A man have some pride, you know. Those men, I don't like how they talk to me. I don't like how they look at me."

"You kill a person because of how they talk to you or look at you?"

"I think you should be happy that I did," he said.

"Happy is not the right word. Grateful, yeah, I am. How did that make you feel? Killing that man?"

He studied me. His blunt was done and he put it down. "How it make you feel, man?" he asked me, knowing what I did to Penko.

"Like shit," I said.

"Even after what they do to your friend? How they treat him? Hurt him? And to the woman?"

"Yeah, even after that. I try to think of the hurt they did to him and Betta to help me deal with what I did. It doesn't help. I still feel like shit. Don't get me wrong, I'm glad he's dead. He deserved that and maybe more. I just wish it wasn't me who did it."

"See, it no bother to me at all," John said. "I see that man about to come at you and kill you, I have no regrets shooting him dead. I lose no sleep. I like you more than I like that man. Like I said, simple as that."

"I guess I'm lucky you did then." I gulped down the dregs of the beer. John got up to get me another and one for himself. I was trying to think of the best way to steer the conversation to why I was really there, but I couldn't. So I just came out and said: "You never told me your father died on 9/11—in the towers."

What I said surprised him. He was not expecting it. He looked down for a moment. "You come here with Levett and ask me to help you and take you to that boat and get that woman. You don't come here to make friends. You don't come see me at my house to find out about my father or anything else about me. So why should I just tell you that he die when the towers fall?"

He was absolutely right. We were not friends. His personal life was not why I came to see him. I used him—paid him—to help me. "I just came from speaking with your stepmother," I said.

He didn't look happy at that. He made one of those hissing sounds, harsher than the kind Tubby would make when I teased him about something. "Why, man, you go speak to her? Why you get into my business? You own that bar up on Windy Hill. What all this about you go snooping around?"

"It's about Lord Ram, John," I said, now realizing I should just get to it. "Any reason you would do him harm?"

His silence after I asked him was telling. He was trying to compose himself—trying to decide what he should say next.

"Why would I hit him on the head when I could just shoot him dead?"

"Did I say anything about hitting him on the head?" I looked at him. He drank from the beer bottle. He knew I caught him. It didn't matter; I didn't want to lose the flow of where I was going. "Is that what you wanted to do? Shoot him dead?"

Again, he didn't answer. He got up, put some cannabis in a pipe, lighted it, leaned back and inhaled deeply. After exhaling, his voice going an octave higher from either weed or emotion, he said, "You know that man, the great Lord Ram, not so great a man. Some people know. Some refuse to believe."

"What's that supposed to mean, John?"

He thought for a moment. And then he got up to turn off the music. "So you talk to she. Why you need to talk to me?" He shook his head and laughed a little. "What she tell you happen to him?"

"She told me she was upstairs when he must have fallen. That Ms. Sparks found him dead and then she came down and saw him lying there."

John shook his head. "No, man, what did she tell you about that man? What did she tell you about her daughter, my stepsister, who die from addiction? What did she tell you about my father who die in the towers?"

"Nothing," I said to him. "Why?" I gripped the bottle of Carib. It was still cold and about half full. I lifted it to my lips and took a gulp.

"You know they have a parade every Labor Day in Brooklyn," John said. "West Indian parade. You from New York. Do you know this parade?"

I was from the Bronx, but with my bars all being in Brooklyn, I did know about the Labor Day parade. It was on Eastern Parkway in Crown Heights. I would see pictures in the *Daily News* or *Post* the day after—usually featuring a politician, the mayor or governor, making nice with the West Indian community, surrounded by men and women in colorful costumes. But along with those pictures was the reporting of sporadic gun violence linked to a long day of alcohol consumption. As a result, I remembered politicians shortening the hours of the parade, hoping that would curtail some of the drinking and ensuing violence. I didn't stick around New York long enough to know if that policy worked or not. St. Pierre had a carnival each December before Christmas and the same kind of costumes were worn—the women displaying what they never did the rest of the year, dancing all day and into the night on Front Street in Garrison. But the St. Pierre Carnival was probably no more than a block or two compared to what went on in Brooklyn on Labor Day. "Yeah, I know it," I said, wondering why he was bringing up the parade.

"Lord Ram the special guest in 2001," John said. "He sing and wave to all he people from a truck. You know it's not only Peteys who love he music."

"What does any of this have to do with what happened to him a couple of weeks ago?"

He was slowly inhaling from his pipe, gathering his thoughts. "My father die two weeks later in the tower," he said. "He work there maintenance."

"I'm sorry about that, John," I said. "I had a few friends, cops and firefighters from my neighborhood, who also died that day." I still wasn't sure what he was trying to tell me.

"Yeah, cops and firefighters go in to try to save people they didn't know."

"No, they didn't know," I said. "They were just doing their jobs."

"Were you just doing your job?"

"What are you talking about?"

"When you went down in that tunnel that day. Were you just doing your job?" He asked again.

I tried to pretend that I didn't know what he was talking about—that he was still on what happened on 9/11. "I wasn't there, John. I was in the Bronx that morning, nowhere near the

Towers."

He snickered. "You know what I am talking about, man. You know I don't mean the Towers. You know I talk about the time you go into the subway to save people."

I took a deep breath. I didn't want to talk about my past. "It's late here. I'm just getting over the flu or something. Can you just tell me, yes or no, if you did something to Lord Ram? I'm tired."

"You think I did something to that man? That Johnny Too Bad must be the one," he said with disdain in his voice.

Was he right? Just because Ms. Blue told me Johnny Too Bad was her stepson, I immediately suspected him of something I really knew nothing about. I hoped that wasn't true. "No, I don't think that, John. As a matter of fact, I don't think Johnny too bad at all." I would never forget how he came back on that skiff when he could have just gone home.

He put the pipe down. "My stepsister on that truck with Lord Ram," he said. "She was fourteen and because she dance so well at her school, she chosen to ride the truck with others."

"Which stepsister?"

"Miriam," he said.

Miriam, Ms. Blue told me, was the one with the drug problem. The one who died. The other sister, Jasinda, was living in Atlanta with her husband.

"Lord Ram think he something." John said. "A man like that famous. He believe he can do anything and no one will say a thing. And he do it many times. I know this. People know this, but they stay silent because he such a great man to many. And my father knew. He knew what he do to Miriam that day. Miriam tell me everything. Everything she can never tell her mother. So she tell me. My father knew. He tell her he was to take care of it. He was to avenge what the man do to his daughter. She even know he get a gun. She know he want to kill Lord Ram for what he do to her, but he die in the tower before he can do it. Miriam come here, but she never forget that Labor

Day and then what happened to our father. She get on with the drugs. Always sick with drugs. When she die, I say I take care of him for what he do to so many. But then I go away—to Fort Philippe."

"So you went there to do what your father and stepsister and, as you say, others never could or would do. You killed him?"

"Man, don't you understand anything? You not a young man. You supposed to be wise and smart. I just tell you what happen to my father when he try to avenge what the man did to his daughter. He die."

"I'm no one to judge, John. I just want to know."

"I think if I go there to kill a man who really already dead, how is that justice? His mind gone. He would not even know who I am and why I kill him. He would not remember what he did to my stepsister. What he did to others like her. He would not know anything. Is that revenge?"

I didn't answer and he didn't expect me to.

"And your stepmother never knew all this?" I asked.

"No, she never know. I tell you already, Miriam never tell her. My father never tell her."

That eliminated any real motive Ms. Blue would have and also explained why she would work for the man who raped her daughter. "What did you do, John?"

I waited for an answer. He rubbed his hands over his face. Johnny Too Bad's eyes were wet. He just shrugged but said nothing. Was that his confession?

"Did anyone see you go to or leave from there?" I was hoping no one did. I was already trying to figure how I would keep this from McWilliams. This man saved my life. Would I turn him in for the murder of a man who raped his stepsister?

I got up from where I had been sitting. My head was spinning, and my legs were wobbly from the beers, lack of sleep, the weed, or from what he just told me. Or it could have been something else. That fragrant scent. That perfume. With the weed gone, it was now the dominant scent in the house. I remember it made me dizzy once before. But it wasn't here where I smelled that perfume. And that was when I remembered where. I needed to get out of there now, I needed to get home and into bed. I didn't need to hear anything else from him.

When I left he was still sobbing.

# 34

The dogs were hungry. I filled their bowls, standing over them as they scarfed down their kibble, making sure the big ones didn't steal from the Puppy's bowl. Once the Puppy was done, I moved away and noticed the dirty dishes in the sink and the pot with the remnants of the cow foot soup. Betta's fragrance still lingered in my kitchen. She wore a distinct perfume, or maybe it was some sort of lotion, something subtle but enough to know it was hers and much different from the stronger scent I detected in John's house. She had left me numerous texts and messages while I had been out. When I left John's I finally texted her back and told her I was fine and heading home. She didn't respond and I wasn't sure if that meant she was angry with me for not getting back to her sooner. The lack of emotion and nuance in a text always puzzled me. And that went for both sides of the conversation. It was as if miscommunication was built into that form of discourse. I can tell if someone is pissed at me when I'm talking to them, but not always by what I read.

I passed out almost immediately and slept through the night. As soon as I woke up, I checked my phone to see if Betta responded to my last text. There was nothing and I wasn't sure what to make of that. She had only been with me for a couple of days, helping out while I was sick. I had to remember who I was to her and not make too much out of it.

And then my thoughts went to my visits to John and Ms. Blue. There were still loose ends, things I wondered about. What John told me—his not-so-confessional confession—bothered me. If he actually did hurt Ram, he had his reasons, but I sensed his tears were for something else. Maybe, I thought, for what he didn't do.

Despite all the doubts and loose ends, I had to go now to see McWilliams. I just wasn't sure what I would tell him.

I drove down to Fort Philippe and entered the police headquarters.

"Is the great man in?" I asked Emmalin Sealy, the police headquarters' receptionist. Despite its grand stone and mortar exterior, inside the police department offices had a distinct 1970s look. There was lots of gray and steel with bad fluorescent lighting.

"We haven't seen you here in too long, Mr. Len," Emmalin said.

"I know, Emmalin, you really missed me, didn't you?" She was married, a grandmother, but that didn't stop her or me from our innocent flirting the few times I would come to see McWilliams.

"Oh yes I did," she said with a grin. "Your visits always have my little heart skipping a beat." She pointed toward the back, which meant he was in and I could go back to see him.

His office was small and ugly, with a gray metal filing cabinet and a matching desk topped with an old desktop computer, harsh bright lighting, and one hard silver metal chair that was so sturdy it could survive a nuclear attack. McWilliams was staring at a computer screen when I walked in and pointed to that chair. I sat. He turned away from the computer. "So? You come here to tell me something?"

"Something? Really not much, McWilliams. I come here to

tell you that your original theory was correct. Lord Ram, as far as I could tell, died from a fall. Well, at least I am pretty sure he did not die from anyone hitting him with anything." I wasn't going to tell him about my chat with John and how he practically confessed to doing something—and then really didn't, leaving me nowhere on this.

He just looked at me. He had a pen in his hand that he was tapping against the desk. "Is that so?"

"It's as deep as I can go, McWilliams. I interviewed the two caregivers and even talked to Queen Sassy. There's no one else to talk to."

"You are an honorable man, Buonfiglio," McWilliams said. "But that you did not tell me you would go see a known criminal like John makes me wonder if I should trust you anymore in our dealings."

More angry than surprised when he sprung that on me, I got up out of that chair ready to leave. "You could have done your own damn investigation."

"Easy now, Buonfiglio. Sit. He is not a suspect. He was never in that house that morning; that has been confirmed. Is there a reason you didn't tell me about talking to John?"

I slowly sat down again. "Because he assisted me in another matter," I said.

McWilliams pushed his glasses up his nose. "How did he assist you?"

"You don't need to know any of the details."

He thought about that for a minute and nodded. "I know that boy's father—Saint John," McWilliams said. "He grow up near me here before he leave the country for New York. A terrible thing. The country mourn for him when it happen. He the only one from St. Pierre to perish in New York on that sad day. Why that boy not use his proper name, I do not understand."

"Sainthood is a heavy burden, I guess," I said, repeating John's assertion for dropping the Saint in his name. "And you also know Saint John had two daughters?"

"Yes. They move here soon after with their mother."

"Ms. Blue?"

He nodded.

"And Lord Ram? You knew? You knew about the things he has done?"

He looked at me and then slowly nodded.

I tried to digest everything. He knew, yet he did nothing? I think I understood why he'd brought me into this. Better me, an outsider, than him to expose the man. "Why did you ask for my help? What purpose did it serve if you already knew everything?"

"But I don't know everything, Buonfiglio. I only know what you already know. I was hoping for something else, but it doesn't matter now. I've decided to leave it be. It's best that way. The man will be buried in two days. There will be a big funeral. The prime minister will be in attendance as will all the members of St. Pierre's government. Banks and schools will be closed. He will be interred as if he were royalty. Whatever else you might learn, I suggest you keep it to yourself. There are people here who also know about Lord Ram. Some have covered up his actions. Others have been directly involved in them. Yet because of who he was, nothing was said. Nothing was done. And that is what you should do too, sir."

"Ah yes, Just go on." I shook my head. I knew the coverup of the doings of an influential person was nothing new. "He's dead. What good does it do to accuse the dead when they can't defend themselves? And in the end, the people will believe what they want to believe about him. Right?"

"Exactly, Buonfiglio."

"So we're okay now, McWilliams? Our business is done? I can go back to what I do best, mix rum punches and open up beer bottles?"

"Yes indeed, Mr. Len." He smiled and his use of the familiar island greeting indicated that he was happy with the results of our arrangement. But I wasn't convinced. He knew something and didn't want me to know about it. I knew in my gut that there was one piece missing. McWilliams knew, but he didn't seem to care. And why should I? I didn't know, but it nagged at me. John never really confessed to doing something to Ram, but he didn't deny it either. He was covering for someone, I thought. The obvious person would be his stepmother, but that didn't make any sense. She never really knew what Ram did to her daughter. No, there was someone else. Or maybe there was no one at all. My gut told me it was the former, not the latter. And maybe those gut feelings meant that I was better at this new business I was involved with than I thought. I hoped not. I had no appetite for any more of it.

# 35

## The Funeral

We closed the bar the day of Lord Ram's funeral. There was no point in opening, and many might have thought it disrespectful, at least according to Tubby. Prime Minister Fitz-Greene Jacobs had declared it an official day of mourning. As McWilliams had said, banks and schools would be closed, as would most businesses aside from hotels and a few restaurants. A big cruise boat was scheduled to dock in Garrison Harbor but was redirected north to St. Lucia instead. There was a brief protest about that by the local taxi owners, mainly Harold Boothe and his crew, but again, it was quickly silenced when public opinion, through social media, loudly voiced its disgust at Boothe and the others for daring to profit on the celebrated man's Day of Mourning.

"Everyone go but you," Tubby said to me when I told him I wasn't going to the funeral. "That not a good thing. People might hold it against us here. They might boycott the bar because you disrespect Ram."

"We are closed for the day, Tubby. You said to do so because being open would show disrespect to Lord Ram. So I agreed. I don't think my not attending the funeral will draw any attention."

I went on to explain that funerals and wakes were not one of my favorite activities. I had been to a few on the island for people I knew or for the loved ones of people I knew. They were long affairs, and I was respectful and did what I had to do, but I was never comfortable being there. What I wasn't going to admit to Tubby was that there was no way I could go to the funeral knowing what I knew about Ram. Despite his acclaim as a Calypsonian, I couldn't disguise my disgust with him as a person.

"Just keep making those rum punches strong, Tubby, and they will return. I'm not worried."

"You joke about it, but I know these people. You will see," he said.

"It's not the same for me. I'm not a Petey."

"You're not?"

The way he asked that made me pause. Was I now finally a Petey? I didn't answer. I just shrugged. I wasn't going.


But in a way I did go. I had promised Betta that I would take her, her mother, and Paolo to the funeral and drop them off there. She also questioned why I wasn't going, but unlike Tubby, didn't press me on it.

They were ready when I pulled up to her mother's house. Paolo was wearing a navy-blue sport jacket, dress pants and shoes. He was a handsome kid. I had never seen him like that. And I had never seen his mother as she appeared that morning, wearing a simple, fitted black dress, her long elaborate braids gathered up on her head, exposing her neck and highlighting the silver hoop earrings and the colorful coral and blue ceramic necklace she wore. I got out of the Jeep to help Mrs. Baptiste up into the front seat while Betta and Paolo slid into the back.

"Thank you, Mr. Len, for driving us," Mrs. Baptiste said to me. "But I do think you should stay for the service."

I peered into the rear-view mirror. Betta was looking at me, waiting for my response. That look almost changed my mind. Almost.

"Yeah, I know, and it doesn't mean I'm not feeling it for all of you here. I know how special the man was to St. Pierre." I couldn't believe what just flowed from my mouth. I looked again into the rearview mirror to see Betta's reaction, to see if she knew I didn't mean what I said. The look this time was different—closer to a cold stare. And then she looked away from me and whispered something to Paolo.

"Yes he was," Mrs. Baptiste said. "He will be dearly missed."

I said nothing. I had to keep my mouth shut.

The funeral was held at the St. Pierre Cricket Stadium in Garrison. Traffic was stalled when we got closer to the stadium, and there was a stream of pedestrians making their way by foot. Cars were lined up on the side of the road adjacent to the stadium.

"We can walk from here, Leonard," Betta said to me, leaning forward from her seat in the back. I could feel her breath on my neck. And I could smell that scent that was almost part of her skin.

Since we were not moving, I got out and opened the door for Mrs. Baptiste. I took her hand as she stepped down onto the curb. I looked at Betta. She looked back at me. "Text me when it's almost over," I said to her. "I'll come get you."

"I will unless we can find a ride with someone else."

"I can get here. Just text me."

She didn't respond, and she took her son's hand as she and her mother made their way toward the stadium with all the others. I got back into the Jeep and waited about ten minutes until traffic finally cleared. A big black SUV pulled in front of me and stopped. I was going to beep but I restrained my New York impatience. I waited and watched as a driver got out and opened the back door to the SUV. My windows were down as usual and when the SUV's door opened, a strong floral smell wafted from it into my Jeep. I remembered it from my visit to Sassy's—how it made me dizzy. I recalled smelling the same thing at John's house after the cannabis cleared. I didn't think John was one to apply floral perfume to his body. It made me wonder if that nose of mine was making a connection.

I watched as Queen Sassy, dressed in black, stepped out. She was alone. Her daughter, the teenage girl who came to see me what seemed like centuries ago carrying cassava pone, was not with her. She was not at her father's funeral. I should have been surprised at that, but I wasn't. And now I had somewhere else to go.

I was back at the stadium just as the funeral ended. There was already a procession forming to head to Garrison Cemetery, the island's largest, situated on a rocky bluff overlooking the city. I could see the hearse carrying Lord Ram's body and behind it the black SUV with Queen Sassy inside. I had to talk to her, but it really wasn't the time or place. I could wait a few hours for that.

I went back to the stadium looking for Betta, Paolo and Mrs. Baptiste. I couldn't find them, and Betta hadn't texted. They must have gotten a ride from someone else and that didn't make me happy. I had to get over that.

I heard a car honk behind me. I looked in my rearview mirror. It was Tubby and his wife, Lysah, in his Camry. I waved but there was nowhere to pull over and get out and say hello to them. Through the mirror, I noticed a rare thing: Tubby had a jacket and tie on. I guess he felt the funeral of Lord Ram was a special enough occasion. Either that or Lysah pressured him to the point he had no choice. In my mind, it was probably the latter.

Both of us were at the roundabout, but I took the southern extension up to Windy Hill and the bar while Tubby continued to his home. I opened up the bar and texted him. *Take that*

*choke collar off and meet me up here at the Place.*
After a few minutes he texted back. *I come soon.*

I'd been in the bar many times by myself opening and closing it, but for some reason, in the middle of a hot, sunny afternoon, the fact that it was empty felt strange to me. And lonely, too. I poured myself a glass of water and walked out to the deck to take in the view that never got old. The Caribbean was shimmering as if there were little fairy lights scattered over the water. There were a number of smaller boats and some bigger ones in Garrison Harbor. The cruise port was vacant; the Prime Minister's edict honored. The copper-colored roofs of the older nineteenth-century structures, homes and offices around the harbor contrasted with the deep blue of the nearby sea. I could see Fort Philippe towering over the city and beyond, and the dormant volcano that was Mt. Hadali. Who could ever complain about what I had here, yet I felt something missing. My phone was in my hand, almost an extension, an added appendage. I looked at the screen. The screensaver was a photo I took when I was back in New York for Kasie's high school graduation in the spring. It was a picture of her in her blue-and-gold gown, hugging her younger brother, Luke. I scanned my emails, and then my voicemails and texts. There were no messages from either of them. Or from anyone. I kept staring at the phone and found myself pushing the contact number for my ex-wife. I held the phone to my ear.

"Len?" she answered, her voice sounding harried.

"Hi? You good?" I asked, not really knowing why I called her. An impulse, maybe?

"Good? Yeah, we are good. Why?"

"You sound...I don't know."

"I'm packing."

"Packing? Where you going?"

"We're all going to the beach. Richard rented a place in Amagansett," she said. "Two weeks before Kasie heads off to Penn."

I thought about that. The family vacation. "Nice. Fancy."

"Whatever," she said, knowing I was poking at her a bit, and the new and financially improved life she was now living.

"You know, you guys can always come down here. Beaches are spectacular. I can set you up with a suite at the Bougainvillea. Kasie will tell you about the snorkeling."

"Kasie's got a college schedule now. And Luke is gonna be busy this school year."

"Well, you and Richard then. If you ever want to get away."

There was silence on the line and then: "Yeah, that's not gonna happen, Len."

"Alright, well..." I knew that last offer was a long shot. I was just trying to think of something else to say to her. I wasn't really sure why I called, but I didn't want to end the call yet.

"Are you okay?" she asked. "You sound off."

"Yeah, I'm fine. I was sick, got a virus or something, but I'm better now."

"You got a virus? *The* virus?"

"I don't know. But whatever, it's gone."

"You aren't getting involved in that other stuff again, are you?"

"What other stuff? I don't know what you're talking about."

"Yeah, sure. Playing John Wick."

"Never," I said. I could hear Tubby's car pull into the parking lot. "Listen, I want Luke at least to come visit. You think he can make it down this year? He's old enough to travel on his own."

"I just told you, Len. Junior year is crazy. He's got lacrosse, SATs, and college visits coming up. This is an important year for him."

She had to remind me of what I was missing in my son's life? But what I was really hearing were excuses—nice ways to say no. "Can you send me his schedule for school and sports? We can see what we can do. He'd love it here."

"I have to finish this packing. Can we talk about this later?"

"Okay, Kathleen. Let's talk soon." I pressed the end button on my phone just as Tubby was entering. I stared at my ex's name as it remained on my screen.

"I tell you keep the bar closed," Tubby said as he came out to join me on the deck. The jacket and tie were gone. He was wearing a T-shirt and baggy shorts.

"It is closed," I said, as I put the phone into my pocket.

"Door is open. Someone think we open for business."

"What someone? No one is around. Everyone is still mourning the death of the great man," I said with derision and Tubby noticed.

"Respect, Mr. Len. I accept that sarcastic tone you sometimes have, but others might take it differently."

"Should I worry about that?"

"I leave my wife and children to come here. Was there a reason you wanted me to come?"

There wasn't. I just wanted his company. "Are you telling me you needed a reason to vacate that crowded home for a few hours?"

He laughed. "Good thing you text. I tell Lysah you need me here and she okay with that."

The sun was hot on the deck so I headed back inside the shaded bar. I walked behind it and picked up the bottle of vermouth we had opened when this whole thing started and that I kept from the others. I looked at the label created by Mimmo. The one I kept had the illustration of the man on the beach playing the guitar. There was a crowd of children around him. He was smiling. The children were smiling. Maybe he was playing them a calypso, I thought. I looked at the cursive script on the label: *Bellezza Nera*. He named the vermouth after the wife he left behind. It reminded me that I never really asked or followed up with Betta about what she said to me that night— about baking bread. It made sense to me now. Despite her quiet manner, I knew she was ambitious. I knew the small room on Front Street was something she never would go back to. She would do anything to prevent that. Maybe she wanted something now in her life to call her own. Did she mean it when she said she wanted me to help her? That was what was fuzzy. I wasn't sure what she meant.

"Are you going to stare at it or drink from it?" Tubby asked.

"Want me to make you a drink with it?"

"Keep that nasty stuff away from me."

"No, Tubby, that was the Campari. This is sweet. Maybe you should give it another try. Work it into one of your rum punch creations."

"No, Mr. Len. That will never happen."

I laughed and went ahead and made myself a Negroni. I needed some of that bitter Campari on this afternoon and in preparation for what I had to do later.

"How was the funeral?" I asked.

"Nonsense mostly," Tubby said. "Jacobs speak and tell a story about how he meet Ram when he was a boy and idolize the man until the day he die."

"What about Sassy? Did she talk or sing?"

"Sassy just up there with the family, some of his other children and grandchildren from other wives he have. She say nothing."

"So no one else spoke?"

"Preacher man preach. He tell us Lord Ram a gift from God to this island. That he make us all proud."

"You believe that?"

Tubby opened a Carib and took a sip. He just looked at me but did not answer. I wondered what he knew about Lord Ram. I wondered if everyone knew about him.

"Anything else I miss?"

"They get St. Patrick Parish secondary school steel drum band to perform Ram's songs, and one of the children sing a hymn, but there was no other entertainment."

I added gin and Campari to the vermouth, shook up the Negroni and poured it into a rocks glass, adding a slice of orange. Tubby watched in horror as I sipped it and made a satisfied face.

"What makes a man drink such a sour thing?"

"As you said, Tubby, because I'm a sour man."

"No, Mr. Len. I said you a bitter man. But maybe you sour, too."


We went out to the deck to watch the sunset. On any other night, there would be no room out there for us. The deck would be packed with tourists and even locals. The sunset was so famous it was featured in travel guidebooks, labeled a must-see when visiting St. Pierre. But on this day of mourning, Tubby and I got to witness the sun sinking into the watery horizon all by ourselves.

Once the sun disappears, darkness comes quick. And I'm talking real dark. And with the darkness comes the sounds of night creatures, tree frogs, birds, and who knows what else chirping and singing out there. I hadn't turned the lights on inside and had to feel my way to the wall switch and flick them on. Tubby was right behind me.

I rinsed out the glass I used for the Negroni. "You want to open tomorrow or should I?"

"You go now?" Tubby asked, not answering my question.

"Yeah, I need to see someone."

I could have said I just wanted to go home and get some rest but now I teased Tubby into wondering who I was going to see. I don't know if I did it intentionally or not. But it came out of my mouth without a thought as to what the consequences might be.

"Tonight? Who you going to see?"

"Are you getting jealous? You worried I'm cheating on you, wifey?"

That deflection got a loud hiss. "I open tomorrow. You sleep in. You getting old now. Hubby need all the rest he can get."

I left with a smile on my face and that was a good thing because I wasn't sure I'd have one after what I was about to do. The Lord Ram business was officially over. But I had put some time into this. I wanted an answer I had not yet gotten.

Devin Cooley was sitting in the dark in a golf cart near the entrance to the gated community of St. Francois. I could see the glow from his cell phone as he stared into it. I pulled the Jeep up next to the cart.

"Devin, don't tell me you're watching that cricket match in Pakistan?" I asked. Whenever Devin came to the bar, he insisted I find cricket somewhere for him to watch on one of the multiple televisions I had. He was not alone in rooting for the West Indies or Windward Island teams. The only thing I knew about cricket was that Tubby officiated youth games and that his friend Rondo was a mighty fine batsman, which I guess meant he was a good hitter.

"Not Pakistan," Devin said. "Sri Lanka."

"I was close." I said, though I had no idea how close Sri Lanka was to Pakistan. "Has Ms. Alexis returned?" I asked.

He looked away from the phone. "She come back from the funeral and service an hour or two ago. She expect you?"

This is where it was tricky. I wasn't going to lie to Devin. "No, but if you want to check and tell her I'd like to come see her, I'll wait until you get her approval."

He smiled. "Let me just call her up now, Mr. Len."

I watched him take out another phone and press some buttons. I could hear him talking, but not what he was saying. He nodded and put the phone down.

"She say come right over." He smiled and waved me past him.

As I maneuvered the Jeep through St. Pierre's most upscale neighborhood to Sassy's villa on the hill, I tried to put together what I would tell her about what I learned that afternoon after my trip to Lavantville and my most recent chat with John. When he came to the door upon my arrival, wearing what looked like the same white T-shirt and shorts from the night before, I could tell by the look on his face that he knew I knew. And it didn't take any coaxing for him to admit what really happened at Lord Ram's house on the morning he was found dead. "No reason to tell you," he said. "Not your business."

But it was my business and he told me anyway. He knew, like we all did, that it didn't matter. The case was closed. Lord Ram was buried. Nothing was going to change that. But I was here at the villa because I wanted to hear it from Sassy. To hear her confirm what John told me. She brought me in on this and I wanted to know why.

There were many lights on as I made my way up the steps to the front door. She was still in her black dress when she opened it for me. As soon the door opened, my nose took over. That perfume. Queen Sassy's perfume. It was the scent that led me back to John's house.

"Mr. Buonfiglio, you do know that today was my husband's funeral, don't you?"

"My condolences. I'm sorry I wasn't able to attend. I hear it was some event."

"Yes it was. The perfect farewell. For my husband and for me."

"For you?"

"Yes, I'm leaving this island. I just want to move on. There's no point in me being here. I'm not from St. Pierre. I thank you for whatever you've done, but I'm done worrying about gossip and innuendo. I don't care anymore."

She led me inside to the expansive living room.

"I was wondering, Ms. Alexis, why your daughter was not at her father's funeral?"

I followed her into the kitchen. She didn't react to my question at first, except for a slight stiffening of her back. Without turning around she said, "I sent her back to Toronto. She started school and it is more important she not miss her studies than be here."

"I guess that makes sense."

She studied me through the heavy lenses of her glasses. "And you just tell me you weren't at the funeral. How do you know she wasn't there?"

"I drove a friend to the stadium and saw you when I dropped her off. I didn't see your daughter."

She studied me and just nodded at what I said. "It's been a long day, Mr. Buonfiglio, so I hope you understand that I'd like to get some rest now. I know I asked you to help me, and I guess you did in a way. What do I owe you?"

"Your daughter brought me that pone and that was good enough. I'm not here for money."

"Yes, but you shouldn't undervalue yourself. Taking food from the ladies here will only get you so far. I believe you are probably good at what you do."

"I'm a very good bar owner, Ms. Alexis." We were back to addressing each other more formally now.

"You know what I mean," she said.

"No, I really don't know if I'm good at this. I guess it's just that I like to learn the truth. When I think something is just not right, I want to know what I'm missing. And, you know, in this case, I think I found out what was not right."

"What do you mean?"

"I guess I just don't understand why you ended up marrying Lord Ram and then living with him all these years. That must have been very unpleasant for you."

"Is that what you learned, Mr. Buonfiglio? What kind of man my husband really was?"

"I did."

"He helped me when I was younger to make this career. I acknowledge that. Without him, I would not have become Queen Sassy. He was the most powerful Calypsonian then. No one was even close. Not even King Delight, Panther, or the Mighty Sparrow."

"How old were you?" I asked.

"I married him when I was nineteen," she said.

"No, I meant how old were you when it first happened to you?"

I noticed a little quiver of her lip at that. She knew where I was going with this.

"Why does this matter?"

"How old is your daughter?"

"My daughter's age is of no concern to you."

"She's fifteen, isn't she?"

"Yes she is. And if you know, why ask me? Now please, can you leave?"

"I'm bad at math, Ms. Alexis, but I checked Wikipedia and I think I figured it out. You know you have your own page there?"

"Mr. Buonfiglio…"

"You are forty-four now and married Lord Ram when you were nineteen and he was already seventy. Your daughter was born almost ten years later."

"I know when she was born. What's your point?"

"He was almost eighty when your daughter was born. I've heard much about the virility of the men here on St. Pierre. Cow foot soup, bois bande, sea moss, and all those other herbal remedies, right? Or maybe just the plain old blue pill? Or maybe he didn't need anything at all?"

"You are talking gibberish now. You make no sense. Why don't you just tell me what you know. Stop being so vague."

She was right. I was being vague. "Yeah, I think that's probably best. And I am sorry. I just want to lay it all out. I don't know why I do, but I do."

"Then do it, man." She threw up her hands and shook her head. I didn't blame her for getting exasperated. I would have, too.

"I know that Teesha is not Lord Ram's daughter. And I also know that you had enough of the old man and the things he did. To you. To others." Her nostrils flared as I spoke. "Did he try to do it with your daughter? Did he start the same thing with her—even at ninety-five and feeble?"

The rage that she had hidden from others was coming. "Yes."

"Yes what."

"He was inappropriate with her. Even at ninety-five, but that man not so feeble as you think."

"What did he do to her?"

"What do you think? Do I have to spell it out?"

I wanted her to but knew she wouldn't. Because I also knew that he didn't do anything to her. That Sassy used his past— what he did to her, not her daughter—to get to John. To get him to act for her.

"I have to live with it always, Mr. Buonfiglio."

"Live with what?

"Knowing he hurt so many."

"Like Miriam Saint John?"

She took a deep breath. "Yes. She was one."

"Is that how you met her half-brother?"

"You talked to him?"

I just nodded. She realized there was no point in denying it anymore. "I was needy, Mr. Buonfiglio. Back then Ram still had control over me. It was hard to have a real life. He could do whatever he wanted, but he made sure I didn't, even with my own success. He tried to control that too. After that poor girl die from drugs, her half-brother confronted me about what my husband did to her. How that trauma wrecked her life. I knew that trauma but dealt with it differently. He and I, we had a bond—something in common. We both despise the man. So it wasn't about love or anything like that. We did it almost out of retribution. To get back at that man."

Retribution—a fancier word for revenge. It was all part of

the same useless response to a wrong. And I fell for it as easily as anyone would. I fell for it without a moment's hesitation.

"You say retribution, but if Ram never knew? If he assumed Teesha was his biological daughter, how could that have satisfied you and John?"

"Because we both know we cuckold the fool. I know and John know too that when Ram die, Teesha taken care of. He think she his blood, he make sure she get what a daughter should when her father die. And she deserves it. I deserve it to put up with a man like that."

John had told me most of what she was telling me now, but there were still blanks to be filled in and she was doing just that.

"When you went to John to tell him about Teesha. That story you made up."

"No...it was true. The man inappropriate. He try to touch her. She tell me so."

"You told John all that because you knew what kind of man John was. You knew he would not let that slide. He would go after the old man. He would get his revenge."

She was trembling now.

"But he wouldn't do it. He even tried to protect you, you know. He wanted to make it seem he might have done something to the man who raped his half-sister. Until I confronted him with what I knew. And the police already ruled him out as a suspect. But you were hoping I might start other rumors. About John Saint John Jr.. That they would take the attention away from you. He was almost willing to go along with it. He was almost going to do it for you. But now you are leaving and your daughter, his daughter, will be gone."

She took her glasses off and wiped at her eyes. Her head was down.

"He agree. He know that is best for Teesha. For all of us."

"You both decided John wouldn't make a great father?"

She looked up at me, wondering what I would do with all I knew.

"I don't like to be judgmental," I said. "I've made some mistakes in my life. Some big bad ones that I regret and haunt me every day. I'm not one to question another's motivations. So I guess I shouldn't ask why, even after what he did to you when you were so young, you stayed with him. You became part of his life, and then continued with that life even knowing what kind of man he was. You did nothing. Said nothing. Is that right?"

She didn't have to answer me. I looked around at the house with all the modern conveniences. The pool was beautifully lit in the perfectly manicured backyard. I knew why she stayed. She was the Lord's Queen. Together they were the royal calypso couple. If that partnership ended, would she continue to have the success she had? Would she remain as popular as she was as his wife? She couldn't risk it and now with his "natural" death, it didn't matter. She was still the Queen of calypso. I knew why she said nothing.

She was crying now and despite what I was thinking on my way over, I felt for her. I didn't like being lied to—misled—even used. I had been angry, but my anger was gone. Seeing her like this—confronting the choices she made, right or wrong—was taking its toll. And had taken enough of a toll for her to finally act.

Driving to her villa, I had wanted to hear Sassy confess to me that she struck Lord Ram with the Dutch pot—that his death was not an accident—that it was she who killed him. But I realized it didn't matter. I didn't care how he died. I didn't need to know. I had no idea what it was like to be her, and I was ashamed of myself now. It was cruel of me to push. I didn't need any other answers. I didn't need to neatly tie up that last loose end. McWilliams didn't care. St. Pierre had done its grieving. The people had their fete and they had their funeral. Who really cared? Why should it matter to me? Nothing would change.

I had to get out of there. I saw a box of tissues on the kitchen counter. I gave her one. She blew her nose and then put her glasses back on. I walked to the door. As I headed down the stone steps, I could hear her sobbing, alone in her big house in the upscale, gated community of St. Francois. I had also heard John sob. And Ms. Blue too. I didn't like what I was doing or who I was becoming. I hustled to my Jeep to get away from those sounds.

From St. Francois, I could have gotten home quickly via the East Road, but I decided to take the longer way back. I was in no rush to get to my house. I knew the dogs needed to eat. I knew they might actually be worried that I hadn't come home yet. A few minutes later, I found myself parked in front of Betta's house. The lights were off. It was late. She and Paolo were asleep. Would she be upset if I woke her so we could talk? But what would I say? Maybe I could tell her how I felt right now, after coming from Queen Sassy's house. I wanted to confess to someone about what I did. I wanted to tell Betta that I made Queen Sassy cry on the day of her husband's funeral. A long ordeal had ended for her and there I was grilling her about it. I made her bring up things she was trying to forget. Why did I have to do that? Maybe I was getting better at what people seemed to be asking me to do; to dig and find out truths. It's not like I considered myself a dinosaur, but with age usually comes wisdom. I was getting good at some things, not so good with others. I needed to learn to be more delicate. I was too blunt—too quick to rush to judgment. And did I really find out anything? "Sassy, she hurt the Lord bad" was what Livingston Harrod said when he was in my Jeep back when all this started. He knew. Maybe everyone knew except me. Was this all just a test, an initiation concocted by McWilliams? Why would he do that? Why would Sassy bring me in on it as well? I had no answers. My hand was shaking as I gripped the steering wheel. What was happening to me? I wanted to talk to Betta. I wanted to try to explain to her how I was feeling now. I wanted to hear that whisper—her voice I knew would soothe me—calm my frazzled brain. But I didn't want it to be all about me. We could talk about her dreams. About baking bread and making an independent life for herself. I would help her do that. Of course I would. We would talk about everything. All I had to do was turn off the Jeep, get out and knock on her door.

But I just could not.

# 36

## Farewell to Mike

The Sporting Place was at capacity. We hired Tony X to bring his DJ skills to the bar for the night. Music was loud. There was food, courtesy of Elfera's, steam trays overflowing with chicken stew, pepper pot, pelau with goat, callaloo, lambi curry, and oil down with pork feet. It was a happy fete, but sad in a way. We were throwing Mike a farewell party—a sendoff for him and his family before heading to North Carolina. His son was already at his new school, training with the soccer team. Mike and his wife and daughters were to follow and soon settle into a new life in the United States.

It had been six weeks since Lord Ram's funeral. Summer had ended—whatever summer was here on St. Pierre. We didn't get the rain we usually get in the summer and the temperatures, which usually only vary a few degrees, winter or summer, I noticed were hotter than usual. But I guess St. Pierre wasn't the only place where that was happening. But summer and fall also meant less business, though that was changing also. We were getting a more consistent flow of customers, and that was a good thing.

I already had a Carib and was handed a rum punch.

"Who made this batch?" I asked Tubby.

He pointed behind the bar to where Mike's replacement,

John Saint John Jr., stood. I sipped and felt the burn of the rum along with the tartness of lime and the sweet guava and mango juice we used. "I tell him go easy on the lime," Tubby said. "But he say lime make the drink. You believe he say such a thing?"

"Tubby, you could take the mango or guava from the punch. You could even use Cockspur Bajan rum instead of our Karime and the punch would be the same. But if you take away the lime, it just is not a proper rum punch. And let him put his own signature on the drink. This way if both of you are working and I'm not here, the customer can choose which one they want." I talked loudly over the din so he could hear, and even after just an hour of the party, my throat was getting scratchy from raising my voice.

"No, I don't like that idea," Tubby said. "The Sporting Place should have only one signature rum punch. You make another it confuse people."

"All right, Tubby, I'll tell John to go easy on the lime. You just keep schooling him on the art of bartending which, you know, isn't always about making drinks. Get him to show some charm. To make nice with the customers."

"I try, Mr. Len, but sometimes a man got that scrunch-up-face attitude he just can't lose."

"Are you implying something about me, Tubby?" I smiled. "Everyone's charm is different. John will find his. I want him to lose that Johnny Too Bad rep and maybe replace it with a new one, like Johnny Be Good, something like that."

"Johnny Be Good? If you say so." Tubby was not sold on John as Mike's replacement. He had lobbied for his friend, Cortell, but I had a hunch about John. Tubby relented, especially after I had to remind him that John saved his butt after that sorry spear-shooting incident out at sea. And he saved mine, too.

The two were slowly getting along and I had no doubt it would work out, despite the disagreement on the proper way to make a rum punch. I didn't want any disagreements on this day. It was a bittersweet occasion, saying goodbye to Mike. I was happy for him, but we would certainly miss him. And though everyone was having a nice time, my usual dour expression was even more so. And Tubby noticed.

"You're not sick again, are you?"

"No, Tubby, I'm fine. Everything's good."

He hissed, and then went back to help out John behind the bar.

I made the rounds, being the best grumpy-genial host I could be. Many found my cranky ways charming. That was my persona: the cantankerous yet accommodating bar owner. I was the June 1st hero who now owns a bar on a tiny remote Caribbean island. That was the legend. That was the myth. Of course, the painful, bad bits like running out on his family because he couldn't take what he did to them, were left out of the legend.

I noticed McWilliams enter. He was in uniform, but he was smiling, and I saw him go to the bar and watched as John, with a cautious smile, made him a rum punch. On St. Pierre, enjoying a rum punch as the superintendent of police did not mean you were on- or off-duty. It just meant that you were enjoying a rum punch.

I made my way over to him. "Tell me, McWilliams, how does our new bartender's rum punch compare with the classic Tubby Levett punch?" I said it loud enough so Tubby could hear—busting his often-busted balls.

McWilliams smacked his lips after a sip. "Mr. John is very adept," he said. "I like the tang of the lime. It lingers and blends with the strength of the rum. He do a very good job."

"Are you sure there's not too much lime?" I again glanced at Tubby with a smirk.

"Not at all. Not at all. Lime is the bedrock of our island's rum punch, is it not? This one has the perfect balance."

"Oh, it is." I turned and grinned at Tubby, who just shook his head.

"I want to give my best regards to Mr. Clarke. We will miss him on the island, but it is a happy occasion for his family."

"You might have to wait your turn. Mike is a popular man." I pointed to Mike and his wife, Sheila, who were surrounded by friends out near the entrance to the deck.

"He is indeed. I can wait. In the meantime, can I have a word with you?"

"Yeah, sure."

"It's loud here, Buonfiglio. Let's chat outside."

Now I wondered what he needed to tell me that required some privacy. He took his rum punch, and carrying a bottle of Carib, I followed him outside to the small parking lot. We walked over to my Jeep and leaned back against it.

"They find some of them out near Union Island," McWilliams said.

"Some of what?"

McWilliams just looked at me and then I understood. When he said "some of them," I wasn't quite sure what he meant. Did he mean some of the three men? Borka, Migos, or Penko? Or did he mean that they find some of what was left of the three? I had tried to put that night out of my head. I wanted more distance from what happened on that boat and what I did there. Now he was bringing it back to me. "Is that something I need to worry about?"

"No. Not from me or from IMPACs. Since they find it so far from St. Pierre, there no reason to investigate here."

"So why are you telling me this?"

"I just want you to be aware. Maybe they do a DNA or dental remain check on what they find. Maybe they identify those men and whoever they work for, or their family might want to do their own investigation. I doubt it, though. It seems to me that might not be worth the expense, and I hear they close some countries for travel because of some sickness over there. They have other problems to deal with."

"Yeah, I heard that too. Okay, thanks for the heads-up."

Now I had to worry about the Swedish mob coming after me? He was right that it was a long shot, but still, the worry was planted in my mind despite the odds.

I heard the slamming of a car door and saw two people emerging from the dark of Windy Hill Road, heading toward the parking lot. My stomach clenched at what I saw. One of the two was Betta, dressed in a clingy white dress with thin shoulder straps. Her slender form was snug in the dress, her skin contrasting boldly with the bright white of the dress. I had never seen her wear it before. I didn't even know she had a dress like that. But where my mind went first was that the man walking very close to her had bought that dress for her. Her body was almost up against him. He was wearing jeans, a white dress shirt, and a blue sport jacket. She was taller than him by an inch or two. The man smiled at McWilliams as he approached and as he came closer, I estimated that he was probably a good decade older than me. Betta saw me and her eyes flitted around, seemingly trying to avoid mine.

"Ahhh, Mr. Steele. Just what is your connection with Clarke in there?" McWilliams asked the distinguished-looking gentleman. He had light brown skin, short gray hair, and was wearing wire-rim glasses. I noticed he had his arm around Betta's waist, almost possessively.

"His son was in one of our honors programs. The parents did a very good job with that boy."

"Buonfiglio, have you ever met Mr. Arund Steele, the Superintendent of Education on the island?"

"Never had the pleasure," I said, offering him my hand. He shook it with a broad, genial smile. I tried to return the smile, but it just wasn't coming. I could feel Betta's eyes studying me, gauging my reaction.

"The pleasure is truly mine, sir. I've heard so much about this establishment. And about you as well. I know you both have met Ms. Baptiste." Steele turned to Betta with a big smile. "Soon she will grace our island with her own bakery, making rustic bread. And pizza too. Isn't that right, Betta?" She nodded with a nervous smile.

"Hello, sir," she said to McWilliams. She looked at me and in her soft voice said, "Hello, Leonard."

*Hello, Leonard.* I felt a chill from that. I hadn't talked to Betta in weeks and I didn't know what to say to her now. Her own bakery—and pizza too, he had said. I wondered what part this man had in that enterprise. Her words to me that night now were clearer than they were at the time. "Will you help me bake the bread," she had asked. It was a question—a request I never answered, and I really had no idea why.

"Let's go say hi to the Clarkes," Steele said to Betta and, with his hand on her lower back, steered her to the loud bar.

I took a sip of the bottle of beer and tried to act nonchalant but nonchalant just wasn't working and it was obvious. Maybe it was that I gritted my teeth. Or that I clenched the beer bottle so hard it almost shattered in my hand. Whatever my body language was, McWilliams was reading it.

"Everything okay, Buonfiglio?" he asked.

"Yeah, all good, McWilliams. You need me for anything else?"

"I wanted to commend you for hiring John. If anyone will keep him straight, it will be you."

"Oh yeah? You give me much too much credit."

"In this case, you deserve the credit, Buonfiglio," McWilliams said. "And did you know that the house in St. Francois has been sold and Queen Sassy has moved out?"

Speaking of obvious, the way he just threw that in there, was his not-so-subtle way of informing me that he most likely knew I went over there the night of the funeral. For a small island cop, McWilliams had a knack for knowing pretty much everything that was going on. He also knew that there were things he couldn't officially handle. The Sassy mess was one of those things.

"Should I care about that?"

"I just thought I should tell you."

"Yeah, well, thanks very much. But what did any of what I did accomplish? Why should I care about all that island drama you had me chase down?"

"Island drama? I don't know what you are talking about."

"Cut the bullshit. Don't tell me you didn't know everything I had to coax out of those people."

He was looking me over.

"You do very good work, Buonfiglio. Remember, we are on the same side. You want what is best for this island as much as I."

He was complimenting me. I wasn't having it. "What I want is this, McWilliams." I gestured to the Sporting Place. "I want to run this bar. Make it a good place for people to come to. To enjoy themselves."

He smiled. "Yes, Mr. Len. You are a very good bar owner. But who knows, maybe we will work together again on something in the future."

"Don't count on it," I said as I drained the bottle. "Now let me get back to my real job."

I left him out in the parking lot and went back inside the crowded bar. I could see that white dress—Betta stood out in it, but it wouldn't matter what she wore. To me, she always stood out. She glanced over her shoulder at me as Steele was chatting with Mike and his wife. I turned away from her and looked for Tubby. I wanted to let him know I was going home. He and John were busy at the bar. I looked again at Betta, and then decided to just leave. I could text Tubby and tell him I left. I would make a trip to Mike's house before they actually left the island to say a proper goodbye. I couldn't stay in the bar any longer. I just was not strong enough for that.

# 37

I was alone in my bed. The Puppy had climbed in next to me. I could hear the waves from the turbulent Atlantic crashing against the rocks. I heard them every night. That sound was a balm for sleep. But then I thought I heard something else. It was a familiar sound and one that was now a permanent part of my psyche. What I heard were bones breaking. It was a distinct, blunt sound. Not quite a crack, more like a quick snap. Once I heard the snapping sound, what followed was something like gurgling water, almost like what you might hear coming from your mouth when you are at the dentist and he/she has that sucking question mark to capture your saliva. I listened as the gurgling, like a clogged drain, slowly receded until there was silence. I sat up in the bed. I had been asleep. It was early; the sun was just rising.

I got out of bed and put on shorts. I made coffee and poured a cup. I had turned my phone off before bed. I went to it and stared at the dark blank screen. I put my earbuds on and looked at my phone, scanning my playlists. I went to the tried and true. I put on "Nura's Island," the playlist I was listening to when all this started that morning I last had the dream. The morning I learned that Lord Ram was dying.

I took my coffee outside and walked to the cliff overlooking the beach as the sun started its rise over the horizon. I was about to head down that steep incline to the beach but instead stood at the cliff's edge. I sipped the coffee, the music playing from the earbuds. I looked down at the water and the rocks on the beach below. It was a good forty-foot drop, almost straight down. There was a brisk wind at my back. I spread out my arms, imagining the wind taking me—pushing my bulk over the ledge—flying. The rising sun was now beginning to glisten over the surf. I noticed the impossibly clear blue water—what those on St. Pierre call "calypso blue," a rich, almost teal, color of water that seems to encircle the island and occurs every year at this time—at summer's end in this two-season land. Why that occurred each year, I didn't know and never inquired. Like many things here, I just accepted it as fact.

I looked down once more at the steep drop. Not unlike other Caribbean islands, St. Pierre was born from the eruption of volcanoes and as a result had numerous cliffs around it. I thought about Freedom Drop, the island's infamous historical site, a steep cliff where indigenous people and slaves would bravely sacrifice their own lives by leaping from it to escape the shackles of tyranny. Not all leaps, however, were so brave. My mind went back to New York and the Throgs Neck Bridge, so close to the house where I lived in the Bronx. And the Whitestone, the Triboro, the Brooklyn, Verrazzano, and the other many bridges around the city. Why did people choose to jump from them? And why did I let thoughts like that get into my head?

Through the earbuds I heard whining. The Puppy was nudging my ankles and panting up at me. Calling her the Puppy was silly. She was getting bigger. I had to find a better name for her. I could call her the Copper one, because of the color of her coat, as I called her older brothers by theirs. But she was still acting like a puppy now as she scurried around my legs. Maybe she wanted to play? Maybe she wanted food? Or maybe she sensed that she and I were much too close to the ledge. I smiled down at her and moved away from the steep incline. I turned back to the ocean, looked once more at the calypso blue water. The sun was fully up now. I breathed in the salty warm air, and with the music still playing, headed back to my house.

The Puppy hesitated, watching me, and then she followed.

# ACKNOWLEDGMENTS

The process of creating a novel has many stages. Along the way to completion there are those who pitch in with help, advice, and just good words of support. In writing Calypso Blue, I would like to thank my early readers, Charles Salzberg, Phil Falcone, Scott Adlerberg, and JB Stevens. Their comments and feedback helped me shape the story as it went through numerous drafts. Christine Pepe's always stellar editing contributed in the early phases of the book. The very intense eyes of my long time friend, and proofreader extraordinaire, Doug Schwartz, detected the usual amount of typos, misspellings, and inexcusable literary blunders. In the process of promoting my work, I thank Lisa Amoroso for creating prototype covers for *Calypso Blue* and its predecessor, *Freedom Drop*. I thank also Lance Wright for his tireless work on getting the books into production for Down & Out Books, my publisher. Finally, I would like to thank the support and patience of my wife, Heather, who got to listen to my whining about agents, and lack thereof, publishers, and lack thereof, as well as endure the many moods I inhabit while maneuvering through the creative process.

# ABOUT THE AUTHOR

**BRIAN SILVERMAN**'s writing career has spanned over thirty years. He has written about travel, food, and sports for publications including the *New York Times*, *Saveur*, *Caribbean Travel and Life*, *Islands*, the *New Yorker*, *New York* and others. From 2004 through 2013 he was the author of the annual Frommer's New York City guidebook series. He co-authored, with his father, Al Silverman, the acclaimed *Twentieth Century Treasury of Sports*. His short fiction has appeared in numerous publications, including *Mystery Tribune*, *Down & Out Magazine*, *Vautrin*, *Mystery Magazine*, *Dark Waters*, and *Rock and a Hard Place*. His stories have been selected to appear in *The Best American Mystery Stories* in 2018, and *The Best American Mystery and Suspense Stories 2021*. He is the author of the novel, *Freedom Drop*. He lives in Harlem, New York.

www.ingramcontent.com/pod-product-compliance
Lightning Source LLC
Chambersburg PA
CBHW052123270326
41930CB00012B/2729